D1478204

HYPATIA

WOMEN IN ANTIQUITY

Series Editors: Ronnie Ancona and Sarah B. Pomeroy

This book series provides compact and accessible introductions to the life and historical times of women from the ancient world. Approaching ancient history and culture broadly, the series selects figures from the earliest of times to late antiquity.

HYPATIA

THE LIFE AND LEGEND
OF AN ANCIENT PHILOSOPHER

Edward J. Watts

OXFORD
UNIVERSITY PRESS

OXFORD
UNIVERSITY PRESS

Oxford University Press is a department of the University of Oxford. It furthers
the University's objective of excellence in research, scholarship, and education
by publishing worldwide. Oxford is a registered trade mark of Oxford University
Press in the UK and certain other countries.

Published in the United States of America by Oxford University Press
198 Madison Avenue, New York, NY 10016, United States of America.

Library of Congress Cataloging-in-Publication Data
Names: Watts, Edward Jay, 1975– author.
Title: Hypatia : the life and legend of an ancient philosopher / Edward J. Watts.
Description: New York : Oxford University Press, 2017. | Includes
bibliographical references.
Identifiers: LCCN 2016033662 (print) | LCCN 2016040747 (ebook)
ISBN 9780190210038 (hardback) | ISBN 9780190210045 (Ebook) |
ISBN 9780190659141 (Ebook)
Subjects: LCSH: Hypatia, –415. | Women philosophers—Egypt—Biography.
Classification: LCC B667.H84 W38 2017 (print) | LCC B667.H84 (ebook) |
DDC 186/.4 [B]—dc23 LC record available at https://lccn.loc.gov/2016033662

1 3 5 7 9 8 6 4 2

Printed by Sheridan Books, Inc., United States of America

To Karen, Amber, Manasi, and Zoe Watts . . .

Contents

List of Figures

Cover Image: Raphael, detail from the School of Athens (c. 1510–1512), once assumed to represent Hypatia (now assumed to be the portrait of Francesco Maria della Rovere). **Credit Line: School of Athens. Stanza della Segnatura, Stanze di Raffaello, Vatican Palace; Photo courtesy of Scala/Art Resource.**

Acknowledgments

My parents, Dan and Karen Watts, are both scientists who have worked in industry and/or taught in universities for more than four decades. I always understood that both of them were accomplished in their fields and passionate about their work—and this is a passion that I believe Hypatia shared. When I was growing up, I had no appreciation for the barriers that this overwhelming love of science and pride in discovery enabled my mother to overcome as a female scientist who began her career in the late 1960s and early 1970s. This makes her successes even more impressive. I see a similar love of discovery in my daughter Zoe and my son Nathaniel (both of whom won their science fairs today). They may or may not decide to become scientists, but, whatever they do in the future, I hope that they share their grandparents' passion for it. This is also a book inspired by my sister Amber and my wife, Manasi, two incredibly strong women with the wisdom to embrace the lives they wanted to lead. Both of them know how much I admire them for making difficult but courageous choices. Manasi deserves particular credit for making this project what it has become. Through many long walks and lunches, her insightful suggestions and probing questions helped me to better understand the person that Hypatia was and pushed me to make her life rather than her death the true centerpiece of the book. I cannot be more grateful to her for the book that resulted from her perceptiveness.

Many other friends and colleagues helped enrich and improve this study. Cristiana Sogno carefully read an entire draft of the manuscript and, through her acumen and advice, made the work much stronger and more tightly argued. Gyburg Uhlmann offered thoughtful comments that helped me refine my arguments about Pappus and Porphyry. Peter

Brown offered suggestions for improving arguments related both to late antiquity and early modern English and French history. Stefan Vranka, Ronnie Ancona, Sarah Pomeroy, and an anonymous reader all offered important advice that made the manuscript clearer and more efficient at the point when it reached the press. Sarah Svendsen helped it move through the production process.

Alex Petkas, Lieve Van Hoof, David Maldonado, and Alan Cameron shared forthcoming chapters with me that helped me think in new ways about Hypatia's students and her larger social world. At a very early point in this project, Gillian Clark was generous enough to send the entire manuscript of her wonderful biography of Monica, a book that is inspiring in more ways than one. At a later point, I was privileged to read David Potter's *Theodora* manuscript and talk at some length about his experiences writing it.

This book also grew out of numerous conversations with many friends and colleagues over the past few years. For these I thank Brad Storin, Oliver Nicholson, Tina Shepardson, Diane Fruchtman, Maria Dzielska, David Brakke, Tudor Sala, Christopher Haas, Ann Hanson, Carly Maris, Susan Harvey, Andrea Sterk, Jorit Wintjes, Cam Grey, Genevieve Gessert, Michele Salzman, Susanna Elm, Elizabeth Depalma Digeser, Shane Bjornlie, Raffaela Cribiore, Michael Kulikowski, Dawn Teresa LaValle, Christian Wildberg, Henriette Harich-Schwarzbauer, Kate Cooper, Alberto Quiroga Puertas, Marco Formisano, Tom Barton, Mark Hanna, Dana Velasco Murillo, Seth Lerer, Denise Demetriou, and Tom Gallant. I am equally grateful to audiences in Kraków, Berlin, Princeton, Minnesota, and San Diego who offered their own responses to material presented in this book. Alexia Anas and the Hellenic Cultural Society deserve special mention for creating a friendly and exciting environment in which to present scholarship about the Greek world in San Diego. As a final word, I want to thank Carol Vassiliadis for her extremely generous support for research into early Byzantine studies at UCSD—support that made the completion of this project possible.

—Carlsbad, California, April 21, 2016

A Lenten Murder

The fifth-century Roman Empire depended on its citizens accepting an intricate illusion. People were encouraged to believe that the state in which they lived and the people who administered it enjoyed such power that ordinary people could not challenge them. Imperial officials, local elites, church leaders, and military officers colluded to manage the empire's cities through a combination of threats, rewards, and personal relationships that hid how precarious a grip they held on public order. Little things went a long way in maintaining this illusion of elite control. The wealthy city councilman who helped arrange the wedding of a client, the governor who pardoned a criminal he could have executed, and the bishop who fed starving migrant workers all, in their own ways, built the individual relationships that sustained the empire. Elites gave enough of their time and money that ordinary people usually felt they had the support they needed to survive in the Roman world. Most of the time, regular Romans who had a problem relied upon the elites with whom they had ties to shepherd them through this system. Most of the time, the system worked.

In the spring of 415, however, the Roman imperial machine in the great city of Alexandria seized up. The trouble began with the election of Cyril as bishop of Alexandria in 412. After the death of Cyril's predecessor, the Christian community in the city split into camps, with one side supporting Cyril and the other supporting a rival named Timothy. It took three days of street fighting and the intervention of Egypt's top military official for Cyril to prevail.[1] The fighting lasted just long enough to create suspicion among elites in Alexandria.

The next three years saw Cyril take action against his opponents. By 415, the confrontations between Cyril and other Alexandrian groups brought the bishop into conflict with the Roman governor Orestes. Cyril first tried to calm things with Orestes in ways that preserved the basic illusion that elites could work together to solve the city's problems. This failed. Cyril then decided to pull back the curtain hiding the messy divisions between Alexandria's elites. Relying on the language of the street, Cyril summoned a mob of monks to Alexandria. He hoped they would intimidate the governor into an agreement. But violent protests have unpredictable consequences. Instead of persuading Orestes to talk, one of the monks hit him in the head with a stone. Orestes had the monk arrested, tortured, and killed.

Cyril's stunt brought the city frighteningly close to chaos. As the conflict with Orestes heated up, Cyril and his associates began to blame their problems on the regular audiences that Orestes had with a female philosopher named Hypatia.[2] The daughter of a prominent Alexandrian mathematician, Hypatia had been Alexandria's leading thinker for nearly thirty-five years. Philosophers had no formal authority in the later Roman world, but some of them enjoyed immense influence. They had historically advised cities and officials about policy while standing apart from the transactions and favors that bound the Roman elite to one another. Concerned only with truth and uninterested in reputation or personal gain, these public intellectuals involved themselves in political life only to the degree that their actions made cities more justly governed.[3] If deployed at the right time and in the right way, their counsel could defuse tension by adding a calm and rational voice to heated confrontations. Her status as a philosopher, then, gave Hypatia's audiences with Orestes tremendous symbolic power in a city that was struggling to hold itself together. Her presence at Orestes's side made the governor appear to be the reasonable party in the dispute. In the language of antiquity, Cyril seemed to be a provocateur whose childish pique now threatened the very stability of the city.

Christians loyal to Cyril saw something much more nefarious in Hypatia's audiences with Orestes. They began to murmur that Hypatia had bewitched the governor and used her magic to keep him alienated from Cyril.[4] In their minds, the system had stopped working because Hypatia had blocked the voices of Cyril and his supporters from participating in the conversations that mattered in Alexandria. She needed to hear the anger of these people directly—and she needed to back down so that the city could again function.

In March 415, this frustration led a member of the Alexandrian church named Peter to gather a crowd of Cyrillian supporters that could confront Hypatia.[5] We do not know what Peter and his associates initially planned to do when they found her. Mobs gathered all the time in the Roman world.[6] They usually screamed and yelled. Sometimes they vandalized property. In rare cases, they even killed. It was, however, quite exceptional for a member of the Roman elite to be physically assaulted by a mob. Most of the time, crowds angry with a member of the elite vented their fury and then dispersed without ever coming particularly close to their target. But this mob was different. It either went out with an uncommonly violent sense of purpose or it had uncommonly canny luck in finding Hypatia teaching in a public classroom or traveling in one of Alexandria's streets.

While the mob may not have expected to see Hypatia, it is clear that she was utterly unprepared for their fury. She was in a public space with few attendants to protect her, and she was without the security of the solid outer walls that secured the homes of Alexandria's wealthy from the noise, smell, and anger of the masses.[7] She was exposed, and Peter and his partisans grabbed her. They shredded her clothes and her body with pottery fragments, tore out her eyes, dragged her corpse through the streets of Alexandria, and then burned her remains.[8]

Most people, both Christian and non-Christian, saw Hypatia's killing as a brutal, unprovoked murder that exploded out of a toxic set of circumstances for which Hypatia bore little responsibility. Few people outside of the immediate circle of Peter and his followers understood why Hypatia had been targeted. They were instead genuinely shocked that the Christian leadership of a major Roman city had manufactured so much popular anger that a philosopher like Hypatia could be murdered. This frightening rip in the late Roman social fabric suddenly suggested that any member of the Roman elite engaged in public life could similarly fall victim to mob violence. They now feared that the illusion of civic order and imperial control on which Roman life depended might dissipate.

This danger meant that the public reacted swiftly to Hypatia's murder. Christians throughout the empire erupted in condemnation of Cyril and the Alexandrian church for the ways in which their leadership had enabled such uncontrolled violence.[9] Because this violence happened on his watch, the murder of Hypatia apparently ended the public career of Orestes. The Alexandrian council became alarmed enough to send an embassy to Constantinople asking for additional imperial intervention. Even the fourteen-year-old emperor Theodosius II was supposedly horrified by her murder and ordered an investigation.

Hypatia's death was so shocking and so frightening that she quickly became a symbol of an older, more functional time that seemed to be slipping away in the early fifth century. Over the next 1,600 years, a wide range of authors, poets, painters, filmmakers, and scholars celebrated or condemned Hypatia and the age she came to represent. She has been defamed as a witch, marked as a feminist icon, and lionized as a martyr. Her death has been used to symbolize the corruption of the Alexandrian church, the end of Greek rationality, and the rise of religious fundamentalism.[10] And Hypatia's example is perhaps even more resonant now than ever before. According to Google search data, she is the world's best-known Neoplatonic philosopher and the fifth most popular Greek philosopher ever—trailing only Plato, Socrates, Aristotle, and Pythagoras.[11] She is now even more popular than Cyril, who would come to be recognized as one of the leading theologians in the Catholic, Greek Orthodox, Coptic, and Syrian Orthodox Churches.[12]

History is full of figures whose unprovoked and undeserved death resonates profoundly. The killing of leaders like Martin Luther King Jr. mark the final sacrifice they made for a larger, noble cause to which they dedicated their lives. Their lives and their deaths are part of the same story, with their murders simultaneously spotlighting the profound injustices against which they fought and showing the need for the struggle they waged. For sixteen centuries, Hypatia has been seen as a martyr for a host of lost causes. In antiquity, she died as a champion of traditional religion and philosophy who fell victim to a hostile Christian regime. In the Enlightenment, she seemed like the last defender of the ways of the ancient world at the moment when superstition overwhelmed Classical rationality. In the twentieth century, she championed the independence of women against a patriarchy that limited women's social roles and career options as a new age dawned.

But Hypatia was a person before she became a symbol. She was brave, but her trials were private. She was a fighter, but her goals were personal. She died in large part because she was in the wrong place at the wrong time, but this does not make her death less significant. Few people can rival Martin Luther King in life or in death, but that does not make their lives unimportant. There is heroism in every story, even if the heroism is not the sort we expect to find.

In death, Hypatia has become a powerful symbol useful for a host of just causes. In life, however, she was an activist for few of them. She was instead a gifted philosopher who went into spaces usually dominated by men, taught ideas usually expressed by men, and exercised authority usually reserved for men. None of these things were without precedent, but none of Hypatia's female contemporaries tried to do them all. Hypatia did. And she did them all very well. As a young philosopher, her work redefined the intellectual dynamics of her city. In her later career, Hypatia became a force for peace and good government in a city that was struggling to maintain trust and cooperation between pagan and Christian communities. While Hypatia fought no large wars for social change, she fought countless small battles to carve out the space necessary to live the life that she wanted. Hers was a life lived with a clear purpose and sustained by the tremendous courage it takes to achieve a personal goal despite significant obstacles. Hypatia the symbol has shaded nearly all of what we know of Hypatia the person. But this person is not entirely lost. This book will tell her story.

A biographer of Hypatia faces a considerable challenge. Our evidence for Hypatia's life is scanty, it is almost entirely written by men, and it is interested in telling only the stories that appealed most directly to male authors. These authors did not understand the particular obstacles prominent women faced, and they were often completely ignorant of the daily courage that a woman like Hypatia needed to show. In Hypatia's case, there is the additional challenge of distilling the details of her life out of the works of authors primarily interested in talking about her death. Much of what these men said about her life served only to set their readers up to view her death in a particular way.[13] Some of these men knew few of the details of her life, and all of them cared little about the daily courage she showed.

Despite this, there is plenty that we can say about Hypatia and the world in which she achieved such prominence. Some of this information emerges from the physical space in which she lived. Further material hides behind the incidental or unmentioned details that lurk within our sources. Male authors thought these things unimportant, but these small comments or stray remarks often show the subtle but significant steps that Hypatia took to build a remarkable set of professional, intellectual, and personal achievements. Hypatia's heroism lies not in the brutality that she suffered at the end of her life, but in the subtle barriers she overcame each day while she lived. This book will tell the story of that remarkable life and the world in which it unfolded.

1

Alexandria

Hypatia lived, worked, and died in Alexandria[1], a city that enjoyed one of the Mediterranean's best physical locations and housed one of the world's largest and most diverse populations. It was a religious center for Christians, pagans, and Jews; a cultural center for Greek intellectuals and the site of the ancient world's most advanced scientific work. In the modern world, we have no trouble understanding that a large city is so complicated that no one individual can experience all of it. The city of San Diego, for example, includes areas that are very different from one another, such as the suburbs of Rancho Bernardo, the beach houses of La Jolla Shores, the Chicano Park area in Barrio Logan, and Naval Base San Diego. The people living in each of these areas may interact with each other regularly, but the parts of the city from which they come, the professions in which they work, and the languages they speak all lead them to experience the city differently. All of their stories are San Diegan stories, but none of them can tell the complete story of the city. And no general profile of the city can fully capture their individual experiences.

Late Roman Alexandria was no different. Hypatia lived largely in an Alexandria dominated by wealthy, well-educated, Greek-speaking city councilors who owned luxurious townhouses and enjoyed urban gardens. She died at the hands of people who lived in a different Alexandria. Theirs was a dirty, dangerous, and often disgusting city that offered none of the space or security that Hypatia enjoyed. These two cities collided violently with one another in the spring of 415, but they had always coexisted uneasily. This chapter explains what these different Alexandrias were like. The rest of the book will show how both

Alexandrias, in their own ways, helped to shape Hypatia, the life that she lived, and the death that she suffered.

The City of Alexander

All discussions of ancient Alexandria must begin with Alexander the Great, the namesake of the Egyptian capital. Alexander founded the city in 331 BCE atop a limestone ridge that marked the place where the Nile Delta, the Mediterranean, and the desert all met. There were few better locations for a major city anywhere in the Mediterranean. Alexandria was shielded from sea storms by a rocky island that would later house the Pharos lighthouse, one of the seven wonders of the ancient world (see Figure 1.1). The city was connected to this island by a long, man-made promontory that divided the water that once separated the Pharos and the mainland into two large, well-protected ports. Alexandria's Great Harbor, from which the famous grain ships left to supply the imperial capitals of Rome and Constantinople, sat to the east of the promontory, and the smaller Eunostos Harbor was to the west.

By the fourth century, Alexandria's Mediterranean ports had been among the world's busiest harbors for nearly 700 years. An even busier

FIGURE 1.1. A Roman coin (Emmett 1002) issued in Alexandria by the emperor Hadrian showing the goddess Isis and the Pharos lighthouse.
Credit line: Courtesy of the author. Photo by author.

(though significantly less famous) port lay to Alexandria's south along the shores of the freshwater Lake Mareotis.² This harbor was linked to both the Nile and the Red Sea by a network of canals, and it handled products, both Egyptian and foreign, that had been transported to the city by ships traveling down the Nile.³ Alexandria is often thought of as an ancient version of the port of Shanghai, a place from which many exports travel but to which far fewer things return. This may have been somewhat true of the Mediterranean port, but the busy docks on Lake Mareotis handled more imports and more exports than Alexandria's better known Mediterranean harbors.⁴

Alexandria was not simply a port city. It was also one of the world's most culturally sophisticated urban centers. Perhaps excluding the Pharos lighthouse, the most spectacular sites in Roman Alexandria were its temples (see Figure 1.2). The city possessed nearly 2,400 of them at the turn of the fourth century, a number that means that there was roughly one temple for every twenty houses.⁵ The thousands of temples scattered throughout the city differed in size and importance. The most impressive seem to have been the Caesareum and the Serapeum. The Caesareum was perched on the shore near the southernmost point of the Great Harbor (see Figure 1.3).⁶ The structure was begun by Cleopatra to honor Julius Caesar and was finally completed under Augustus. For the next 400 years, the Caesareum served as the Alexandrian center of the imperial cult. Then, around the time of Hypatia's birth in 355, it was given to the bishop of Alexandria to become the city's most prominent church.⁷ This means that Hypatia would never have remembered the Caesareum as anything but a Christian church.

The Serapeum, called the most impressive sacred compound in the Eastern Mediterranean by one of Hypatia's contemporaries, stood out as the pagan counterpart to the grand Christian Caesareum.⁸ This monumental temple was dedicated to the god Serapis, a Hellenized Egyptian deity who was the consort of Isis and whose attributes combined the supremacy of Zeus with the healing powers of Asclepius. It sat atop Alexandria's highest hill and, like the Athenian Parthenon or the Roman Capitolium, was visible from much of the city (see Figure 1.4). Ornate statues decorated with gems, colorful marbles, precious metals, and rare woods adorned the temple's interior, and at its center was a huge statue of the god made of gold and ivory.⁹ This temple was merely the centerpiece of an even more imposing complex. Long porticoes raised on huge columns surrounded auxiliary chapels, housing for

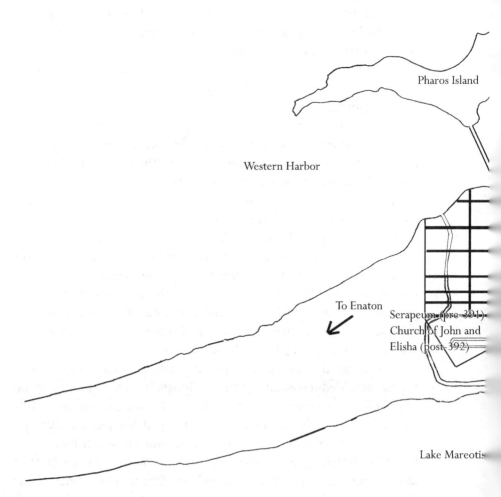

Mediterranean Sea

Pharos Island

Western Harbor

To Enaton

Serapeum (pre-391)
Church of John and
Elisha (post-392)

Lake Mareotis

FIGURE 1.2. Late antique Alexandria.
Credit line: Map prepared by author.

**Late Antique
Alexandria**

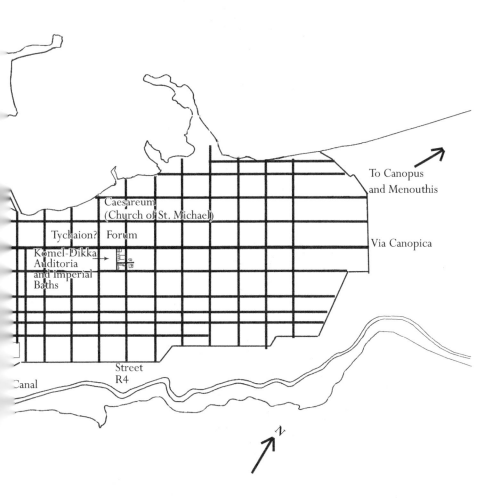

To Canopus
and Menouthis

Caesareum
(Church of St. Michael)

Tychaion? Forum

Kom el-Dikka
Auditoria
and Imperial
Baths

Via Canopica

Street
R4

Canal

FIGURE 1.3. A Roman coin (Milne 2158) issued in Alexandria by the emperor Antoninus Pius depicting the Alexandrian Caesareum.

Credit line: Courtesy of the author. Photo by Nate Watts.

FIGURE 1.4. A Roman coin (Emmett 1668) issued in Alexandria by Antoninus Pius showing the Serapeum and statue of Serapis.

Credit line: Courtesy of the author. Photo by Zoe Watts.

resident priests, meeting rooms in which business could be conducted, and hidden chambers in which religious rituals could be performed. There was also a library that supported the activities of teachers whose schools were based on the site, though the cries of tens of thousands of people from the hippodrome located just down the hill likely made scholarship a challenge on race days.[10]

During Hypatia's early life, the Serapeum library served as Alexandria's most important center of scholarship, but it contained the fragmentary remains of an even greater collection of scholarly resources. Until the last decades of the third century CE, the Alexandrian Royal Library and the city's Museum dominated cultural life.[11] The Museum is the better attested of the two institutions.[12] Although *Mouseia* had served as ritual centers devoted to the cult of the Muses and as centers of literary activity in many classical Greek cities, the Alexandrian Museum seems to have been modeled instead on Athenian philosophical schools like Plato's Academy and, especially, Aristotle's Lyceum.[13] Like the Lyceum, the Alexandrian Museum possessed a common meeting room in which a meal was served. It had space devoted to the worship of the Muses, and its leaders encouraged research on a range of literary, philosophical, and scientific topics. The Alexandrian Museum had far greater resources than the Lyceum, however. Ptolemaic rulers from Ptolemy I until Cleopatra VII funded its activities, with additional support coming from an endowment backed by donations from distinguished families.[14] These funds attracted scholars to Alexandria and provided them with support while they were in the city. In return, Museum members conducted research using its facilities, gave public lectures from lecture halls within the compound, and taught classes.[15]

Government support for the Museum continued after the Roman absorption of Egypt in 30 BCE. Roman emperors assumed responsibility for providing the stipends paid to scholars, paying for the common meals held in the institution, and selecting Museum members.[16] The emperor Claudius even paid for an expansion of the building.[17] Later emperors, however, came to regard membership in the Museum as a prize to be given to favored intellectuals and civil servants who were no longer required to live in Alexandria.[18] This change diminished the quality of research done at the institution, but the Museum remained an important center of culture both within and beyond Alexandria well into the third century.

The Royal Library, the other great center of scholarship in Ptolemaic Alexandria, was located on the grounds of the Museum.[19] It housed the world's largest collection of Greek manuscripts that, at its peak, held nearly 500,000 papyrus rolls.[20] The Royal Library began to decline in the late second century BCE, but the first significant damage to the collection occurred only in 48–47 BCE when Julius Caesar burned the Ptolemaic fleet as it lay docked in the harbor. The fire spread into the city and ultimately destroyed a large number of books belonging to the Royal Library.[21] The Library building itself seems to have survived the fire, and the collection was replenished when Mark Antony gave to Cleopatra VII the holdings of the great Hellenistic library of Pergamum.[22]

Little is known about the Library between the time of Cleopatra VII and the late third century CE. Because the Museum continued to exist, one must presume that the Library did as well. Its collections, however, seem to have grown too large to be housed on site. By the end of the first century CE, there were apparently major libraries within the precincts of the Caesareum and the Claudianum temples stocked with surplus materials from the old Royal Library.[23] The most important annex library was located within the precinct of the Serapeum (see Figure 1.5).[24] In the later Hellenistic period, the Serapeum "daughter library" held nearly 43,000 papyrus rolls.[25] It grew much larger in the

FIGURE 1.5. Wall niches that may once have held books, located in a tunnel beneath the site of Alexandria's Serapeum.

Roman period until, at the end of the fourth century CE, we are told, it contained over 700,000 works.[26]

The physical Museum and the Royal Library both disappear from the historical record in the mid-third century. The last reference to members of the old Museum appears in materials dating from the 260s.[27] By the year 300, it appears that both the original Museum and the Royal Library had been destroyed,[28] probably during the emperor Aurelian's campaign against the Palmyrene queen Zenobia in 272 CE.[29] Sometime in the fourth century, the Museum appears to have been re-established on a different site.[30] The last two members of the Museum about whom we know anything were Alexandrian teachers of the fourth and fifth centuries. Despite these few scattered mentions of Museum members, nothing is known about the exact characteristics of the institution in its final phase. The Museum could legally have retained the sacred connection with the Muses until anti-pagan legislation in the 390s made such a thing untenable, but it must have changed into something less overtly sacred by the fifth century.[31] Indeed, the Museum's last member, Horapollon, may have joined it after his conversion to Christianity.[32] The fate of the Library after the third century is equally mysterious. By the fourth century, however, the Serapeum and its library had become the biggest repository of literature in the city. Whatever dedicated bibliographic resources the Museum still possessed during Hypatia's life did not compare either to those available to its predecessor or to what the Serapeum held.

Alexandria's People

The intellectual life of late Roman Alexandria is often compared to that of Athens, its great rival as a center of scholarship and teaching, but the cities themselves were very different.[33] Unlike fourth-century Athens, which had shrunk into a university town of 20,000 people and an unofficial museum to the classical Greek heritage, later Roman Alexandria pulsed with the energy of a living, breathing ancient megacity. Within a few decades of its foundation in the fourth century BCE, Alexandria surpassed Babylon as the most populous city the world had ever known.[34] It would lose this title to Rome in the first century BCE, but at the time of Hypatia's birth it remained the Mediterranean's second most populous city, with somewhere between 300,000 and half a million inhabitants crammed into its ten square miles.[35]

The population of this metropolis was extremely diverse. Many of its inhabitants were Greek speakers born in the city or Coptic speaking Egyptians, but Alexandria also housed smaller enclaves of immigrants from Lycia, Phrygia, and, presumably, other parts of the Mediterranean world.[36] The members of these communities dwelled in ethnic neighborhoods that were geographically distinct. A large community of Alexandrian Jews, for example, lived in the Delta quarter, one of the five sectors into which the Hellenistic and early Roman city was divided. A smaller, though still significant, community of native Egyptian weavers is known to have lived in Rhakotis, an area located in the extreme southwest of the city near the Serapeum.[37]

Alexandria's population was incredibly dynamic. In antiquity, a city of Alexandria's size could never hope to sustain its population through births alone. Some of this was due to an appalling rate of child mortality and terrible obstetrical care. Nearly half of all children born in the Roman world failed to live until their fifth birthday.[38] Women had a 2 percent chance of dying for each child they delivered—a dramatic danger when women who lived until menopause would normally be expected to give birth to six or more children.[39] When the death toll from childbirth is combined with the particular urban dangers of poor sanitation, risk of accidents, and overcrowding, it is estimated that the average Roman city may have lost nearly 3 percent of its people each year.[40]

This meant that Alexandria required constant immigration from the countryside and other regions of the empire just to keep its population stable.[41] Many of these migrants undoubtedly came to work in Alexandria's ports.[42] Alexandria was a major commercial and transportation hub, but no cargo was more important than the grain shipped from the city. Every year, 650 large transports carrying more than 5.5 million sacks of grain sailed from Alexandria to the new capital of Constantinople.[43] The voyages of these large Mediterranean ships were the final steps in a long, labor-intensive process through which men and women harvested the grain, took it to the large granaries that lined the Nile, and loaded it onto barges bound for Alexandria. When these barges began to arrive in Alexandria in the late winter, a large population of laborers went to work moving the grain they carried from the Nile Canal to the Mediterranean. The first task was to unload the Nile barges into giant warehouses on the city's south side.[44] The grain would then be stored until the beginning of April, when the Mediterranean was safe enough for sailing. Once ships could sail north and west, the grain would then be moved to the Mediterranean ports, either by carts moving through the city or by barge along a canal.[45] Longshoremen would then load the grain on the sea vessels and send it on its way, a process that continued until at least the end of August.

Alexandria's ports provided a huge amount of back-breaking work. The workers were overwhelmingly male, and, because their jobs were seasonal, these men would have been in the city without much to do at various times of the year. One can imagine, for example, that dock-workers would have little work between November and April, when few ships left port. And some men who began the year as migrants with the idea of returning to their villages inevitably would also have decided, by the fall, to escape village life and stay permanently in the big city.[46]

Alexandria was densely populated, but its people lived in a range of conditions. Most Alexandrians in the fourth century crammed in three- or four-story apartment blocks.[47] There is some evidence to suggest that many of the people who worked in a certain profession would have clustered together in a particular part of the city. This seems to have been the case with glassworkers, whose workshops have been excavated near the modern city's train station.[48]

But not all Alexandrians lived this way. As in modern New York or Singapore, one of the greatest markers of one's status was ownership of some of the city's rare open spaces. Only the richest Alexandrians could afford this, but there is both literary and archaeological evidence that some of the land in the city was used not for housing but for "gardens in the midst of the city belonging to great people."[49] Indeed, the register of early fourth-century buildings in Alexandria suggests that some districts were much more densely populated than others. The Gamma quarter, for example, had less than half the number of houses found in any of the other four quarters of the city but twice the number of baths and nearly half of the city's temples.[50] One suspects that it may have been a part of the city filled with monumental buildings, urban gardens, and luxurious townhouses.

Historians writing about Hypatia have tended to focus on fourth- and fifth-century Alexandrian religious dynamics, but spatial and socioeconomic divisions mattered far more than religious differences to Hypatia's contemporaries. Most fourth- and fifth-century Alexandrian Christians and pagans did not understand religious differences in the same way that modern religious communities do. They did not see stark divisions between Christians and pagans and would not have naturally been hostile toward people with different beliefs.[51]

Much of this had to do with the social and economic relationships that inextricably tangled the lives of Alexandrian pagans, Christians, and Jews of all backgrounds. Alexandria was filled with *collegia*, associations of individuals who worked at a common craft, including sailors, shopkeepers, and even gravediggers.[52] These groups had a developed hierarchy that spread out beneath the collegial elders and their stewards. Individual members, regardless of where they ranked, were often quite proud of their involvement in these associations, and this pride in membership crossed religious lines. *Collegia* put up collective dedications to emperors, and from the fourth century forward they were required to perform certain public duties.[53] Indeed, their collective identification was so important that worshippers in the main Alexandrian synagogue were seated according to *collegia*. The Christian teacher Arius even penned songs that explained his theology in individually tailored melodies that corresponded to the rhythms of the work done in different professions.[54]

Cultural bonds were equally strong among members of Alexandria's upper classes. In the same way that similar interests cemented ties between members of the city's *collegia*, a common literary culture nurtured by the city's great institutions of learning provided educated Alexandrians of all faiths with a set of shared interests and a universally accepted pattern of behavior. As leaders of their individual communities, upper-class men and women knew and became friendly with their peers of other faiths. This was the tribe into which Hypatia was born. Like her peers, Hypatia recognized her public influence, understood the responsibilities that came along with her position, and acknowledged the importance of fulfilling her social obligations.[55]

The common interests of Alexandria's educated elite were not solely defined by events in the political arena. Indeed, many of the Alexandrian elite shared a great interest in rhetoric, philosophy, and the ways in which religious traditions could be understood philosophically. As one might expect, the same sort of networks that had been established to foster political cooperation also encouraged intellectual exchange. Word of the latest compositions of prominent rhetoricians, philosophers, and doctors would have passed along the same channels as society gossip and requests for favors. As we will see, Hypatia belonged to this Alexandrian garden and townhouse set, a group whose wealth the city helped create and whose cultivation its cultural institutions perpetuated.

Hypatia's Alexandria was real, but it did not exist as a fourth-century Green Zone, cut off from the rest of the city. The Alexandria of the elite sat beside and folded into the Alexandria of migrant workers, mule drivers, sailors, and longshoremen. For centuries, elites in the Mediterranean world had served as patrons and protectors of their poorer, less fortunate neighbors. They continued to do so in the later Roman period.[56] But this civic-minded concern for fellow citizens was not always joined with an ability to treat those fellow citizens with respect. In fact, fourth- and fifth-century authors marveled whenever a philosopher or rhetorician was able to carry on a conversation with a shopkeeper.[57] It was even rarer for an intellectual to actually seek out a regular person and initiate a conversation. When most intellectuals went out, they traveled the city in carriages or litters born by attendants so as to avoid the filth of the streets and the stench of the city air. Most of the time they probably thought little of the people whose shops they passed, whose labor they may not even have observed, and whose daily lives they did not really understand. The laborers, too, must have reacted to the passing of the entourage of yet another member of the elite with a degree of disinterested indifference. Some of Alexandria's wealthy teachers were probably known to regular people by reputation, and some teachers may have served as patrons who helped lower-status individuals, but most of these men and women had no more individual identity to a member of the urban crowd than the average worker or porter in the streets had to a member of the elite. They shared the same city, but they were from another world.

The gap between these two worlds mattered very little to Hypatia during her life, but it would contribute dramatically to her death. This is why most of the next few chapters will focus on Hypatia's Alexandria and the ways that she learned how to navigate it. The discussion will leave this wider city to the side for the time being, but we will return to it soon enough, once Hypatia begins to play a larger role within it.

2

Childhood and Education

Hypatia was born in Alexandria to the philosopher and mathematician Theon and his wife around the year 355.[1] Although Theon is one of the best-attested intellectuals of the mid-fourth century, no source says anything at all about Hypatia's mother. It is possible, though, that she was from a family of intellectuals. We know of many other marriages that joined accomplished male philosophers and rhetoricians to the daughters of their colleagues around the time that Hypatia's parents married. The philosopher Themistius, for example, married the daughter of another philosopher in the 340s, and the rhetorician Himerius married into a long-established Athenian intellectual dynasty at roughly the same point in time.[2]

The boys born of these types of marriages were often educated in ways that prepared them for the intellectual careers that had become the family business.[3] This is not surprising, but the female children of intellectuals also needed to be educated. Some of these young women trained to be teachers as well, but even if a female child of an intellectual did not want to teach, she still needed to have enough training to manage the education of her own children. Roman wives were often much younger than their husbands, and the demographic realities of ancient life meant that women would often be left to arrange the education of their children after their husbands died.[4] If their children were to take up the family profession, their mothers needed to be able to recognize whether or not a teacher was capable.

We cannot say how much education Hypatia's mother received, but it is clear that Theon and his wife raised Hypatia to be a mathematically and philosophically literate young woman. This meant that Hypatia's education differed greatly from the functional training that most Egyptian women received. Women from poor and middling families who lived in rural areas may have acquired basic training in letters, but they did not need anything more advanced.[5] It was perhaps a little better among the urban poor. They were more likely to have some schooling, but it often consisted of nothing more than learning to recognize and reproduce letters.[6]

Upper-class daughters had more opportunities, at least in theory. Elite education in the fourth century was a multistage process. It began in the home with a basic introduction to proper modes of speech, followed by the analysis of memorable stories that taught lessons about appropriate behavior. Much of this initial training came from the wet nurses hired by the families to take care of babies until they reached the age of six or seven.[7] When a girl of privilege turned seven, she often began to study language and the rules of basic conduct that would mark her as a member of the elite.

In early adolescence, she would advance to grammatical training. This focused on exercises that helped her learn correct grammatical rules, develop the skills to express herself eloquently, and master the basic content of some of antiquity's most famous works of literature.[8] This training was doubly important because the Greek in which Egyptian elites were expected to write was different from what most people spoke. Almost 700 years had passed since the time of Plato, and while literary Greek remained more or less the same across those centuries, the spoken language had evolved significantly. The Greek of the classical period was spoken with a different sort of accent than the Greek of the fourth century CE, a change in pronunciation that made it difficult for late Roman Greek speakers to understand classical Greek poetic meters (and even many individual words).[9] This meant that even a native Greek speaker like Hypatia had to learn this literary Greek.

Grammatical training served as a primer for how to read, write, and understand classical Greek, but it also had a more subtle purpose. Teachers of grammar designed their lessons around the group reading of texts. They would stop at each mention of a significant event or person within the text and explain its importance to the students.[10] As the girl progressed in her training, she would begin working on exercises called *progymnasmata*. These pushed her to elaborate upon well-known stories, poignant sayings by famous historical figures like

Diogenes the Cynic or Isocrates, and defined themes using the linguistic skills she had earlier acquired.[11] All of this helped her to develop writing and reading skills, but the training also served as a moral education. The texts read, the stories analyzed, and the historical figures discussed were chosen because they helped young members of the elite understand appropriate behaviors.

The *progymnasmata* exercises divided grammatical training from the teaching done in the schools of rhetoric. In her early teens, a student moved from grammatical to rhetorical training.[12] Students who made this transition often did so gradually either by continuing to take half of their classes with a grammarian or, at the very least, continuing with the *progymnasmata* under the supervision of a teacher of rhetoric.[13] Male students occasionally could continue studying rhetoric until sometime around the age of twenty, but most stopped well before then.[14] The girls who began rhetorical training likely either completed or dropped out of it in their teens.

In a few cases, we know of women who moved on to the formal study of philosophy, the highest stage in late Roman elite education. The student of philosophy needed to master such things as astronomy, geometry, arithmetic, and the texts of Aristotle and Plato. The training was intensive and progressive. Students began with math and ended with the most advanced elements of theology. In all cases, though, philosophical education was text based. The teacher and students would go through a text written by a major thinker line-by-line and discuss its contents extensively.[15] This collaborative reading encouraged the student to appreciate all of the text's distinct elements, the ways in which they fit together, and the larger significance of the entire work. By the end of the full course of study, a student would appreciate not only the contents of individual texts, but also the ways in which they fit together to make up the school's philosophical system.[16]

A late antique philosopher was not primarily measured by her command of the details contained within canonical texts. People instead evaluated the degree to which her life and conduct embodied the philosophical principles those texts taught. This meant that an aspiring philosopher needed to listen to stories about her philosophical ancestors and the ways in which they put the abstract philosophical ideas presented in the curriculum into practice in the world. These stories were shared both formally in classrooms and informally in social settings with both male and female students present.[17]

Even the wealthiest and most powerful late Roman men did not usually complete this education. Some of this had to do with what education meant in late antiquity. For male members of the Roman elite, education served as a means of social and financial advancement. In the early years of the fourth century, the Roman government created tens of thousands of well-paying jobs in imperial and military administration open only to men.[18] By the time that Hypatia entered school, the male recruits for these administrative positions were drawn largely from the schools of rhetoric and law based in the empire's major cities. The recruitment process was formalized in the 370s when the emperors Valens and Valentinian mandated the creation of a centralized record of student performance so that they could see which men had the potential to serve in the administration.[19] The students who got those jobs hit a sort of late antique lottery, but those seeking imperial positions tended only to get the training that the jobs required. Rhetoric and law grew extremely popular because bureaucrats could use that sort of training. Philosophy and advanced mathematics had no practical benefits for government workers. They thus became elective courses taken by a small fraction of students.[20] If students took them at all, these courses were either squeezed into a gap year between the school of rhetoric and the beginning of law school or pursued for as long as other personal and financial obligations permitted.[21]

This happened because the education that got one to the top of the imperial registry of student performance was long and extremely expensive. Families needed to pay student fees, provide bonuses to teachers when a student advanced in school, and, unless they lived in a major educational center like Athens or Alexandria, cover the living expenses of the attendants who went along with the student.[22] This was not an investment that always paid off. Although the fourth century saw the creation of many new jobs in imperial administration, there were not enough positions for every member of the elite who wanted one. In fact, in the majority of cases, male students who matriculated in a school of rhetoric did not complete their training.[23] Some had to return home to manage the family estates following the death of their father.[24] Others left school after their families arranged a marriage for them.[25] In most cases, it seems, the families either decided that they could no longer afford the gamble that their son would make it big, or they determined that their investment in him would never pay off. These schools gave no diplomas and held no graduations. One completed them when he felt he had done so. If an imperial position looked unlikely, a male student could deem himself sufficiently educated and go home.

Women participated unevenly in this educational process. Some highly trained female authors show up sporadically across the fourth and fifth centuries. Fabia Anconia Paulina, the wife of the Roman senator Praetextatus, authored a long, extremely sophisticated poem honoring her husband that was inscribed on a funerary monument on their property. It later circulated publicly as a stand-alone text.[26] Given the quality of the poem, she must have had a very good rhetorical training. The future empress Eudocia, the daughter of an Athenian professor, wrote an epic poem celebrating her husband Theodosius II's victory over the Persians. She was so well versed in Homeric texts that she also composed an even more impressive cento that refashioned lines of Homer into a biblical narrative.[27] In an earlier period, the city of Pergamum regularly awarded prizes to young women who won competitions for the best recitations of elegiac and lyric poetry.[28] Egyptian papyri reveal other upper-class women who were both literate and conversant with literary culture. This includes one papyrus that preserves a joke that a mother made about her son that uses a subtle but unmistakable reference to a passage from the second-century satirist Lucian.[29] Other papyri show clear evidence of female teachers of grammar active in Egypt and North Africa in the Roman imperial period.[30] These women must have themselves been educated above the level of a grammarian if they were to properly teach the *progymnasmata* that bridged grammatical and rhetorical training.

A number of factors converged to ensure that this sort of functional and cultural literacy was far from universal even among the most privileged women. First, and perhaps most importantly, elite women married in their late teens, roughly at the point where they would have been engaged in rhetorical education, while men often married in their late twenties or early thirties.[31] Marriage likely ended the formal educations of many men and women, but it would have ended those of women at an earlier stage. In addition, while some men are known to have resumed their educations after marrying, we have no evidence of a similarly fortunate woman.[32]

Another factor also influenced the sort of education that women received. While it seems that the growth in administrative jobs in the fourth century pushed more men to pursue a specific type of literary education, none of these jobs were open to women. There was no financial incentive for a family to pay for the education of a daughter. The value that was returned from her training was cultural, not economic. Educated women better understood the manner in which members of the elite behaved, they were better able to take care of the education of their children, they could take pride in their schooling, and, like Fabia Anconia Paulina and Eudocia, they could even show off their erudition by creating and publishing original literary compositions. However, because elite women could not have a career in administration, they could study whatever they wanted for as long as their family would pay, without it having any impact on their earning potential. It is therefore not surprising that we hear nothing about late antique female lawyers or sophists, but we know of a number of highly educated female philosophers in late antiquity.[33]

Hypatia's Education

This survey of educational practices in the later Roman world points to the range of possible ways in which Hypatia could have been educated. Unfortunately, we know a lot more about the comprehensiveness of Hypatia's education than we do about the actual process through which she acquired it. We are told by our sources that she was "fully trained in the mathematical sciences" by her father and that her interests eventually expanded into the study of "other forms of philosophy" to such a degree that she surpassed her father "in many ways."[34] This suggests that she acquired a clear mastery of language, grammar, and philosophy (in its most expansive sense), but it says nothing about her ever having studied with any teacher other than her father.

This leaves us to guess about much of her early education. Her early training in reading and writing is a complete mystery, but it was probably done in the household. Such a thing was so unremarkable that none of the authors who wrote about Hypatia would think to mention it. Although our sources similarly say nothing about Hypatia's training in grammar, we can at least hazard a guess at how it might have occurred. By the middle years of the fourth century, the boundaries between the disciplines of grammar, rhetoric, and even philosophy had begun to break down. Because the demand for training in rhetoric and especially grammar far outstripped that for philosophy and mathematics, many philosophers taught lower-level classes in grammar in order to support themselves. This was true even of quite prominent philosophers like Chrysanthius, a former philosophical teacher of the emperor Julian who, by the 350s, was teaching grammar to paying students in Sardis while providing free philosophical instruction on the side. Around the year 400, the famous philosopher Syrianus did the same thing, though his interest in grammatical teaching was serious enough that he authored commentaries on two grammatical treatises by Hermogenes of Tarsus.[35] By the last decades of the fifth century, the philosopher Horapollon, who was a Museum member like Theon, also ran a grammar school in Alexandria.[36]

It is possible, then, that Hypatia may have moved directly from the home language instruction of a tutor into the school of her father. If this is true, then Hypatia may never have left Theon's circle of followers. She could have done her grammatical training there in a classroom with boys (and perhaps other girls), probably under the supervision of one of Theon's teaching assistants. It is unclear if she ever did any formal training in rhetoric, but, if she did, this might have been either in Theon's school or, potentially, in the school of a rhetorician who had a relationship with Theon's school.[37] It is notable, however, that no contemporary mentions Hypatia ever having any rhetorical training at all. Although the lower levels of rhetorical training taught useful skills like formal letter writing,[38] the rhetorical curriculum was designed ultimately to train students to make powerful and persuasive public speeches that conformed to established rhetorical genres. Women could not serve as advocates in a court and, to our knowledge, did not offer public rhetorical performances. Much of this training would then have been completely useless to Hypatia. This raises the possibility that she may not have spent much time studying rhetoric, but might instead have moved quickly into mathematics after some basic study of the *Progymnasmata* and exposure to other essential practicalities like effective letter writing. This would be a surprising choice for a male student, but it is certainly a decision that Hypatia could make if she wanted.[39]

We are on firmer ground once we turn to Hypatia's mathematical and philosophical education. She likely began this under her father's direction when she was in her late teens or early twenties. Although they could not seem more different in a modern university setting, mathematics and philosophical teaching were linked in antiquity. Platonic philosophers often taught mathematics as an introductory module designed to prepare students for the study of Aristotle and Plato, but Theon's school placed more emphasis on mathematics when Hypatia was a student.[40] Her training involved the systematic reading of a group of mathematical texts organized specifically so that she would develop increasingly more sophisticated mathematical skills. No surviving work defines the precise curriculum that she would have followed, but sixth-century curricula for the study of philosophy and medicine give an idea of how it may have been structured. Students of philosophy worked through a curriculum made up of Aristotle's *Organon* followed by a series of Platonic dialogs read in a specific order and designed to help them develop a set of philosophical virtues.[41] Medical students followed a similar curriculum made up of eleven works of Hippocrates and fifteen or sixteen treatises of Galen, each read in a specific order and corresponding to particular areas of medical instruction.[42]

It is very likely that men and women studying mathematics would have seen their curricula similarly structured. The Alexandrian mathematician Pappus authored a work called the *Collectio* in the early fourth century CE that treated a range of different mathematical topics in eight books, including calculation, geometry, astronomy, and mechanics.[43] It served as a compendium of mathematical instruction that was organized so that its more difficult material built upon topics treated earlier.[44]

The *Collectio* also gives a sense of how mathematical teaching was done. Book 2 of the *Collectio* treats calculation by offering arithmetical proofs of propositions once proved geometrically by the third-century BCE mathematician Apollonius of Perga.[45] Like Platonic philosophers and Alexandrian doctors, Pappus seems to have assumed that the students would read Apollonius's text and consult it as they worked through this part of the *Collectio*.[46] An even better sense of the close pairing of Pappus's instruction and a recognized canon of mathematical texts appears in Book 7. This focused on techniques that one could use to solve geometrical proofs by working through the steps backwards. In the book's preface, Pappus mentions the three mathematicians on whose work his discussion will be based. He then lists thirty-three texts written on the topic, a canon of texts containing nothing composed after the third century BCE. The book summarizes many of the works contained within this canon in order to allow the student to develop the skills they collectively taught.[47] It then served as a comprehensive introduction to the topic.

Mathematicians also organized their teaching so that students worked through basic theorems and calculation techniques before they encountered any higher-level material. Book 6 of the *Collectio* offers material related to the heading "Little Astronomy," a discussion of things evidently designed to prepare students to read Ptolemy of Alexandria's *Almagest* (which was sometimes called the "Big Astronomical Collection").[48] Writing in the sixth century, Cassiodorus suggests that what he calls the "Minor Astronomy" and the "Major Astronomy" had become so closely linked in the curricular sequence that they were then both seen as works by Ptolemy himself.[49] The second-century mathematician Nicomachus of Gerasa's exotic *Theologoumena Arithmeticae*, an arcane work about the properties of numbers, also follows his much more accessible *Introductio Arithmetica*. This leaves the clear impression that, while we have no text that lays out the complete mathematical curriculum from the fourth century, mathematicians usually would have moved students progressively through individual texts that were carefully chosen to develop particular skills. The study of math, then, closely resembled that of philosophy and medicine.

Hypatia was not content with only a standard mathematical training. She quickly proved more capable than her father and developed competencies greater than his. At some point, Hypatia moved from being a mathematics student at her father's school to being one of his colleagues. In the modern world, this sort of transition is clearly demarcated. Students formally become colleagues with their teachers when they complete their dissertations, significant works of original scholarship that demonstrate their intellectual creativity and scholarly command of their chosen field.

The late antique equivalent of a doctoral dissertation was much more of a collaborative project than its modern descendant. The first "publication" of the philosopher Proclus, for example, consisted of the material contained in three notebooks he had assembled when reading Plato's *Phaedo* with his teacher, the fifth-century Athenian Platonist Plutarch.[50] The ideas in Proclus's publication derived from their joint reading of the text and were, in all likelihood, more Plutarch than Proclus. Plutarch, however, made it clear to Proclus that the published text would be "written by Proclus," and Proclus took great pride in the book.[51] Proclus's fellow student, the Alexandrian Hermeias, wrote a *Commentary on the Phaedrus* in the 440s that seems to have been based almost entirely upon his notes from lectures given by his teacher Syrianus.[52] The sixth-century Alexandrian philosopher, mathematician, and grammarian John Philoponus offers perhaps the most extreme example of this tendency. Not long after arriving at the school of Hermeias's son Ammonius, Philoponus began publishing a sequence of commentaries that drew heavily upon the teaching of Ammonius and his assistant teachers. Between about 510 and 517, Philoponus wrote a commentary on Nicomachus's *Introductio Arithmetica* that was based upon an earlier commentary written by Ammonius's student Asclepius,[53] and he also recorded Ammonius's teachings in commentaries on Aristotle's *De Anima, De Generatione et Corruptione, Categories,* and *Physics.*[54] All of these were seen as Philoponus's work, despite the fact that many of the ideas in them originated from other thinkers.

The connection between Hypatia's work and that of Theon is less immediately apparent than, say, the link between Philoponus and Ammonius, but it is still discoverable. Hypatia would eventually author commentaries on the third-century CE mathematician Diophantus of Alexandria's *Arithmetica* and the *Conic Sections* of Apollonius, neither of which now survive.[55] These commentaries do not overlap with any known works of Theon and are thus unlikely to be her earliest projects. Two other projects that Hypatia completed do relate intimately to publications attributed to Theon. Hypatia edited the manuscript of Ptolemy's *Handy Tables*, the astronomical tables that accompanied Ptolemy's thirteen book, *Almagest.*[56] Theon authored two different commentaries on the *Handy Tables*. The first, a one-book "small" commentary designed as an introductory text, set up his five-book "large" commentary. It is possible that Hypatia's editorial work on the *Handy Tables* was designed to support her father's commentary. This may then represent one of her earliest projects.

While Hypatia probably collaborated with Theon when preparing her edition of the *Handy Tables*, another editorial project seems more likely to be her earliest publication. In the heading of Book 3 of Theon's thirteen-book commentary on Ptolemy's *Almagest*, he wrote that this is the "Commentary by Theon of Alexandria on Book Three of Ptolemy's *Almagest*, an edition revised by my daughter Hypatia, the philosopher." Alan Cameron has recently suggested that this notice means that, beginning in Book 3 of his commentary, Theon was commenting on Hypatia's edition of the text of Ptolemy's *Almagest.*[57] It is possible, then, that the text of the next ten books of the *Almagest* that Theon uses were also Hypatia's edition. This is even more likely because the method of long division used in Books 3–13 differs from that found in Book 2.[58] Unlike Hypatia's later work, her edition can be placed chronologically alongside an ongoing project of Theon. She clearly began it after Theon had started writing his *Almagest* commentary but before he had completed it. This suggests that Hypatia may have first acquired the technical skills necessary to do this work while Theon was in the middle of the project. If this is true, the text of Books 3–13 of the *Almagest* that we now have may be the equivalent of Hypatia's dissertation.

Hypatia's edition of Books 3–13 of the *Almagest* was no simple project.[59] Unlike, say, a literary text whose words were fixed by the original author, ancient mathematical texts were designed to teach skills and demonstrate truths. The editor's work consisted not in making sure that the manuscript corresponded to the actual words written long ago by the text's author, but rather in making the mathematical processes outlined in the text as clear and elegant as they could be. The editor added intermediate steps in proofs that moved too quickly, simplified elements of the argument that were unclear, and, above all, worked to make the text easier to understand.[60] Because numbers represented a sort of immaterial element that contrasted to the changeable physical world, a skilled and careful editor of a mathematical text could think that her work brought readers closer to truth. This meant that Hypatia and her contemporaries would have understood her edition to be a quite significant scholarly contribution.

Hypatia and Philosophy

The fourth century was a revolutionary time in the intellectual life of Alexandria, during which mathematicians and philosophers worked to piece together an intellectual system that blended philosophical ideas about divinity with numerical theories. At least since the time of Ptolemy, Alexandrian thinkers had been arguing about whether mathematics or philosophy ultimately led one to the highest-level grasp of truth.[61] The concentration of intellectuals in Alexandria encouraged regular debates between philosophers and mathematicians that required each side to know enough about the texts and ideas of their competitors to frame effective arguments against them.

Two intellectual trends that first emerged at the end of the second century CE further complicated these conversations. At this time, the mathematician Nicomachus of Gerasa and the philosopher Numenius both authored works that helped to spark a revival of interest in Pythagoreanism, a philosophical system that drew heavily upon mathematical roots.[62] Each man approached Pythagoreanism differently. Numenius constructed a philosophical history organized around the idea that Plato was effectively a Pythagorean. Plato himself, Numenius argued, had more or less held true to Pythagorean principles, but Platonism had strayed from its roots when dissention arose within the Academy following Plato's death.[63] The Academy's new leadership then pulled Platonic teaching away from its ultimate Pythagorean origins. Like the Pythagoreans, Numenius understood that mathematics played a fundamental role in the proper functioning of a philosophical system, and his work aimed to bring Platonism back to its true origins.

Nicomachus of Gerasa, Numenius's slightly later contemporary, shared Numenius's view that mathematics and Platonic philosophy were inherently complementary.[64] Nicomachus also revered Pythagoras and even wrote a biography of him, but all of what we would immediately recognize as philosophical works written by Nichomachus have been lost. What we have instead is Nicomachus's *Introductio Arithmetica*, a text that lays out the approaches one needs to master in order to understand the numerically based theological system that Nicomachus developed in a second, longer work called the *Theologoumena Arithmeticae*. This work contained ten books, each of which focused on a specific number and discussed the relationship between its mathematical properties and nonmathematical subjects like ethics and theology.[65]

Third- and early-fourth century intellectuals across the empire worked hard to understand the implications of this Pythagorean revival. Outside of Alexandria, thinkers like the Syrian Iamblichus crafted a sophisticated philosophical system that combined the Pythagoreanizing mathematics of Nicomachus with the innovative philosophical approaches of the Alexandrian-trained philosopher Plotinus and ritualistic elements inspired by the third-century Chaldean Oracles. This intricate philosophical system ultimately promised to lead its followers to a higher level of interaction with the true, divine principles of the universe.

Within Alexandria, though, it seems that these issues were hashed out in a different way. Most Alexandrian philosophers of the third century seem to have stood aside from the Pythagorean revival. Plotinus, who came to Alexandria to study under the "the leading celebrities of the time," was thoroughly disappointed in their teaching.[66] He instead turned to Ammonius Saccas, an intellectual outsider in Alexandria who was neither a Museum member nor a part of the Alexandrian establishment.[67] A lapsed Christian, Ammonius seems to have been a thoroughly unconventional philosopher who taught a philosophy derived in some way from the teaching of Numenius.[68] While Ammonius's ideas ultimately helped to shape the way that Platonism was understood for much of the next millennium and a half, the Alexandrian intellectual establishment resisted them. This may be why Plotinus, who was a native Egyptian, ultimately decided to set up his own school in Rome rather than in Alexandria.

Alexandrian mathematicians apparently offered the strongest resistance to the teaching of Ammonius and his students, a new breed of Platonic interpreters modern scholars now call Neoplatonists. In his *Collectio*, Pappus makes three significant critiques of philosophers who, he felt, were making claims based on unsubstantiated interpretations of Plato's *Timaeus*.[69] One of these involved reworking an assertion made by Plato in the *Timaeus* that there were only five types of convex solids, a point that Archimedes proved to be false. Pappus calls the bluff of these philosophers and claims that they "fail to provide proofs" for the points that they make.[70] At another point, Pappus criticizes "the philosophers" who misidentified the Demiurge, the divine figure to whom Plato attributes the creation of the cosmos.[71] He never names these philosophers, but the view that he ascribes to them is a minority opinion found in none of the works of third- and fourth-century Neoplatonists like Plotinus, Porphyry, or Iamblichus. It did circulate in Alexandria in the early fourth century because of the work of Origen, a student of Ammonius Saccas who wrote a treatise that evidently caught the attention of Pappus.[72] Pappus was then stepping in to a peculiarly Alexandrian argument about the relationship between mathematics and philosophy that played out in a particularly Alexandrian way.

Even more interesting is the way that some of Pappus's critiques are presented. In one of them, Pappus pastes together small pieces of the writings of Nicomachus of Gerasa to prove that Plato misunderstood the number of solids.[73] He refers to Nicomachus by name, but he classifies him as a Pythagorean. In another critique, in which he describes Plato as "most divine among philosophers," Pappus demonstrates a thorough knowledge of Plato's *Timaeus* that can only have come from close study of the text.[74]

These exchanges reveal the messy border between mathematics and philosophy. While Pappus may not have claimed the title philosopher for himself, he evidently had read deeply in both the Platonic and Pythagorean traditions. He not only knew their core texts, but he was also keeping up with contemporary interpretations of these texts. When Pappus responded to contemporary philosophical ideas with which he disagreed, he critiqued them using mathematics, but he did so in a way that both clearly appreciated the philosophical implications of his points and asserted that he could "outdo the philosophers" with his greater intellectual rigor.[75] Indeed, it is no surprise that later Byzantines marked Pappus as a philosopher, not a mathematician.[76]

In truth, Pappus was first and foremost an Alexandrian. Even at the turn of the fourth century CE, the great Alexandrian intellectual institutions continued to foster a sort of interdisciplinary conversation and interaction that most modern scholars would envy. And what was true of the school of Pappus was equally true of the school of his younger contemporary Theon.[77] Like Pappus, Theon is marked by later Byzantines as a philosopher.[78] Probably like Pappus, too, Theon may have disputed this identification as inaccurate, though his work about divination called "About signs and the examination of birds and the croaking of ravens" and his commentary on *The Cynic Epistle* might suggest otherwise.[79] At the same time, Theon likely followed Pappus and Nicomachus in understanding that numbers and the mathematical study of them enabled one to engage with a higher order of reality than theoretical philosophy permitted.[80] In the end, though, Theon came from the same Alexandrian environment that produced Pappus and fueled interactions like the one that Pappus had with Origen.

All of this suggests that Hypatia received her first exposure to philosophy in her father's school in a way that put philosophical texts in dialogue with mathematics. Hypatia quickly surpassed the level of philosophical teaching her father could provide, however, and she seems to have decided that her father wrongly subordinated philosophy to mathematics.[81] In the sixth century, the philosopher Damascius emphasizes that, because Hypatia was more intelligent than her father, Hypatia moved beyond his mathematical training and devoted herself to philosophy.[82] If we read Damascius in a modern context, it seems that he is here contrasting two very distinctive disciplines. Hypatia seems almost to be rebelling against her father by embracing a very different thought system from anything that he knew or understood. But Damascius does not mean this at all. Damascius was a devoted admirer of Iamblichus and, like all late Platonists, he understood that mathematics and philosophy were intimately related. What Damascius implies is not that Hypatia turned her back on mathematics in order to embrace philosophy but that she recalibrated the balance between the two. A philosopher like Damascius differed from a mathematician like Nicomachus neither because he read different texts nor because he disregarded the utility of the discipline embraced by his rival. They simply privileged different things. For Damascius, mathematical concepts were useful tools that helped one to better understand more important philosophical concepts. For Nicomachus, philosophical concepts helped one to understand the true significance of numbers.

Hypatia, then, did not abandon mathematics for philosophy. Damascius suggests that her study of philosophy convinced her to shift the balance between them. She learned enough philosophy to come to the conclusion that math served philosophy. In the view of a later philosopher like Damascius, this allowed her to push beyond the intellectual limits of her mathematician father. This was likely less of an intellectual conversion than it was a gradual epiphany born of Hypatia's reading of philosophical texts, but it was nonetheless extremely important. Hypatia's connection to Theon meant that privileging Platonism over the mathematical approach of Pappus and Theon would have had real significance. It signaled that Hypatia was prepared to move Alexandrian intellectual life in a new direction.

3

The School of Hypatia

Hypatia had already established herself as a formidable intellectual force in Alexandria by the time she reached her thirtieth birthday. She had been trained by her father, Theon, perhaps the foremost mathematician of his generation, and had worked under him to edit the mathematical texts of Ptolemy. She was Theon's best student and stood out to the Alexandrian intellectual establishment as the most promising mathematician in the city. However, she had also developed a sophisticated understanding of contemporary trends in philosophy. This had been true of other Alexandrian mathematicians in the fourth century, but it seems that, unlike her father, Hypatia saw in philosophy a better, more comprehensive way to understand truth. Before Hypatia, fourth-century Alexandrian philosophers seem to have been second-rate characters whose impact paled in comparison to the important mathematicians who presided over what has sometimes been called the "Silver Age" of ancient mathematics. With her mathematical bona fides beyond question, Hypatia's embrace of philosophy had the potential to shift the intellectual balance in the city from one that favored mathematicians to one that privileged the ideas of philosophers.

To do this, Hypatia needed to teach students to combine the mathematical rigor characteristic of the teaching of fourth century Alexandrian mathematicians like Pappus and Theon with the philosophical system of the Neoplatonists Plotinus and Porphyry. No one doubted that Hypatia had the necessary intellectual talent, but she needed an institutional structure in which to do this sort of teaching. Her father's school provided this. Theon turned the role of primary instructor over to Hypatia sometime in the early or mid-380s. The shift appears to have been a gradual one as Theon slowly stepped back into a sort of emeritus professorship.[1] Theon was around campus, but he had no regular instructional responsibilities.[2]

Theon's phased retirement followed a model that appears to have been common in late antiquity. Many teachers who were approaching old age gradually turned over more and more of the teaching in their school to their assistant teachers. In Athens in the 360s, for example, the teacher Prohaeresius held on to his civic chair in rhetoric well into his eighties, but he appears to have led none of the classes that the sophist Eunapius sat through during his years enrolled in at his school.[3] Three generations later, the Athenian philosopher Plutarch would interrupt his retirement only to teach the most promising pupils. Proclus, a brilliant student who would one day head Plutarch's school, was able to convince the nominal head of the school he had just joined to lead two tutorials on individual Platonic dialogues. Outside of those classes, however, Proclus studied under Plutarch's deputy Syrianus.[4] Even Libanius, who fought doggedly to continue teaching some classes until his death at age seventy-nine, seems to have entrusted most of the actual instruction of students to his deputies in his later years.[5]

While we do not know Theon's exact age when Hypatia took over the school in the 380s, it seems unlikely that he was much more than fifty-five at the time. This would make him the youngest professor known to have made the choice to become an emeritus. Although it is of course possible that Theon retired because of an illness from which he later recovered, there is a more likely, more interesting possibility.[6] Theon may have simply realized that Hypatia could offer a more innovative and comprehensive teaching in mathematics, astronomy, and philosophy than he could. If this is true, Theon stepped aside simply because Hypatia was better. Given Theon's age at the time, Hypatia may have assumed responsibility for managing the instruction given at the school while Theon remained the legally recognized teacher in charge until he was sixty. This arrangement would allow Theon to continue to claim the professorial exemption from the financial obligations to the city council that had shielded him for the past few decades. As a woman, Hypatia was not eligible for council service and would have been exempt from any of the financial obligations attached to her family property for as long as Theon lived.[7] After Theon turned 60, however, he became too old for council service, meaning that neither he nor Hypatia needed a professorial exemption.[8] This suggests that Hypatia became the effective head of the school in the 380s and its nominal head at some point in the 390s, at the very latest.

The Teaching of Hypatia

The school began to offer a much more comprehensive instruction in the teaching of Plato, Aristotle, and other philosophers under Hypatia's direction. To this point, we have discussed philosophy primarily as a system of thought that built upon and interacted with mathematics. This point of disciplinary intersection was real, but one must be careful not to overemphasize it. In the fourth century, philosophy was, in its most basic form, a system designed to inculcate specific virtues in an individual. If done correctly, philosophical education created a well-ordered soul that enabled the philosopher to form a close connection with the divine. At its pinnacle were theological ideas like those developed by commentators on Plato's *Timaeus*, but the pyramid these topped was quite broad at its base. From at least the time of Plotinus, there had been an emerging sense among Platonists that philosophical virtues were found in different forms depending upon the level of development of an individual soul.[9] This would, by the fifth century, develop into a scale of philosophical virtues that guided a philosopher's progress from the basic physical virtues all the way to those associated with pure understanding of the divine.[10]

This full system came after Hypatia, but the basic ideas behind it were well known to her.[11] The education of a philosopher represented the way in which she developed each of the specific virtues necessary for her to ascend to philosophy's highest peak. A student could not skip ahead. She needed a comprehensive training in logic, math, and other preparatory subjects that taught social and political virtues. This gave her the skills to do a high-level reading of Platonic theological texts. More importantly, she needed not just to understand these texts, but also to learn to organize her life according to the virtues that they taught.

The early philosophical education of Proclus gives a sense of how this training worked in practice. It followed a text-based curriculum that required the student to do close readings of philosophical texts, primarily those of Plato and Aristotle, under the supervision of a professor who explained their meaning by drawing on an old, extensive, and ever-expanding interpretative tradition. Although Proclus's higher-level instruction occurred in Athens, he started studying philosophy in Alexandria perhaps a decade after Hypatia died. His first course in philosophy consisted of "Aristotelian philosophy alongside of the philosopher Olympiodorus.... He also turned himself to the study of mathematics with Heron, a religious man, who had the perfect background for teaching."[12] Proclus would eventually move to Athens to study the rest of Aristotle's *Organon* and the dialogues of Plato, but the Alexandrian preliminary work he did on Aristotle and mathematics remained fundamental. Without it, he could never have properly understood the higher level Platonic training he received in Athens.

The place of mathematics in this lower-level philosophical instruction explains why Hypatia's teaching proved so appealing. As Theon's successor and most important collaborator, Hypatia had already established herself as an heir to the great Alexandrian mathematical tradition.[13] By deciding to teach both mathematics and higher-level philosophical texts in the same school, Hypatia could instruct students who wanted only a basic training in mathematics as well as those who sought a deeper, more integrated mathematical and philosophical education. Unlike Proclus, who needed to attend lessons in mathematics offered by Hero and classes in Aristotle offered by Olympiodorus, a student of Hypatia could stay in the same school for classes in mathematics, astronomy, Aristotelian logic, and Platonic theology. This would allow him or her to more clearly appreciate the interconnectedness of the two fields of mathematics and philosophy.

Hypatia's curriculum can only be reconstructed in an imprecise way, but it is clear that she offered a thorough and sophisticated training. Her own mathematical work suggests that she followed in Theon's footsteps when determining the mathematical curriculum. The philosophical texts that her students read show that her teaching in that area combined the discussion of canonical philosophical texts and the more recent interpretative traditions that had developed around them. Her students exchanged copies of philosophical commentaries written by the early third-century CE Aristotelian commentator Alexander of Aphrodisias, which helped them to craft a Platonic understanding of Aristotle's work.[14] They became familiar with Pythagorean concepts, an unsurprising thing given the way that Hypatia's interests blended mathematics and philosophy.[15] Her students also knew the *Life of Plotinus*, a text written around 300 CE by Plotinus's student Porphyry as an introduction to Porphyry's edition of the collected works of his teacher.[16] Because the *Life of Plotinus* circulated along with Plotinus's collected works, this suggests quite strongly that Hypatia's students also read Plotinus's *Enneads*.

Hypatia and the Neoplatonic Tradition

It is worth pausing for a moment to consider where Hypatia fits in the history of late antique philosophy. As the reading list of her students suggests, the Neoplatonists Porphyry and Plotinus provided the philosophical framework on which Hypatia based her teaching. Plotinian and Porphyrian teaching centers on the basic question of how the human soul departed from the immaterial world, the manner in which it descended into the world of matter, and the mechanisms through which it can find a path back. Plotinus, who lived from 204 to 270 CE, is often seen as the author whose writings first shaped Neoplatonism. In order to explain this process through which the soul departed, descended, and returned, Plotinus mapped a reality that emanates from the One, a transcendent first principle. According to Plotinus, the Intellect, an entity that derives from the One but exists as its perfect image, is the highest order of reality that the human mind can access. It is less than the One simply because it derives from the One. The Intellect bears responsibility for the organization of the material world. Beneath it is the Soul. A perfect image of the Intellect from which it derives, the Soul relates to the Intellect in the same way that the Intellect relates to the One. The Soul is responsible for the generation of the material world (Matter in Plotinian terminology). Unlike the Intellect and the One, the Soul has the power to interact with Matter in a way that enables it to serve as an intermediary between the corporeal world and the immaterial realm. The human soul is a fragment of the Soul that forgets its origin and dwells in the body, which is a product of the material world. The human soul can return to the immaterial reality through a process of developing higher-level virtues that permit it to remain unaffected by Matter and begin to again contemplate the One. If it develops these virtues, the soul then withdraws into its own immaterial being and rises to the world of the Intellect. At its most profound, this process can lead to the human soul seeing the One.

Porphyry (who lived from 232 or 234 until 305) did a great deal to develop and explore the practical implications of Plotinus's system. For Porphyry, the One of Plotinus came to be equated with a notion of a supreme God.[17] The Intellect and Soul could also be designated as Gods in Porphyry's theology, though Porphyry always affirmed the primacy of the One over these two others by identifying it as "First God" or "God over all."[18] The lines between the Soul and Intellect are even blurrier for Porphyry since, in his conception, both are associated with each other even in such fundamental acts as the creation of matter.[19] Even more confusing is Porphyry's apparent tendency to use the name "Father" to refer at different times to the One, the Intellect, and the Soul.[20] Although Porphyry's philosophical system worked off of the basic architecture charted by Plotinus, he was much more interested than his teacher in seeing it as enabling a sort of salvation through which the soul returned to its divine origin. For Porphyry, this was a religious undertaking, but it was one in which traditional pagan religious practices like sacrifice were essentially useless. Sacrifices were material acts performed in the material world that had the effect of pulling a soul away from the transcendent philosophical life it sought.[21] This points to another aspect common to the thought of both Plotinus and Porphyry. The materiality of the body and its concerns are things to be overcome. If they cannot be, the soul can become bound to the matter of the material world, confused, and unable to achieve the pure contemplation that leads it to union with God.[22]

Iamblichus, a Syrian philosopher and former student of Porphyry who lived from 245 to 325, represents the next step in the process of development. In a career that bridged the third and fourth centuries, Iamblichus brought together a number of the most important trends in mathematical and philosophical thought that had emerged across the previous two hundred years. At its highest level, Iamblichan Neoplatonism emphasized the study of the divine and functioned as a sort of pagan philosophical and religious training. It placed great emphasis upon the practice of theurgy, a set of rituals designed to make it possible for a person to purify her soul and enable her mind to ascend for a time to the heavenly world of pure thought.[23] These active elements were linked to a theoretical understanding of the divine expressed in the *Chaldean Oracles*. This work, said to be a set of divine teachings revealed to a Syrian named Julian the Theurgist, was seen by Iamblichan Neoplatonists as a holy book that provided clear statements about the divine and its relationship to the world.[24] To many Neoplatonists, the Chaldean texts even offered a clear theoretical explanation of how theurgy enabled divine ascent.[25] As a result, Iamblichans held that any true philosopher needed to understand Chaldean teachings.[26]

The importance of theurgy in the highest levels of the Iamblichan system impressed contemporaries and has led to a tendency among modern scholars to emphasize this element of Iamblichus's teaching.[27] This is undoubtedly one of the features that defined the Iamblichan system, but Iamblichus's thought was much fuller and more nuanced than the intense focus on theurgy suggests. Iamblichus taught the texts of Plato, Aristotle, and Pythagoras as well as elements culled from quasi-philosophical religious works like the *Chaldean Oracles* and the Orphic writings. Indeed, Iamblichan teaching had such appeal that by the end of the fifth century it had grown into the dominant philosophical approach across the eastern Mediterranean. It would ultimately help shape Byzantine and Renaissance Platonism. This is why modern histories of late antique philosophy tend to take a linear view of philosophical evolution, in which Platonism progressed steadily from Plotinus to Porphyry, from Porphyry to Iamblichus, and, ultimately, from the fourth-century disciples of Iamblichus to the Iamblichan-inspired Platonists of the later fifth and early sixth centuries. Along the way, it absorbed or outlasted the once distinctive teaching traditions of Aristotle and the Stoics.

Hypatia has always been an awkward fit in this story. What we can reconstruct of Hypatia's philosophical teaching seems to place her and her students firmly within the Plotinian and Porphyrian interpretative traditions but outside that of Iamblichus. Writing a generation after her death, Socrates Scholasticus anoints her the "heir to the Platonic interpretative tradition handed down from Plotinus" who explained "all philosophical doctrines to those who wished to hear." She was a popular teacher, he continues, whose instruction attracted "people from everywhere who wished to philosophize."[28]

Socrates is here being quite deliberate in the way that he describes Hypatia's teaching. Modern scholars often equate later Roman philosophy with the Neoplatonic tradition taught in Athens in the later fifth and early sixth centuries CE.[29] Socrates, who wrote before this Athenian tradition had taken form, understood a different philosophical ecosystem.

Philosophy in the fourth century was much more heterogeneous and diverse than we usually imagine. Indeed, it more closely resembled the intellectually robust world of the Hellenistic and Roman imperial periods than it did the Athenian Platonism of the early sixth century.[30] When Hypatia began teaching Platonic and Aristotelian texts in the last decades of the fourth century, philosophers in the empire still used a variety of approaches. In Constantinople, for example, Themistius presented an Aristotle-centered ecumenical philosophical training that included elements from the Platonic, Stoic, and perhaps even Epicurean traditions.[31] Other teachers based what they taught in part around the ideas of Platonists like Porphyry or even an integrative philosophical system developed by the mathematician Ptolemy that probably differed little in practical terms from the teaching of Pappus.[32] As late as the end of the fifth century, there are also mentions of a philosophical system based upon "the writings of Plato, Aristotle, or Plotinus," a system that sounds very much like that which Socrates attributes to Hypatia.[33]

As Socrates Scholasticus suggests, Hypatia was very much a transitional figure. When she received her philosophical instruction in the 370s, knowledge of Plotinus and Porphyry was widespread across the Mediterranean, but only the relatively small groups of philosophers who had either learned from Iamblichus himself or from Iamblichus's own students seem to have absorbed his system. Iamblichan ideas spread to new locations only when one of these individuals physically brought books and ideas with him or her. So, for example, the Iamblichan system first reached the city of Athens in the luggage carried by a nephew of the philosopher Iamblichus in the 360s.[34]

No Iamblichans are known to have been in Alexandria at such an early date, and this makes it highly unlikely that Hypatia would have been exposed to Iamblichus's ideas when she was studying philosophy in the 370s. By the time of Hypatia's death, however, things were very different. Iamblichan teaching had become entrenched in the Athenian school of Plutarch—the site from which it would eventually colonize much of the Eastern Mediterranean. In Alexandria, too, Iamblichans begin appearing in our sources perhaps as early as the 380s and are known to have been teaching in the city by the early 390s.[35] While it is unlikely that Hypatia would have been exposed to Iamblichan ideas when she was a student, she certainly would have known Iamblichans and had access to their texts during her teaching career. This access does not mean that Hypatia necessarily became an Iamblichan, however. There is a big difference between a teacher learning of the ideas of Iamblichus while still a student and a teacher who later adapts her ongoing teaching in light of them. Porphyry, for example, taught Iamblichus and knew a great deal about the system that Iamblichus later developed, but this knowledge made him a critic of it rather than a devotee.[36]

There is no evidence to show that Hypatia engaged with Iamblichus's work either as a devotee or a critic.[37] Her surviving editorial work betrays no Iamblichan influence, but one would not really expect to find such a thing in an edition of Ptolemy's *Almagest*. Her pupil Synesius is often used to try to reconstruct what Hypatia's philosophical system might have been like, but he too makes no mention of the Syrian philosopher, and his works show little notable Iamblichan influence.[38] In his treatise on dream divination and in his hymns, Synesius does show some familiarity with the *Chaldean Oracles*, but this text was known to Porphyry as well as Gnostic Christians.[39] Engagement with these materials in a non-Iamblichan context was common in the late antique cultural environment and Synesius's knowledge of them cannot be conclusive evidence of Iamblichan sympathies.

It is tempting to imagine that Hypatia would always seek to incorporate the most cutting-edge, Iamblichan readings of such a text into her courses but professors can be hesitant to embrace new textual approaches. Often, established teachers simply do not believe that a new approach to an established curriculum is correct. Even professors who see the merit of some new interpretations of a text may decide not to make radical changes to classes they have already been teaching. Synesius's use of the *Chaldean Oracles* may suggest that Hypatia worked from an Iamblichan paradigm. It is equally possible that she continued to approach Chaldean texts in a Porphyrian manner that takes seriously the theological implications of the text but denies the utility of theurgy and sacrifices.[40] Synesius's references to the text do not represent definitive evidence for either point.

In the end, we must come back to Socrates Scholasticus's assertion that Hypatia headed the Plotinian tradition of Platonic teaching. He says, in essence, that Hypatia was a Plotinian Platonist and not an Iamblichan Platonist, a Themistian Aristotelian, or any other breed of philosopher.[41] Given the range of philosophical approaches still possible during Hypatia's lifetime, this remained a meaningful distinction to make. It is also one that Socrates was qualified to appreciate.[42] Elsewhere in his *Ecclesiastical History*, Socrates mentions that he studied under the

teachers Ammonius and Helladius, two Alexandrians who had participated in religious mysteries organized by the Iamblichan Neoplatonist
Olympus in 392.[43] Socrates knew the difference between Hypatia and
an Iamblichan Platonist. His classification of Hypatia as the heir of the
Plotinian Platonic tradition should therefore not be seen as an ignorant
comment to be disregarded but as a detail that he deliberately mentions
to define her.

Christians in Hypatia's School

Hypatia's Plotinian- and Porphyrian-influenced teaching may seem out
of step with cutting-edge late fourth-century philosophical interpretations, but her approach proved to be particularly well-suited to the
needs of Alexandrian students. By the 380s, Alexandria was a Christian
majority city, and most of the students who entered Hypatia's school
from Alexandria and neighboring regions would have been Christians.
This is not as surprising as it might first seem. While most of the best-
known philosophers of the fourth and fifth centuries were devotees of
traditional religion, philosophy remained a vital part of the ancient
world's cultural inheritance. While they could disagree about specific
philosophical points, both Christians and pagans saw value in the virtues philosophy cultivated.

In Hypatia's case, the Christians in her school included figures
such as the Libyan aristocrat Synesius and his brothers Eutropius and
Alexander, the sophist Athanasius, and Synesius's friend Olympius.[44]
It is important to emphasize, however, that these students understood
their confessional identity in their own individual ways. Although most
of Hypatia's students would probably classify themselves as Christians,
this did not mean that they shared the same beliefs or religious practices. Not only were there major divisions within Christianity in the
later fourth century,[45] but self-identified Christians attended festivals
dedicated to the gods, experimented with Jewish dietary practices,
and persisted in celebrating holidays in ways that church leaders condemned as improper. As this suggests, people who identified themselves as Christians in the fourth century still did and believed a broad
range of things that their clergy condemned.[46]

It is here that the real strength of Hypatia's teaching becomes clear.
Christians remained deeply interested in philosophy in the later fourth

century, but the theurgic ritual practices that represented a key part of Iamblichan Platonism were unmistakably pagan. This likely prevented most Christians from pursuing high-level study under Iamblichan-influenced teachers when an alternative existed. Hypatia offered this alternative. The tradition of Plotinus and Porphyry frowned upon the ritual elements that Iamblichus championed.[47] It instead emphasized that unity with God could be achieved through contemplation rather than ritual. The appeal of this teaching went beyond simply offering Christian students a philosophical system that did not inherently conflict with the basic commandment against sacrifice. Porphyry also conceived of the Platonic divine hierarchy in ways that could be seen as quite close to Christian ideas of the Trinity.[48] Christian students of Hypatia could then practice Platonic philosophy in a way that was philosophically sound and not radically inconsistent with Christian theology.[49]

Some of the hymns written by Synesius in the years immediately following his departure from Hypatia's school show the relatively seamless ways in which the Platonism of Hypatia could blend with Christian ideas. *Hymn* 1, for example, asserts the necessity of exchanging worldly concerns for divine contemplation. It works equally well as a Platonic call to philosophy and as a Christian invocation of God "the Father of all things." Its opening lines contain a series of metaphors that compare the glory of divine contemplation with the folly of pursuing gold, honor, and treasure. There is nothing particularly pagan or Christian about these themes; they are equally at home in the philosophy of Porphyry and in the work of Synesius's Christian contemporary John Chrysostom.[50] *Hymn* 1 changes in its fifty-second line from Synesius's yearning to unite with God into a description of God's nature and the path through which the soul can return to God. Synesius then lays out a version of the cosmos that again works for both Platonists and Christians. It is a divine reality headed by a transcendent God with three distinctive aspects. The first of these turns the heavens, the second presides over the angels, and the third takes an earthly form in order to look after mortal things. The hymn ends by affirming that the soul can reunite with God only if it is sufficiently purified by philosophy.[51]

This hymn draws heavily on Platonic concepts of divine emanation developed by Plotinus and Porphyry, but the cosmic structure it describes also works as a philosophical model of the Christian Trinity. *Hymn* 1 was not written simply to lay out this divine structure, however. The discussion of God's nature explains why union with God is possible and why Synesius seeks it so earnestly. Synesius also speaks about what philosophical union with the divine is like. It was available only to a small, elect group of philosophical initiates and achieved, "through mysteries without rites," a clear indication that this was not an Iamblichan union arising from theurgy but more of a Plotinian and Porphyrian union achieved through contemplation.[52] Average people could neither aspire to this union nor could they take a ritual short-cut to reach it. Perhaps just as importantly, one's philosophical attainments, not one's confessional identity, made this union possible.

While *Hymn* 1 celebrates philosophical union with God, it contains no explicit reference to the Trinity or any other clearly Christian concept. Other Synesian *Hymns* do contain these Christian markers, but they are not any less philosophical than *Hymn* 1. *Hymn* 4, for example, begins with an appeal to a God who grants "a life which earthly care, mother of griefs, mother of sufferings, does not trample." This resembles the call to a life without earthly concerns found in *Hymn* 1.[53] Like *Hymn* 1, *Hymn* 4 also asks that God enable Synesius to keep his life "purified" of earthly concerns so that he will not "be turned away from God by delusions that lead one astray."[54] Synesius then proceeds to describe how God's help compels demons to flee from his "pure prayer" that "the happy servants who occupy the depths and heights of the universe" bear up to their Creator. As in *Hymn* 1, the body of *Hymn* 4 lays out the structure of the cosmos. The language used, however, is more clearly Christian. Synesius sings to the Father who is the Creator, his "Offspring, the First-born, the First-appearing," and the Holy Spirit, whom Synesius describes as the "Center of the Creator and Center again of the Son." This is, Synesius claims, a Unity and a Trinity at once. It also has the power to wall Synesius's soul off from demons and permit him to live "a life purified of matter" and devoted to contemplation.

While the terms used to describe God and the three forms in which He is manifested are recognizably Christian, there is no real structural difference between the cosmology that Synesius develops in *Hymn* 1 and that which appears in *Hymn* 4. Both are, in their ways, Platonic variations on a Porphyrian idea of a single divine principle with three aspects present in the same reality.[55] For modern readers, however, the concept of the Trinity and Christian markers like the Son and Holy Spirit flag *Hymn* 4 as something different. Although there is now a growing consensus that Synesius was always a Christian, for many years it was supposed that *Hymn* 1 reflected a moment in Synesius's life before he had converted to Christianity and *Hymn* 4 represented a moment after his conversion.[56] But this is not the natural way to understand these works. *Hymn* 1 was, after all, a poem celebrating a philosophical union with God. It could have done this in unmistakably Christian language, but the *Hymn* succeeds perfectly well as a call to philosophical union with a Christian God even without any explicitly Christian language. Similarly, there are plausible (though, admittedly, not particularly likely) ways to read *Hymn* 4 as a non-Christian composition. We miss the point if we try to use Synesius's *Hymns* to trace his confessional development or mark the moment of his supposed conversion to Christianity. Synesius's *Hymns* showcased his status as a philosopher rather than his confessional identity. They were not written to mark his membership in a Christian community. They instead celebrated a philosophical union with God that Synesius learned was possible through the teaching of Hypatia.

None of this suggests that Hypatia's teaching pandered to Christians or diluted Platonism to make it palatable to them. Hypatia offered her students a rigorous philosophical education that moved progressively through the scale of virtues a philosopher was expected to master. Synesius clearly understood this. He repeatedly represented himself as a philosopher concerned primarily with living a life that remained true to philosophical principles. Synesius developed this absolute fidelity to philosophy under Hypatia and it was to his fellow students that he most eagerly proclaimed it.[57] This seems to have been the true hallmark of the philosophical instruction that Hypatia provided. Hypatia encouraged her students to develop an identity as philosophers rooted in the promise of union with the divine. She emphasized to them that philosophy was an all-encompassing pursuit, and that union was possible only if one organized his or her life according to philosophical virtues. While Hypatia's readings of individual Platonic and Aristotelian texts may be lost to us, we can still see the larger message of her teaching. We can also understand its broad appeal to both pagan and Christian students in the 380s and early 390s.

Hypatia took over as the primary teacher in her father's school at a transformative moment in the intellectual history of both Alexandria and the wider Mediterranean. When Hypatia began her education, mathematicians and scientists dominated the Alexandrian intellectual landscape. The city's philosophers seem to have been reduced to sniping ineffectively at powerful mathematicians like Pappus whose philosophical knowledge rivaled theirs but whose reputations far surpassed them. Hypatia provided a recalibration of the city's intellectual dynamics. Her school offered a mathematical instruction that rivaled the best of what Pappus once provided, but it broke from Pappus and his successors by marking the Platonic philosophy of Plotinus and Porphyry as the peak of its training. We know of no Alexandrian teacher who would ever again see mathematics as anything but a lower-order training for Platonic philosophy. Hypatia deserves a great deal of the responsibility for this shift.

Hypatia also began teaching at a profound moment of change in the intellectual direction of the Hellenic world. Her generation was perhaps the last to be able to experience anything approaching the diverse and heterogeneous marketplace of philosophical ideas typical of the Hellenistic and Roman imperial periods. She overlapped with the last teachers known to privilege Aristotle over Plato as well as the last who admit to teaching Epicurean ideas in their classrooms. Her younger contemporaries were instrumental in ensuring the fifth- and sixth- century dominance of Iamblichan Platonic thought. Hypatia sat very much between these two worlds. She was a Platonist like all other celebrated philosophers who came after her, but she was not interested in the ritualized elements of Iamblichan philosophy that would come to dominate the tradition in the decades after her death. Instead she taught a sort of retro-Neoplatonism based on the ideas of Plotinus and Porphyry that emphasized contemplation over ritual.

Hypatia's Platonism may not have been the Platonism of the future, but it was perfectly pitched for the time and city in which she lived. The emphasis that Hypatia's teaching placed on a contemplative union with the divine ensured that both Christian and pagan students could benefit from it. This enabled the rapidly growing population of Christians in and around Alexandria to access a philosophy that did not conflict with their ideas about appropriate religious practices. Like Synesius, they could become philosophers and remain Christians. Developments in religious life and philosophical thought in the fifth century eroded the long-term effect of her work, but, for the better part of a decade, Hypatia stood on the empire's intellectual cutting edge. Few men or women can make a more impressive claim.

4

Middle Age

As the 380s gave way to the 390s, Hypatia faced many of the same professional and personal challenges encountered by midcareer professionals in the modern world. By her thirty-fifth birthday, Hypatia had created a distinctive brand of philosophical teaching that combined the rigor of the leading Alexandrian mathematicians with the sophistication of Plotinian and Porphyrian Platonism. Hypatia's impeccable training and tremendous skill in mathematics enabled her to shift the balance between mathematics and philosophy in the Mediterranean's foremost center of mathematical and scientific scholarship. Indeed, Hypatia's career marked such a point of division between two intellectual eras that one could say that she was both the last great Alexandrian mathematician trained in the tradition of Pappus and the first Neoplatonist to be accepted by the Alexandrian intellectual establishment.[1]

Even the most intelligent and impactful scholars often struggle to find their second act. This was no less true of Hypatia. While she achieved a great deal in the 380s, the world around Hypatia began to change dramatically as the 390s dawned. The steady expansion of Iamblichan teaching into leading centers of scholarship like Alexandria and Athens meant that Hypatia's Plotinian- and Porphyrian-inspired teaching began to look increasingly dated. While she had prevailed over the mathematicians in the 380s, she looked dangerously out of step with the direction in which philosophy was moving in the 390s. The emergence of a militant anti-pagan tendency among some Alexandrian Christians in the early years of the decade presented a different sort of challenge. The nonconfessional intellectual middle ground that

Hypatia cultivated continued to draw elite Christian students like Synesius who valued traditional education. The wider world, however, became increasingly polarized in the 390s as a toxic combination of anti-pagan imperial legislation and aggressive actions against pagans by Alexandria's Christian leadership destabilized the city. Both developments proved challenging for Hypatia.

After a lull following the death of the pagan emperor Julian in 363 and the arrest of some of the Iamblichan teachers who advised him, Iamblichan teaching began to regain momentum in the 380s. This took place in many cities of the Eastern Mediterranean, but in no place was the growth of Iamblichanism more consequential than in Athens. This was because Athens had a unique identity as an educational center in late antiquity.[2] While the expansion of government and the growth of well-paying administrative positions had begun to transform the schools of many cities across the Roman world, Athens stood apart. It continued to attract significant numbers of students who sought to be trained as educated gentlemen, and, because of this, it was somewhat immune to the economic tides that forced newer, less prestigious centers of learning to adapt their teaching to meet the needs of the empire's aspiring bureaucrats.[3]

Athenian schools could do this because their city enjoyed a particular sort of cachet that other cities lacked. Athens was, after all, the birthplace of the Academy, the Lyceum, and the Stoa Poikile, as well as the home of luminaries like Plato, Demosthenes, Lysias, and Socrates. Students chose to study in Athens in part so that they could commune with the ghosts of these legends, in the very spaces in which these rhetorical and philosophical giants once walked. But Athens was more than a museum to the Hellenic past. Athenian teachers and their students traded on the particular sense that the place was special and distinctive. The sophist Libanius claimed that, as a youth in the 330s, he was intoxicated by tales of the greatness of the teachers of Athens and the exciting student culture they nurtured.[4] Other former Athenian students spoke about ritual initiations in which they were led them into a bathhouse in the center of the Agora before being permitted to don their academic gowns.[5] Athenian students also developed a culture of hazing that reinforced one's sense that studying in an Athenian school made one truly distinctive.[6]

All of this fostered the notion that a person who had studied in Athens owned a cultural pedigree that give him greater standing than someone who had studied in another city. The dynamic was not that different from the modern idea that a degree from Oxbridge or the Ivy League somehow attests to the qualities of a person. As one would expect, people who had not attended schools in Athens tended to push back against this in much the same way that a Berkeley graduate pushes against the conceit of Harvard. Synesius once wrote to his brother that he felt compelled to visit Athens so that he would "no longer have to prostrate himself before those who went there for their education. They differ in no way from us mere mortals."[7] They understand Plato and Aristotle as well as we do, Synesius continues, yet they "raise themselves above us as demigods because they have seen the Academy, the Lyceum, and the Stoa Poikile."[8]

For most of the fourth century, this attitude about Athenian superiority concerned mainly students who pursued rhetorical study there. Athens had been a philosophical backwater since the middle of the third century. Longinus, the leading Athenian philosopher of the third century, had once trained Porphyry before Porphyry abandoned his school for the more intellectually stimulating circle of Plotinus. After Longinus's execution by the emperor Aurelian in 273, no Athenian philosophers of note appear in our sources for over a century.[9] While Longinus knew of the ideas of Plotinus, there is no sign of Iamblichan Neoplatonism reaching Athens before the 360s. When Iamblichan teaching arrived, its first devotees were was a small group of wealthy eccentrics. They included a man named Nestorius who is said to have used theurgy to prevent an earthquake[10] and deployed Iamblichan-influenced psychotherapy to cure a depressed woman of memories of her past lives.[11] Nestorius was certainly an interesting character, but he was not the sort of man to start an enduring philosophical school.

The historical prestige of Athenian philosophers meant that the city had considerable untapped potential as a center of Iamblichan philosophical study, if an innovative and effective teacher could establish himself or herself there. It was not until the 390s that such a figure emerged. His name was Plutarch and he was either the son or grandson of Nestorius.[12] But Plutarch was not an oddball like his ancestor. He was a skilled philosopher who combined an acute understanding of Platonic texts, a well-developed understanding of theurgy, and a natural charisma.[13] Plutarch was also from a prominent Athenian family that had long played a public role in the civic life of his city.[14] He was the perfect figure to revitalize Athenian philosophy through the introduction of Iamblichan ideas.

The combination of Plutarch's philosophical skill and Athens's reputation quickly made his school a viable rival to the circle of Hypatia. This is not to say that the schools were identical. They were not. Hypatia offered a purely contemplative path to the divine and had no interest in theurgy at all. While Hypatia's training had a distinctive attraction to elite Christians in Alexandria, Plutarch had no interest in appealing to that population. He offered his most advanced students a Platonic education that joined the study of text and the perfection of rituals to allow students to approach the divine in an Iamblichan fashion. This had no appeal to Christian students, but Athens did not have a particularly prominent or powerful Christian community in the fourth century.[15] Even if it did, Plutarch, who three times sponsored the Panathenaic procession, would have cared little about appealing to Athenian Christians anyway.[16] His philosophical program was unapologetically pagan, and it thus provided the very sort of education that a certain group of pagan students craved. These were students like the Alexandrians Syrianus and Hierocles as well as Proclus, a native of Constantinople who would defect to Plutarch after finding Alexandrian teaching inadequate.[17]

Hypatia had little to offer pagan students like these, but her disciples clearly felt that the school of Plutarch represented a new sort of challenge to which they needed to respond. Upon his return from Athens, Synesius wrote to his brother about how inferior the place and its teachers were to Hypatia's Alexandria. The letter is a delightful takedown of the place and the pretensions of those who taught and studied there. Synesius begins by saying how much wiser he feels for having visited Athens. The proof, he continues, is that he has learned that "Athens now has nothing worthwhile but famous names."[18] The city, he continues, is like a burnt carcass from which all living philosophy has disappeared.[19] Thus, "in our time, Egypt nourishes the fruits it receives from Hypatia, but Athens, which used to be the city of the wise, now has only its beekeepers to bring it honor." This is the case, he concludes, with "the pair of Plutarchans, who attract young people to their classrooms not by the reputation of their arguments but with pots of honey from Hymettus," the mountain on which Athens's famous beehives were located.[20]

Synesius's wonderfully biting letter shows that Hypatia's students understood the Athenian school of Plutarch to be a real rival to that of their teacher. It also reveals that Synesius refused to recognize Plutarch and his Alexandrian-born assistant Syrianus as serious philosophers.[21] In his mind, they were not philosophers but sophists, a term he uses deliberately in a way that does not reflects its contemporary fourth-century usage but the old Platonic distinction between true philosophers like Socrates and scholastic profiteers like the sophist Gorgias.[22] His choice of this term was quite deliberate. It emphasized that Plutarch and Syrianus peddled ideas that had no substance and attracted students who wanted easy rewards instead of intellectual challenges. This implicitly criticized the flashiness of Plutarchan-sytle teaching and the magical shortcut to divine union that Synesius felt that theurgy promised. But Synesius was also acknowledging that Plutarch's teaching had an easy and powerful appeal to certain types of students who did not respond to Hypatia.

While Plutarch was the most formidable of Hypatia's Iamblichan rivals, he was not the only one. Iamblichan-influenced teachers began appearing in the area around Alexandria probably by the middle of the 380s. The first such figure about whom any information survives is Antoninus, the son of the female philosopher Sosipatra.[23] An eccentric, Antoninus did not lead a school or an organized circle of disciples. Instead, he apparently practiced philosophy on the grounds of the temple of Serapis in the Alexandrian suburb of Canopus and answered the philosophical questions posed by visitors to the temple.[24] He "displayed no tendency towards theurgy," however, and would refuse to speak to anyone about religious rituals.[25] While it is likely that Antoninus introduced some Alexandrians to the philosophical interpretations of Iamblichus, it is hard to imagine that his influence was particularly pronounced or long-standing.

Antoninus died at some point before 392 but other Iamblichans had set up schools in Alexandria by the time of his death. The most notable among them was a teacher named Olympus. Like Antoninus, Olympus was a transplant from Asia Minor. Unlike his circumspect contemporary, Olympus had no problem teaching "the rules of divine worship, the ancient traditions, and the happiness that accompanied them" to students within the city of Alexandria.[26] Olympus ran a conventional school in classrooms located on the site of Alexandria's Serapeum.[27] It seems likely that he also instructed at least some of his students in theurgy. Olympus lacked the intellectual credentials of Hypatia and his teaching had little appeal to the Christian students who found a home in her school, but he did offer students a credible and more modern interpretation of Plato. While Olympus's emphasis on pagan rituals meant that he could not pose a serious threat to Hypatia's primacy in Alexandria, his relative success did point to the fact that some Alexandrians sought a different sort of philosophical training than that which Hypatia provided.

Outside events prevented Alexandrian Iamblichan teachers like Olympus from seriously challenging Hypatia in the 390s. Hypatia had grown up during a period that might be called the "little peace of the temples." This era between the accession of the pagan emperor Julian in 361 and the mid-380s saw pagan temples opened, the legal toleration of sacrifices, and imperial officials who first encouraged and then essentially tolerated many traditional religious practices.[28] It was also a perfect moment for Hypatia to develop a nonconfessional philosophy that offered a contemplative path to union with the divine without explicitly specifying the Christian or non-Christian character of that highest divine power.

By the mid-380s, the changing religious climate in both the city of Alexandria and the empire at large made it harder to imagine a nonconfessional approach to divinity. The change began with a law issued by the Eastern emperor Theodosius in 381 banning nighttime sacrifices and making it illegal for people to approach a temple for the purpose of sacrificing.[29] This law was followed up in late 382 with another effectively banning worshippers from entering temples in the East and a set of Western initiatives through which the emperor Gratian removed the financial support that the state had long provided to traditional Roman religion.[30]

The last years of the 380s saw the assault on traditional religion take a different form. In the East, a party of monks and bishops traveling alongside the praetorian prefect Cynegius destroyed temples in Mesopotamia and Syria and sacked shrines in Egypt between 386 and 388.[31] These same years saw bishops, monks, and imperial officials take other actions against temples in Syria and Mesopotamia.[32] These individual temple destructions made little tangible difference in an empire that had once contained perhaps one million temples, but the symbolic effect of these actions was undeniable.[33] By the later 380s, devotees of traditional religion understood that the public practice of their religion was now facing an existential threat—and they feared that the private practice of it might be the next target.

The situation for pagans within Alexandria was even more dire. The city had seen remarkable and sustained growth in the size of its Christian population throughout the fourth century. At the same time, conflicts within the Christian community about how to interpret the Council of Nicaea and whether or not to accept its findings meant that Alexandrian bishops had been mostly unconcerned with taking actions against traditional religion in the city. This changed with the selection of Theophilus as Alexandrian patriarch in 385.[34] Theophilus came into office as a young Nicene Christian patriarch who served under a young Nicene Christian emperor. This had significant advantages for him because, unlike many of his predecessors, Theophilus faced no threat of being deposed by an emperor who favored a different creed. But it also brought with it significant challenges. The regular liturgical celebration of Alexandrian martyr bishops and the commemoration of the multiple exiles of the bishop Athanasius had conditioned Nicene Christian Alexandrians to measure the quality of their bishop in part by looking at the way that he fought for Christian principles against hostile imperial officials.[35] Theophilus served under a friendly emperor who agreed with his Christology, and this meant that he could not define his Christian piety by taking a dramatic stand against the imperial court.

Theophilus chose instead to demonstrate his Christian bona fides by going even further than the emperor in acting against traditional religion.[36] As the religious restrictions of the early 380s and the anti-pagan actions of the later years of the decade began to bite, it seems that Alexandrian pagans began to engage in regular public protests.[37] These likely intensified in late 391 when a new set of imperial laws reiterated the bans on public sacrifice and entry to pagan temples for religious purposes while adding to them a severe punishment for officials who failed to observe these earlier prohibitions.[38] Christians appear to have occasionally egged the pagans on during these years, but in early 392 Theophilus ratcheted tensions up further.[39] In that year he asked for and received imperial permission to renovate an imperial basilica. This civic building had been given to a non-Nicene bishop of Alexandria in the 350s, but it had since fallen into disuse. When the renovations began, Theophilus's workers found the remains of an old underground shrine that contained disused pagan cultic objects.[40] Seeing this as an opportunity to mock traditional religion in public, Theophilus led a parade of "tokens of the bloody mysteries" and used them to make fun of "the dens of iniquity and caverns of sin" that pagan shrines represented.[41]

The laws banning traditional religious activities, the random temple destructions, and the parades in which pagan ritual objects were mocked in public would no doubt have irritated Hypatia. She was a pagan, and she certainly understood that these new laws impinged on traditional religious practices. At the same time, Hypatia's philosophy promised a purely contemplative path toward union with the divine. Because this required no rituals or temple visits, the new laws did not threaten her philosophical or religious practices. They were objectionable, and Hypatia may have believed them to be unjust, but they did not threaten her. This was not true of Iamblichans like Olympus. For a follower of the Iamblichan tradition, rituals and even temple visits were integral parts of the path to philosophical union with the divine. Iamblichans could not practice their philosophy properly under these new conditions. In Alexandria, they and their students refused to accept the restrictions the empire now placed upon them.

Theophilus's provocation took things even further. Not only did the philosophers and their disciples find their religious practices restricted, but they now had to suffer the indignity of being publicly mocked. The frustration that had been building for years finally boiled over into an open riot. Christian sources describe pagan mobs that "began to behave violently and to vent their fury in public." "They used weapons, battling up and down the streets so that the two sides (pagan and Christian) were at open war."[42] It is unclear whether Olympus, his colleagues, and their students instigated this violence, but they quickly assumed control of it. After seizing a number of Christian prisoners, the rioters retreated to the Serapeum hill, the monumental temple and classroom complex that could be likened to the Acropolis of Alexandria.[43] They then blocked the entrances, used the temple mount as a base for guerilla operations, transformed parts of it into a prison to hold Christian captives, and snuck through its tunnels to make occasional raids into the city.[44]

The Serapeum hill proved impregnable to the forces available to the civilian and military administrators of Egypt. This led to a standoff during which the Serapeum defenders deferred to the leadership of Olympus. He exercised such power that a later philosopher wrote of him that "nobody's soul was so inflexible and barbarous that it was not persuaded and charmed by the words which flowed from his divine mouth."[45] A devotee of Serapis in particular, Olympus "used to gather together all of those around him and teach them the rules of divine worship, the ancient traditions, and the happiness . . . sent by the gods to those who defend them."[46] Traditional religion may have been suppressed and mocked elsewhere in the empire, but the violent resistance of the Serapeum defenders had carved out one small island on which Iamblichan-tinged, philosophically inspired religious rituals could still be conducted.

It would not last. When imperial officials in Alexandria failed to resolve the standoff, they wrote to the emperor Theodosius for guidance. The emperor's response made it clear how he hoped the situation would be concluded. A Christian source says that Theodosius issued a blanket amnesty to the pagan rioters, declared the Christians killed in the violence to be martyrs, and ordered the pagan cults in the city "to be done away with (so that) the reason for the conflict would disappear."[47] While the last provision is unlikely, it is reasonable to imagine that the emperor's letter contained either an implicit or explicit condition that amnesty for the rioters would be contingent on their departure from the temple compound. With a military siege of the Serapeum mount the likely consequence if the pagans failed to disperse, the defenders quietly melted away. A Christian crowd then swarmed the temple, seized the property in its treasury, and hacked apart the monumental statue of Serapis that was the most prominent representation of his cult (see Figure 4.1).

Many of the pagan teachers who had defended the Serapeum fled the city soon after this.[48] After leading his followers in a daylong service worshipping Serapis "according to the ancient custom," Olympus prophesized that the god would abandon the temple.[49] Olympus apparently followed the god; he is never heard from again in any of our sources. Other teachers involved in the Serapeum defense also fled the city. The grammarians Helladius and Ammonius moved to Constantinople, where they would both teach the future ecclesiastical historian Socrates Scholasticus. Socrates said that both men spoke proudly about their roles in the Serapeum siege. Ammonius complained about the abuse done to traditional religion before the violence started, and Helladius bragged about killing nine men with his own hands during the defense of the temple.[50] Despite the emperor's amnesty, some of the pagan intellectuals who remained in the city may have lost their jobs in the riot's aftermath.[51]

The next few years saw a dramatic refashioning of the sacred space of both Alexandria and the empire. In the fall of 392, Theodosius

FIGURE 4.1. Theophilus standing atop a bust of Serapis. Marginal illustration from an early fifth-century Alexandrian chronicle.

Credit Line: From Bauer and Strygowski, *Eine Alexandrinische Weltchronik* (Vienna, 1905), Fig. VI verso.

issued a law banning both public and private sacrifices throughout the empire.[52] The Serapeum settlement emboldened Theophilus to undertake a campaign to transform Alexandria. Using the money taken from the treasuries of the temples of Serapis in Alexandria and Canopus, Theophilus built a "massive" and "very much decorated" shrine housing the remains of John the Baptist and the prophet Elisha on the site of the Alexandrian temple.[53] He built a monastery on the Serapeum site in Canopus and may well have added one in Alexandria, too.[54] Theophilus also turned the richly adorned Alexandrian Tychaion into a wine shop and even sponsored a campaign of organized vandalism through which images of Serapis were ripped from the walls of Alexandrian buildings.[55]

The Serapeum destruction killed the community of Iamblichans emerging in Alexandria in the later fourth century. In its aftermath, their leadership scattered, and their students presumably did as well.

While some of the classroom space on the site may well have survived the battles of 392 and the subsequent construction projects undertaken by Theophilus, whatever was left undamaged could never again serve as the evocative location that, in Olympus's hands, once so powerfully blended the sacred and the philosophical.[56] Perhaps even more importantly, the fervor and enthusiasm of the Iamblichans had done real, serious, and irreversible damage to the religious infrastructure of Alexandria. It is unlikely that very many Alexandrian pagans had an appetite for more.

Hypatia could have dealt with the elimination of her Alexandrian Iamblichan competitors by co-opting elements of their teaching, adapting the content of her own instruction to reflect at least some of the ideas of Iamblichus, and attempting to draw some of the former students of Olympus into her classes. This would, however, carry significant risks and uncertain rewards. Not only would Hypatia have to retrain herself in the middle of her career, but she was unlikely to keep these radicalized pagan students even if they did enroll initially. She did not share the Iamblichan idea that a connection with the divine required theurgy, and she did not teach the rituals that Olympus and his counterparts practiced. Although Olympus was gone, the school of Plutarch in Athens still beckoned pagan Alexandrian students who wanted this sort of training. In addition, the prominent role played by Iamblichans like Olympus in the Serapeum riot had significantly discredited them. It is likely that only the most militant pagan Alexandrians would now seek this sort of training.

Hypatia instead decided to embrace more deeply some of the distinctive elements of the philosophy she had already been teaching. As the next chapter will show, Hypatia privileged the philosophical love that her students felt for her and for each other above the cultic rituals and theurgic training that had become the hallmark of the school of Olympus. The deep affection that this created between members of the school bound them while they studied, but it was also strong enough that their friendships endured after they returned home. As Chapter 6 will discuss, Hypatia also embraced the idea that a philosopher needed to play a public role in the life of her city. She was a philosopher who could work well with both the emerging Alexandrian Christian majority and the city's political establishment. After a pagan rebellion led by a very different sort of philosopher, the city seems to have welcomed her moderation. We know nothing about her relationships with Christian clergy, but her Christian students seem to have gotten along well with them. Theophilus even officiated at the wedding of Synesius.[57]

By the middle years of the 390s, Hypatia's school had taken on a distinctive profile defined more by the close relationships its members built with one another and the role they played in the world than the confessional identities they claimed. This was a natural outgrowth of the teaching she offered, but it was also a welcome antidote to the violence and division that had gripped Alexandria in the early 390s. Philosophy no longer needed to serve as a wedge that drove pagans and Christians apart. Under Hypatia's direction, philosophy instead offered a set of principles according to which all Alexandrians could better organize their lives and their city. She then offered a way forward in which Alexandrian philosophers could help the city, its leaders, and its intellectuals move on from the catastrophe of 392 in a fashion that preserved both the Christian character of the city and its role as a major center of scholarship. This was probably the most important service an Alexandrian philosopher could provide her home city in the mid-390s.

5

A Philosophical Mother
and Her Children

The eruption of pagan-Christian violence in 392 and the prominent role that pagan teachers played in it forced Alexandrians to confront, for the first time, the challenges that accompanied their city's position as both the home of one of Christianity's most influential bishops and a prominent center of Hellenic culture. Hypatia offered Alexandrians a vision for how the city could continue to be both things. She showed Alexandrian elites that philosophy, if practiced correctly, pointed the way toward a better-governed and more cohesive city in which Christians and pagans could both coexist and cooperate. But Hypatia's teaching could only succeed if people had access to it. Many intellectuals in the later Roman Empire had the capacity to develop exciting and innovative teaching programs, but they still needed to find a way to reach students. Hypatia's gender made this even more challenging for her.

The sixth-century Platonist Damascius explains how Hypatia presented her ideas to the public. He says that Hypatia "wrapped herself in the philosopher's cloak and advanced through the middle of the city, explained in public to those who wished to listen the philosophy of Plato or Aristotle or any other of the philosophers."[1] The key phrase "explained in public to all who wished to hear" has sometimes been understood to mean that Hypatia drew a public salary. At first glance, this seems plausible. The Museum membership that Theon enjoyed was a financial reward doled out by imperial officials—and, a century later, we know of a teacher who was both a chair of philosophy and a member of the Museum.[2] We also know that, by the mid-fifth century, Alexandria was home to a complex of more than twenty classrooms that included a theater able to seat hundreds.[3] This proto-university provided the space for the sort of large-scale instruction that Damascius implies Hypatia offered (see Figure 5.1). This makes it tempting to think that Hypatia was a public teacher in a fifth-century University of Alexandria.

This attractive picture falls apart upon closer examination, however. The large classroom complex in Alexandria was not built until after Hypatia's death.[4] In fact, it may well have been designed to replace some of the classroom space lost when the Serapeum was destroyed. Hypatia also probably did not belong to the Museum. While Theon seems to have held a Museum membership, such honors were not hereditary, and there is no indication in any source that Hypatia was similarly honored. Even Damascius's description of her teaching does not actually support the conclusion that Hypatia had some sort of publicly funded teaching position.[5] When Damascius elsewhere speaks of publicly funded teachers, he uses the term "public allowance" to mark a public professorship.[6] This is very different from what Damascius says

FIGURE 5.1. Late fifth-century classroom, Kom el-Dikka, Alexandria.

Credit line: Photo by Manasi Watts.

about Hypatia. Damascius does not say that Hypatia received a public salary. He simply says that she taught the works of Plato, Aristotle, and other philosophers in public to all who wanted to listen. Hypatia did not need to have an imperially endowed chair to do this, nor did she need an imperially provided classroom. Roman teachers are known to have taught in spaces as diverse as temples, city halls, cemeteries, and even their own homes.[7] Hypatia could have taught anywhere. But it is most likely that she just took over the teaching her father did in whatever space he had used.[8]

At the same time, Hypatia seems to have been a particularly welcoming professor. Damascius's comment suggests that Hypatia made herself much more accessible than most late antique teachers. Indeed, it is possible that she did this deliberately in an effort to rehabilitate the reputation of Platonism within the city in the 390s. While teachers like Plato and Plotinus ran relatively open classrooms, such things had become less common in the fourth century.[9] Hypatia's older contemporaries, the rhetoricians Libanius and Himerius, seem to have interviewed and recruited potential students before they were allowed to enroll, and their Athenian colleagues even taught in closed lecture rooms in their homes.[10] Similarly, when Proclus arrived at the school of Plutarch in Athens in the 430s, he was interviewed by his teachers before he was allowed to join the school (which apparently also met in Plutarch's house).[11] Hypatia, however, seems to have taught in public and permitted whoever wished to attend her lectures to do so without any screening process.

Teachers and Students in Hypatia's School

This did not mean that all parts of Hypatia's school and its teachings were open to the general public. Since at least the time of Plato, philosophical schools contained a hierarchy of members. In Plato's Academy, for example, Plato supervised public demonstrations of the school's method of inquiry that were open to anyone who happened upon them, but he also ran nightly discussion sections in his home devoted to deeper and more complicated philosophical ideas that were restricted to his disciples.[12] Indeed, it has even been proposed that the Platonic dialogues were composed to serve as the basis for these private conversations.[13] As the Academy developed, Platonists began to consider their teachers as fathers and their fellow students as brothers. They even theorized and explained this notion of intellectual family ties in the pseudo-Platonic dialogue the *Theages*.[14]

By the Roman imperial period, the division between the inner circle of a school and its less capable or less dedicated students had become a standard feature of education. Some enterprising rhetoricians charged one fee for simple attendance at the school and another, higher fee for the increased access and personal attention that membership in the school's inner circle brought.[15] In schools led by more idealistic rhetoricians and philosophers, membership in the inner circle had an emotional rather than financial component. A host of later Roman authors speak about invitations to dinner parties and intimate conversations with their teachers as rewards bestowed only upon the most skilled and dedicated students.[16]

Philosophers saw profound differences between "those students who came simply for listening (*akroatai*)" and those who came "to be disciples (*zēlotai*) and companions in philosophy."[17] The *akroatai* (or "listeners") received a more basic type of training while the *zēlotai* (or "disciples") learned the most advanced material the teacher could teach so that they could "model their life upon philosophy."[18] This advanced material was not thought to be something that even average students could understand. Because it formed the basis of a philosophical life, philosophers feared that ignorant people would be harmed by higher-level teaching if they tried to apply it to their lives. Consequently, some refused to speak about these advanced ideas to the uninitiated.[19] Plotinus and the other members of the inner circle of Ammonius Saccas, for example, even took a vow to never share any of the teachings of their master with outsiders.[20]

Hypatia's student Synesius suggests that, like Plato, Plotinus, and most other ancient teachers, Hypatia convened an inner circle of students to which access was restricted.[21] This was the group that became most familiar with her full philosophical system. Synesius studied under Hypatia from around 390 until a little before 395, and he certainly belonged to the circle of philosophical devotees who received the most advanced training that she offered. Nothing survives that was written by Synesius while he was enrolled at Hypatia's school, but we do have 156 letters written by him that range in date from the months just after he left Hypatia's school in late 395 until his death in 413.[22] Seven of these were addressed to Hypatia and many others were addressed to fellow members of her inner circle. Collectively, they show a great deal about the way that Hypatia's inner circle worked, the relationships that Hypatia had with these students, the bonds that her intellectual children developed with one another under her supervision, and the powerful notion of a philosophical love that bound them.[23]

The relationship between Synesius and Hypatia, his intellectual and spiritual mother, becomes clear from the preserved letters that he sent to her. It is important to understand what these letters are. Published versions of ancient letters belong to collections often made up of revised texts that showcase particular aspects of their writer's character or literary skill.[24] While they may not preserve the exact words of the original conversation between the author and addressee, they usually do convey much of its essence. More importantly, they allow modern readers to understand what an author wanted his literary interactions with other figures to show about himself.[25] This makes the letters exchanged between Synesius and Hypatia particularly valuable documents. In them, Synesius simultaneously shows off his literary skill and advertises his devotion to his intellectual mother. He quite clearly felt that both things were worth displaying and that each in its own way helped to define him in a particularly positive fashion.

The manuscript tradition for Synesius's letters is messy, and this makes it impossible to reconstruct exactly how they were originally organized. It is clear, however, that they were never published in chronological order.[26] This means that Hypatia's first appearance in the collection actually consists of a group of four letters (now numbered 10, 15, 16, and 81) that were among the very last that Synesius ever wrote. They all date to 413, just after Synesius had lost his wife and children to illness and when he was, apparently, also battling the illness that would take his life. If we read these letters as a group, we get a sense of both the intense affection that Synesius felt for Hypatia and the institutional structures of her school that helped to nurture these feelings.

The earliest of the three (*Letter* 15 in the collection) begins bluntly: "Things have gone so very dreadfully that I need a hydroscope." The hydroscope was an instrument used to measure the density of liquids, and Synesius evidently required it because he was looking to precisely measure the ingredients to be included in medicines he hoped to prepare to treat himself or his relatives.[27] As the letter now stands, Synesius's request is a rather blunt one without the careful, respectful greeting that one normally would expect to precede such a request. The letter instead contains a detailed description of the object that Synesius hopes Hypatia will send, a feature that displayed Synesius's technical mastery of this particular scientific instrument to readers of the letter collection.[28] This suggests that the description of the hydroscope may have been added later when the letter was edited for publication.[29] What Hypatia actually received was probably a much briefer and more polite letter with a normal, respectful greeting, rather than the curt introduction and ostentatious display of technical details we now read.

Two young friends of Synesius named Nicaeus and Philolaus carried the next letter in the group (*Letter* 81) to Hypatia in 413. These men were engaged in a lawsuit that they hoped would resolve their claim to family property, and Synesius wrote this letter to serve as an introduction that would put them in touch with Hypatia. He hoped that she would help the young men make connections with people who could influence the outcome of their case. This is, however, another epistolary set piece in which the request for help sits amid a meditation on the nature of Fortune. Synesius begins with the news that Fortune has just taken his son from him. The death of his son is a blow but, Synesius continues, Fortune still could not pull him away from his concern for philosophy and his desire to safeguard justice. This, he continues, is why he writes. Hypatia knows that he cannot bear injustice, and she appreciates that Fortune has prevented him from stopping it in his home city. Only she can still aid him in righting the wrong done to Nicaeus and Philolaus. The letter then moves from this meditation on philosophical principles to a request for specific, tangible help that Hypatia could provide the men.

The next letter in the group, *Letter* 10, suggests that Synesius had not yet heard back from Hypatia about either of the two previous requests. Synesius fashioned *Letter* 10 into an elegant composition that gently chastised Hypatia for her silence. Synesius begins it in an appropriate fashion: "I greet you yourself and, through you, oh fortunate mistress, I greet the most fortunate members of the inner circle of your school."[30] The rest of the letter artfully speaks of the pain that he felt because of the recent death of his three children and begs Hypatia to write back lest he remain deprived of her "most divine soul." Only a response from her, he concludes, can help him overcome all of these difficulties.

This letter is a performance piece that was as much a work of art designed to impress a later audience of readers as it was a missive designed to elicit Hypatia's response. It works on both levels, however, because Synesius is able to convey that Hypatia has not responded appropriately to the deep, personal devotion that Synesius rightly has for his teacher. Hypatia thus owes him a letter not just because he sent her a message and got no response, but also because her role as Synesius's teacher and the head of the group of students to which he belonged obliged her to respond.

If *Letter* 10 offers an artful but gentle chastisement of Hypatia, the final letter in this group, *Letter* 16, serves as a miniature masterpiece of literary passive-aggressiveness. It blends allusions to Synesius's physical ailments with descriptions of the mental anguish Hypatia's silence caused him. It does all of this in a way that ostensibly reminds his teacher of the mutual obligations that bound teachers and students. It begins powerfully. "Bedridden," Synesius writes, "I have dictated this letter which you receive while healthy, oh mother and sister and teacher and benefactor for all things."[31] He continues: "My life has lost its sweetness. I wish that I might stop living. . . . But you keep yourself in good health and greet the most beloved members of the school's inner circle, beginning with the father Theoteknos and the brother Athanasius, and then the others."[32] He also calls upon her to pass along his greetings to any new people who have joined the school. He then concludes the letter with a final comment: "If anything of my affairs concerns you, you will do well; but if this does not concern you, none of it will concern me."[33] This letter, the most impressive of the group, powerfully contrasts Synesius's sickness and devotion with Hypatia's health and negligence. The force of this contrast comes from Synesius's subtle play on the convention that an intellectual parent should care for and assist her student whenever possible, but especially when all he requests is a simple letter.

This group of letters collectively reveals a number of things about how Hypatia maintained the inner circle of her school. Synesius's address of Hypatia as his "mother" followed the convention first described by Platonists almost 800 years earlier through which the student of a philosopher saw his teacher as the parent of his soul. Synesius also suggests that the intellectual family involved more than just Hypatia and a group of "descendants." Synesius identifies an intellectual father named Theoteknos, perhaps a reference to Hypatia's father Theon, and also mentions an intellectual brother named Athanasius.[34] These letters also suggest that Hypatia related to her intellectual descendants in a range of ways. She could provide tangible things like the hydroscope that Synesius requested. She could also grant favors like the introduction of Nicaeus and Philolaus to magistrates who could help them resolve their court cases. But, most importantly, Synesius relied upon Hypatia for intellectual and emotional support.

While these late letters give a general sense of the relationship between Synesius and Hypatia, the earlier letters that he wrote to his teacher add further nuance to the personal and intellectual ties that bound them. *Letter* 46, written in 399, reaffirms both the philosophical connection between Synesius and Hypatia and the mutual exchange of favors their relationship entailed. It responds to a letter sent by Hypatia with an evocation of Plato's *Crito* before offering her the recommendation of a man named Alexander.[35] *Letter* 124, written in 405 while Synesius's home region of Libya was beset by barbarian attacks, speaks graphically of the stench of death that descended on his city during this warfare and reminds Hypatia that she alone has the power to induce him to leave his homeland.

The longest and most complicated of these earlier letters, *Letter* 154, serves as a masterpiece of self-representation. Written in 404, *Letter* 154 trades on Synesius's relationship with Hypatia in order to validate the philosophical propriety of a range of literary projects that seemed to some to be too superficial (or sophistic) for a philosopher.[36] The letter ostensibly accompanied three books, two of which Synesius had written during the past year. One book, a discussion of the meaning of dreams, Synesius claimed was motivated by God. As we have seen, this book drew upon Porphyrian philosophical concepts that Hypatia probably taught.[37] The other, the *Dion*, offered a defense of the particular sort of philosophy that Synesius practiced (and, by extension, that Hypatia taught).[38] It was, Synesius wrote, his response to charges that his concern with style and harmony, as well as his references to Homer and Greek rhetoricians, diminished his credibility as a philosopher. He frames these charges as things motivated by two different groups of jealous rivals. One group, made up of second-rate philosophers, attacks Synesius's work while hoping that he will come and refine his studies under them. The second set of attacks come from rhetoricians who are jealous of Synesius's literary style. Synesius briefly describes the contents of the works and then asks Hypatia to review them. "I wait for your judgment about all of these things. If you reckon that it ought to be distributed, it will be put out among the rhetoricians and philosophers."[39] He then continues, "If it does not seem to you worthy of the ears of Greeks and you, like Aristotle, place truth before friendship, a close and profound shadow will cover it and it will never be mentioned among mankind."[40]

This letter had two lives, each of which reveals something important about Synesius's relationship with Hypatia. Its first life consisted of the actual epistolary conversation in which Synesius asked for Hypatia's reaction to his texts in 404. This conversation reveals how much Synesius valued Hypatia's judgment as a philosopher and scholar. Synesius particularly wanted her input on the *Dion*, a complicated work that helped to define his public literary profile, because he thought that Hypatia alone had the philosophical background to offer him a proper critique. This was, then, a letter from an intellectual son to his intellectual parent in which Synesius sought Hypatia's honest reaction to works that he hoped would gain her approval. Although we do not have Hypatia's response, we can tell that it pleased Synesius; the *Dion* appeared later that year.

The second life of this letter is, in some ways, even more interesting. When the letter appeared in the collection of Synesius's letters, any reader of it would know that the *Dion* was not, in fact, buried beneath a dark shadow but instead became one of Synesius's most celebrated works. This letter then reveals to later readers that the *Dion* appeared in the world only because Hypatia had signed off on its quality. The letter may once have done even more than this, however. *Letter* 154 is, right now, the third to last letter in the collection and is followed only by two relatively nondescript letters to a lawyer named Domitian. Thematically, however, *Letter* 154 parallels the way that Synesius discusses his written works in *Letter* 1, a letter of 405 that introduced readers to the literary aims that Synesius pursued throughout his career. *Letter* 1 was addressed to Nicander, a prominent sophist in Constantinople, and it once served as a cover letter for a manuscript containing work that Synesius sent to him for review. Synesius begins the letter this way: "I have given birth to verbal children, some from most holy philosophy and the poetry that shares a temple with her and others from common rhetoric. But anyone would know that they are all from one father who sometimes inclines towards the serious and other times towards the playful."[41] Synesius says that the audience would decide in what category the work belongs but, for his part, he "would be as happy as possible if it was claimed by philosophy and judged one of its legitimate offspring."[42] He then invites Nicander to pass judgment on it and, if he deems it acceptable, to distribute it among the intelligentsia of Constantinople. If he does not, however, he is asked to return it to Synesius without distributing it.

Letter 154 to the Alexandrian philosopher Hypatia and Letter 1 to the Constantinopolitan sophist Nicander work together to place Synesius's writings at the intersection of poetry, philosophy, and rhetoric while simultaneously defining their character as fundamentally philosophical. Both letters make this claim explicitly and then invite the addressee to agree or disagree with Synesius. If they disagreed, Synesius said that he would destroy the works that he had sent without publishing them. But the ancient audience reading these letters knew that all of the works that Synesius sent to Hypatia and Nicander were widely disseminated. These letters then trade upon the reputations of the leading philosopher and rhetorician in the two most important cities in the Eastern Empire to offer powerful endorsements of the literary quality of Synesius's work and the philosophical credentials of its author. They form a set of thematic bookends to Synesius's collection of letters that defined him as a rhetorically gifted philosopher of the greatest integrity. His status as an intellectual disciple of Hypatia was, of course, essential in making this picture compelling.

Relationships among Hypatia's Students

The seven published letters that Synesius sent to Hypatia allow one to see how Hypatia interacted with members of her inner circle after they left her school. Another group of letters sent by Synesius to his fellow student Herculian offers a precious glimpse into how Hypatia taught her inner-circle students to understand their relationships with one another. Although these are now Letters 137–146 in the modern edition, they collectively represent a meditation on the theme of living philosophically outside of the environment of Hypatia's school. Indeed, their thematic coherence suggests that they comprised a sort of mini-dossier of letters that potentially could have once circulated separately from the main collection.[43]

Letter 137 sets the tone for this discussion. It begins with a passage from Homer that likens the respective journeys of the two men to and from Alexandria to the wanderings of Odysseus. Their voyages, Synesius affirms, resulted in something even more spectacular than that which Odysseus found, for "we ourselves saw and heard the legitimate mistress of the mysteries of philosophy."[44] Because of this, Synesius continued, he shared with Herculian a bond that ran deeper than the human attachment between friends. "Since we live the life of the mind," he wrote, we are bound by "a divine law that requires us to honor one another." This meant that, although Herculian and Synesius were physically distant from one another, Synesius's mind remembers Herculian's image and the sweetness of his voice. He asks his friend to be sure that they both continue to study and practice philosophy, because this will ensure that they live in a way befitting their philosophical friendship.

Letter 137 establishes the existence of the divine love between these fellow students of Hypatia. The next three letters allow one to further appreciate what this idea of philosophical love meant. In *Letters* 138 and 139, Synesius plays with the idea of a letter serving as a medium for philosophical discussion and a tool for finding solace when one is separated from one he loves. In *Letter* 140, a text probably written in 403, Synesius expands further on the nature of this philosophical, divine love.[45] He writes: "Among loves, the type which has its beginnings from the earth and men is loathsome and fading because it only exists when the beloved is nearby." This is a bodily love based in the physical world, and because it grows out of an attachment to matter, it is inferior to a love grounded in the soul. This second type of love "is another sort which God oversees and directs." It belongs to the soul, not the body, and functions on a higher level that does not distract the soul from Truth. "There is nothing," Synesius continues, "which can prevent souls who seek each other from coming together and becoming interlaced. Our affection should be this type if we are not to dishonor the philosophical training we have received."[46] Synesius goes on to emphasize that this divine, philosophical love for a fellow philosopher means that Herculian should not be upset that the two of them are physically separated. Physical separation should not matter if, as a true philosopher, Herculian and Synesius keep their "eyes fixed on heaven and give themselves over completely to the contemplation of what is real." If Herculian were to do this, he would regain the "courage of the soul" that philosophy promises and would triumph over the emotional weakness that Synesius's absence made him feel.[47]

The divine, philosophical love that Hypatia's students enjoyed with one another also provided a mechanism through which they could police one another's unphilosophical conduct. In *Letter* 143, a letter written in 399, Synesius reminded Herculian that some philosophical doctrines are not to be shared with people who were not members of Hypatia's inner circle. Herculian had told non-initiates about these doctrines and, in doing this, had failed to "uphold the things that we agreed upon and did not keep hidden the things that deserved to be."[48] Synesius learned of this only when people coming from Herculian asked him to interpret a doctrine that had been one of those that the inner-circle students had agreed to keep hidden. This was a problem, Synesius continued, because people who are unable to understand the most complicated elements of Hypatia's philosophy will believe that they know something that they do not. This harms the uninitiated and adulterates the sanctity of Hypatia's doctrines themselves.

Hypatia's Virginity

Synesius's letters reveal a tight inner circle of students who were all intensely loyal to their intellectual mother, deeply protective of the content of her teaching, and tightly bound to one another. These intense, loving relationships developed outside of the public space in which Hypatia taught most of her students. Synesius understood that these intellectual relationships grew out of a divine, nonphysical, and nonsexual love that Hypatia and her students developed for one another. Indeed, physical intimacy with other members of the circle would have been seen as the expression of the lesser sort of love that Synesius classifies as inferior and distracting in his letter to Herculian.[49] It would have run counter to the basic goal of divine union that Hypatia's philosophy helped one to achieve.

Hypatia's inner circle shared Synesius's idea that a divine, nonsexual love bound them together, but a mixed-gender philosophical circle set up in this way could arouse suspicions among the uninitiated who wondered what went on outside the public eye. This curiosity about the private lives of Hypatia and the members of her school probably explains why later authors speak at such length about Hypatia's sexuality. Socrates Scholasticus emphasizes her temperance and prudence, qualities that he said left everyone "awestruck and admiring her even more."[50] Writing a century after Socrates, the philosopher Damascius discussed Hypatia's sexuality at even greater length. She was "just and prudent" and "remained a virgin," Damascius wrote, but "because she was extremely beautiful and good-looking, a certain member of her inner circle of students fell in love with her."[51] This student "was not able to control his lust" and made it obvious to Hypatia. It was rumored, Damascius continued, that Hypatia used Pythagorean music to cure him of this unphilosophical yearnings, but the real story was much more impressive.[52] Hypatia tried to cure this student with music, but when this failed, "she brought forth a menstrual rag." This, she told him, represents the impurity of the body, and "it is this that you love, not something beautiful."[53] The young man then became ashamed and his soul turned its attention to more prudent things.

Stories like this helped to fend off any rumors about improprieties that could have occurred between a female teacher and her student. The way in which Damascius tells this story suggests that it also had a deeper significance. In Damascius's telling, Hypatia first tries to address the improper, physical attraction that her student felt by trying to calm his soul with music. This was a proper, philosophical remedy that had Pythagorean roots, but this student had apparently fallen so far from the heights of philosophical contemplation that this remedy could not work. Since he was now overcome with bodily passions, Hypatia had to resort to a display that used physical objects to make an impression on him. Her display of the menstrual rag shocked this student and enabled him to remember that bodily love was ephemeral and far inferior to the proper, divine love that she and her students were supposed to share. This was, then, not just a story that insulated Hypatia against malicious gossip; it was also an anecdote that reinforced the idea of divine, philosophical love that she taught.[54]

Hypatia's philosophical ideal of divine love likely also helps to explain her decision to remain a lifelong virgin. In some ways, her embrace of a celibate life can seem quite similar to the asceticism embraced by increasing numbers of elite Christian women in the later fourth and early fifth centuries. In principle, both these Christian ascetics and Hypatia saw their chastity as something that freed them from the impure, bodily concerns of the world.[55] But the traditions that inspired this embrace of virginity were quite different. Celibate Christian women in the fourth century could draw upon a tradition reaching back to the Gospels that idealized the sort of choice that they were making.[56] Hypatia, however, drew upon a much more complicated tradition that produced some figures who shared her embrace of celibacy and others who did not. Like Hypatia, the fifth-century Platonists Proclus and Marinus refrained from any sexual relationships for their entire lives.[57] Proclus, for his part, was even buried in the same tomb with his teacher Syrianus and ordered it inscribed with the wish that their souls would be reunited in a common place.[58] This inscription perhaps suggests that he understood his philosophical connection with Syrianus to be similar to the connection Synesius claims to have shared with Herculian.

Proclus and Marinus were exceptions, however. Philosophers more commonly saw sexual relationships as something in which one could engage not for pleasure but in order to conceive children. After their families were complete, the physical intimacy would cease.[59] The fifth-century Alexandrian philosopher Theosebius offers an even more interesting case. "The most temperate of all men," Damascius writes, Theosebius had married and "agreed to have intercourse with his wife in order to have children." When it became clear that they were infertile, Damascius continues, Theosebius gave his wife a ring of temperance. He told her that, when they married, he had given her a wedding ring because they were to live together to produce children. Now, he said, "I give this ring of temperance which will prepare you to live a temperate domestic life, if you are able and willing to live with me in a purer manner" that did not include sexual relations. If, Theosebius concluded, his wife was not able to do this, he gave her the option of leaving him for a more conventional marriage to another man.[60]

Damascius writes about Theosebius's arrangement with his wife in order to show the degree to which the temperance he taught corresponded to the way in which he lived. For Damascius, this anecdote distills the very essence of Theosebius's teaching and emphasizes that the philosopher lived within the system he taught. Hypatia's desire to live in accordance with what she taught likely had as much to do with her virginity as it did with Theosebius's embrace of a life of chastity. Synesius's letters emphasize the important role that temperance and philosophical love played within the intellectual family that Hypatia headed. As the head of a philosophical circle, she could teach best by living the life that she believed to be most philosophically pure. Hypatia's decision to refrain from sexual intercourse illustrated a key part of the philosophical system that she taught. It also was a lifestyle that even Synesius, her most notable student, did not decide to adopt.

Hypatia's celibacy served as a powerful and tangible reminder of the particular emphasis that her teaching placed on temperance. It also had very real implications for her school. Hypatia's well-known decision to remain a virgin obviously precluded her ever marrying or having a sexual relationship with a student. This choice insulated Hypatia from any suspicion that sordid things happened in the private meetings that she held with her male students. But it also meant that Hypatia would never have any children who could take over the school should something happen to her. Schools could survive under those sorts of circumstances, but most did not. Even the intellectual circles headed by Plotinus and Iamblichus seem to have dispersed after the death of their head, with the students taking the ideas of the master to new cities. The rare schools that survived in the same city for multiple generations without a clear family connection were headed either by a succession of publicly supported professors or by professors who took particular care to line up and train a specific successor during their lives.[61] The lack of a partner and an heir risked the success of the institution Hypatia headed in Alexandria as well as the long-term intellectual legacy of her teaching.

On the other side of the ledger, however, Hypatia lived according to the principles she taught. This offered an extremely powerful endorsement of the quality of her teaching. In late antiquity, a philosopher was measured as much by how she lived as she was by her mastery of a textual tradition. The catalogue of fifth- and sixth-century philosophers that Damascius provides in his *Life of Isidore* judges these men and women on both the caliber of their thought and the purity of their actions.[62] The philosopher Ammonius Hermiou, for example, is considered the best Aristotelian textual scholar who ever lived, but he is also judged a terrible philosopher because he abandoned his principles in the face of Christian pressure.[63] By contrast, the philosopher Serapio is held out as a particularly inspired sage because he lived as "a model for the golden age of Cronus" despite owning only two books and being unable to bear technical philosophical discussions.[64] Although Damascius ultimately had a mixed judgment of Hypatia, he appreciated the degree to which the prudence and temperance that shaped her life corresponded to proper philosophical principles. Later fourth-century students, colleagues, and peers likely had an even kinder assessment of her ability to serve as both a teacher and a philosophical exemplar.

It is important to also understand the community that Hypatia built, and her own conduct within it, against the larger background of Alexandria in the 390s. Hypatia taught a philosophy that was sophisticated, consistent with Platonic traditions, and remarkably accessible to both Christians and pagans. Her teaching also provided the philosophical foundation for an intellectual community to which both pagans and Christians could belong. Even more important, Hypatia and her students lived according to the community's philosophical principles both when they were at the school and after they left it. These philosophers modeled pagan and Christian harmony to Alexandrians who lived in a city scarred by the confessional battles of the 380s and 390s. The wisdom and intellectual affection that bound them to a common philosophical project in Hypatia's school then offered a model for religious cooperation to a city struggling to move forward. As we will see in the next chapter, this success also gave Hypatia a particularly resonant public voice that she could use to guide political affairs in her home city.

6

The Public Intellectual

The prudence and temperance that defined the teaching of Hypatia had benefits beyond increasing the popularity of her philosophical school. In antiquity, philosophers claimed for themselves a particular sort of social position through which they provided frank, public advice to rulers and other influential people. They were given a freedom to speak freely that few others enjoyed because, the theory went, the pursuit of philosophy obliged philosophers to speak truth to those in power regardless of the consequences.[1] Since philosophers lived the life of the mind, power, wealth, and the threat of physical punishment supposedly had no ability to sway their convictions or limit their freedom to speak plainly. The executions of philosophers such as Socrates, the early followers of Pythagoras, and the first-century Stoic Thrasea Paetus lent considerable credibility to the notion that genuine philosophers held true to philosophical principles even if that stance led to their death.[2] Reason alone backed the voice of a philosopher when it was raised publicly. Nothing in antiquity rang more true than his or her counsel.

Many philosophers took this social role very seriously.[3] They believed that they had an obligation to make the state function better and to bring the behavior of its citizens into line with the principles of philosophy. Philosophers could do this best when they governed the state themselves, but late ancient philosophers recognized that they were unlikely to achieve such power.[4] If philosophers could not rule, they could still serve the state as magistrates, generals, judges, or public advocates who used philosophy to guide their individual actions and state policies.[5] This was a full-time job. Writing in the sixth century, the Platonist Simplicius argued that the philosopher needed to be a father, teacher, corrector, advisor, guardian, and helper in every conceivable situation, while sharing the joy and grief of every member of his community.[6] This meant that philosophers had to try to direct state policy while simultaneously steering every individual in the city toward philosophical behaviors in his or her own life.[7]

Philosophers could not, however, succumb to any of the temptations that people with a public career sometimes encountered. They could involve themselves in the personal lives and disputes of prominent people, but they sought no reward for the services that they provided. While they could hold office, they could not desire it, nor could they be seduced by the honors that accompanied it.[8] Similarly, while philosophers could pay for public works or construction projects, they should not do so in order to be recognized or celebrated by their fellow citizens. All of the public activities that these men and women undertook needed to be motivated solely by the desire to make the people of their city better. As if to underline this point, some philosophers argued that a philosopher could honestly play no public role in a state in which the authorities showed active hostility toward philosophy. Such efforts would, at best, be a waste of time, and, at worst, be simultaneously ineffective and dangerous to her or his philosophical practice. In such circumstances, the appropriate action for a philosopher was either to leave the city or lay low and offer whatever small interventions were possible on an individual level.[9]

False Philosophers in the Public Sphere

The authority often granted to philosophers meant that people without the purity of mind a true philosopher possessed sometimes claimed the title of philosopher and rose to offer counsel in public. Late Roman literary sources are full of stories of pseudo-philosophers whose actions belied their claims of immunity to the comforts and luxuries of the physical world. These characters ranged from philosophical dilettantes like the wealthy Athenian senator Theagenes to poets like the Egyptian Pamprepius and sophists like Uranius. All of them preyed upon the ignorance of the powerful and profited greatly from their usurpation of the status philosophers could claim. Indeed, philosophers actively policed their communities and worked hard to discredit such characters. The Athenian philosopher Marinus, for example, publicly took

Theagenes to task for his lack of seriousness, an action that opened a rift between the two men that alienated Marinus's school from its most important financial backer.[10] Damascius compared Pamprepius to Typhon and mocked him for claiming a philosophical pedigree only when he was sure no actual philosophers were present.[11] Drawing upon an account likely provided by one of Damascius's students, the historian Agathias exposed the philosophical pretenses of Uranius as attributes that Uranius showcased in order to gain favor with the ignorant king of Persia.[12]

Figures like these were easy for philosophers to shun, but the situation became trickier when, unlike Pamprepius or Theagenes, the person in question appeared to have legitimate philosophical credentials. Hypatia's older contemporary Themistius offered just such an example.[13] Themistius was the fourth century's most influential commentator on Aristotle, but he became more famous for his public activities than he was for his teaching. The son, grandson, and son-in-law of philosophers, Themistius received his philosophical training under his father in Constantinople in the late 330s and early 340s.[14] Themistius's first job was in Nicomedia, a position that he won sometime around his twenty-seventh birthday in 344, but Themistius seems not to have wanted to stay in what was then a beautiful but sleepy city located some distance from the capital.[15] He earned a return to Constantinople in early 348 by delivering a unique and powerful panegyric of the emperor Constantius II when the court stopped for a short time in Ancyra.[16] This speech saw Themistius mix the standard biographical elements of an imperial panegyric with the explicit claim that, as a philosopher, he could only speak truth.[17] He proceeded to praise Constantius as the embodiment of all of the philosophical virtues that Plato and Aristotle attributed to an ideal ruler, a claim that had additional power because Themistius ostensibly made it without any desire for honors or rewards.

The problem was that Themistius very much desired rewards from those he praised. Themistius hoped to use his oration to earn a teaching position in Constantinople, the new imperial capital that he loved. Constantius quickly granted this to him. The speech that Themistius gave in 348, however, was the beginning of a long and distinguished public speaking career in which the philosopher repeated this performance for four more emperors across the better part of four decades.[18] Each speech traded on Themistius's identity as a philosopher to offer what he claimed was sincere praise for his subject, but each speech also brought tangible rewards. In 355, as a prize for the philosopher's continued efforts to build support for his regime, Constantius added Themistius to the Constantinopolitan senate.[19] Then, after Themistius gave an important speech praising Constantius before the Roman senate in 357, he was placed in charge of the recruitment of new senators.[20] By 361, Themistius held such a high position that a law was issued that required him to be present in the chamber before any new junior magistrates could be appointed.[21] Eventually, after Themistius served as a philosophical spokesman defending Emperor Theodosius's controversial peace treaty with the Goths in 383, he was even appointed prefect of the city of Constantinople.[22] He was the last philosopher to hold so high an office for nearly 100 years.[23]

Themistius's rivals did not shy away from pointing out the wealth and honors that he received in exchange for these "philosophical" orations.[24] They also took him to task for offering the same sort of praise to five different emperors, some of whom he described as philosopher kings while they lived and villains after their death.[25] These sorts of inconsistencies were acceptable for rhetoricians. Everyone knew that they offered disingenuous panegyrics and gladly accepted whatever remuneration was offered in exchange. Philosophers, however, were not supposed to lie and could not expect any reward for telling the truth.[26] Indeed, some of Themistius's correspondents even suggested that, despite his great philosophical learning, Themistius could often seem more like a rhetorician than a philosopher.[27]

Philosophers who took on a high-profile public role after having once lived philosophically faced a great risk that their new prominence and access to political power could pull them down from philosophical purity. The case of Hypatia's older contemporary Maximus of Ephesus provided a frightening illustration of this sort of fall. Maximus's story was often retold in the 380s, 390s, and early 400s in order to show how the authority that the public granted to philosophers could corrupt even the most philosophically talented individuals.[28] A talented theurgist, Maximus was seen as the most gifted Iamblichan disciple of his generation. Not only was his philosophical teaching among the most sophisticated of any of his peers, but he had an ability to commune with the divine that was rivaled perhaps only by Iamblichus himself.[29] In the mid-350s, Maximus became one of the future emperor Julian's primary teachers of philosophy after the emperor heard of a time when rituals performed by Maximus caused a statue of Hecate to smile.[30] Maximus remained close to Julian after Julian was made Caesar and, when Julian assumed full imperial power in 361, Maximus was summoned to court along with some of Julian's other teachers. Maximus and his colleague Chrysanthius both performed sacrifices together to see if it would be a good idea to go to Julian. They received inauspicious omens. Chrysanthius then behaved philosophically and declined to travel to the emperor, despite repeated summons from Julian. Maximus, however, was so excited by the prospect of joining the court that he continued to offer sacrifices until he got the answer that he desired.[31]

After his summons to court, people honored Maximus for his philosophical achievements, but they also flattered him because his intimacy with Julian enabled him to influence the emperor. Maximus evidently had difficulty differentiating between the respect his philosophical accomplishments deserved and the flattery that now accompanied his position as an imperial associate. Maximus changed significantly while at court. He began to receive crowds of adoring people, took to wearing fancy clothes, and became increasingly unphilosophical in his behavior and demeanor.[32] After Julian's premature death on campaign, Maximus's descent continued. He was imprisoned under the emperor Valens and seriously considered suicide.[33] He was rehabilitated in the late 360s and began a second career as a public speaker before again falling victim to the conspiracy that finally resulted in his execution in 372.[34]

Hypatia and Public Service

Hypatia was perhaps seventeen when Maximus died, and she was just beginning her teaching career when Themistius resigned the Constantinopolitan urban prefecture under pressure in 384. Both of their examples would have been well known to her and likely helped shape the public role that she chose to play. She understood that a philosopher who played a social role needed to guard against the lure of earthly rewards that had tripped up both men. It seems that by the 390s, Hypatia had found a comfortable way to exercise political influence without disrupting proper philosophical practice. All of the sources that speak at any length about Hypatia's career indicate that she became a high-profile advisor to imperial and local Alexandrian officials. Unlike

Themistius, she did not seek out a public role and, unlike Maximus, she did not seem to want the material rewards that came from it. She undertook these activities solely as part of her practice of philosophy.

Socrates Scholasticus explains that Hypatia's public prominence was backed by "her education." She displayed a "personal moderation towards magistrates," a phrase that likely means that she asked for and expected none of the honors or rewards that some of her peers sought.[35] Not only did Hypatia impress people with her learning and bearing toward those in power, but, Socrates continues, "everyone was awestruck and admired her more because of her overwhelming prudence."[36] This led her to hold frequent meetings with the governor of Egypt. In time, she came to be one of his most important local advisors.

Writing almost a century later, Damascius says something quite similar: "Because she was skilled and articulate in her speech and wise and politically virtuous in her actions, the city seemingly loved her and particularly prostrated itself before her and the governors always greeted her first when they came into the city."[37] Like Socrates, Damascius describes the combination of learning, wisdom, and virtue that Hypatia possessed, and he explains that this brought her the sort of public honor that philosophers customarily enjoyed. Damascius makes clear that both members of the public and the governors based in Alexandria extended this degree of respect to Hypatia because they continued to respect philosophy.[38] Damascius's comment suggests that some people may have visited Hypatia so that they could be seen to be appropriately reverential to philosophy rather than because they valued her counsel, but he also makes clear that Hypatia's impact extended beyond these high-profile public interviews. Hypatia, he continues, had regular visits with petitioners and others who sought her advice. She hosted great crowds of people "coming, going and standing around" outside her house like the clients of a great patroness.[39]

Damascius provides few more details than this, but the picture that he paints of Hypatia's public activities broadly corresponds to what Socrates described earlier. It also matches what ancient philosophers were traditionally expected to do for their fellow citizens. Hypatia's wisdom, temperance, and articulateness caused prominent Alexandrians to seek her philosophically inspired counsel. It also led her to have regular meetings with the imperial governors of Egypt, who were based in Alexandria. These high-profile activities were paired with more frequent audiences in which she offered private advice and assistance to her fellow citizens, probably including those of lower social status. Socrates and Damascius both suggest that Hypatia participated in the public life of her city in exactly the way that a philosopher was supposed to, but she never fell into the traps that tripped up men like Themistius or Maximus of Ephesus. She managed to remain publicly engaged while continuing to live philosophically.

Neither Damascius nor Socrates gives us any more details about how Hypatia managed this, but we can again get a sense of how she might have established this balance by looking at the letters of her student Synesius. His letters addressed to Hypatia detail the sort of help he thought that she would provide to those who asked for it. Even more interesting are the letters in which Synesius describes his own public activities and the ways in which he understood them to be consistent with or limited by his practice of philosophy. While these activities differed from what Hypatia could do, Hypatia provided Synesius with the philosophical rationale for the actions that he took. These letters then show how Hypatia may have taught her students to balance the demands of public life with the commitment philosophy required.

All of the letters that Hypatia received from Synesius have been discussed earlier, but two of them are particularly useful for understanding the actions she took on behalf of her friends. Around 405 or 406, Synesius sent Hypatia a letter that introduced her to a man named Alexander.[40] The text is now so short that it may well be an abridgement of what had once been a longer letter of introduction, but the letter itself served merely to give Alexander an opportunity to get a meeting with Hypatia.[41] Synesius clearly hoped that Hypatia would be impressed enough by Alexander that she would introduce him to other possible friends and help him to get established in Alexandria. This letter, then, gave Alexander an excuse to join the crowd of people that Damascius describes as coming, going, and standing around outside Hypatia's house. Like Alexander, many of these people would have been calling on Hypatia armed with letters of introduction from her friends or associates who lived in other cities. It was Hypatia's duty as a philosopher and as a friend to listen to the letters and greet these visitors, but she would often have been more helpful than this. Others who traveled to large cities armed with letters of reference could expect to be hosted and entertained by the recipient of such a letter.[42] In some cases they even found themselves regularly invited to attend gatherings at the home of their new patron, occasions that, at the very least, formed excellent networking opportunities.[43] Hypatia likely spent a considerable amount of time hosting visitors and new residents of Alexandria.

In 413, Synesius sent Hypatia another letter, *Epistle* 81, in which he introduced the two brothers Nicaeus and Philolaus, two of his relations from Cyrenaica. This letter asked much more of Hypatia than the earlier *Epistle* 46. Nicaeus and Philolaus were engaged in a lawsuit connected to their inheritance of family property. They had come to Alexandria to contest the suit. Synesius provided a letter introducing them to Hypatia in the hope that she might connect them with private individuals or magistrates who could help with their case. Synesius sent Nicaeus and Philolaus to Hypatia because she is "always empowered and able to make best use of this power."[44] They are, Synesius explains, "good and noble youths" who would benefit if "all of those who honor Hypatia" would help them regain possession of the property they rightly owned.[45]

Synesius here carefully asks Hypatia to use her influence in order to ensure that Nicaeus and Philolaus will succeed in their lawsuit, while not suggesting that she abandon her integrity as a philosopher. The two young men are, Synesius swears, the best sort of people, and the property they seek to recover belonged to them all along. Because their cause is just, Hypatia should serve justice by appealing to the private individuals and magistrates who honor her dedication to philosophy. Synesius then emphasizes that this aid is not unphilosophical influence peddling. It is instead a philosopher serving philosophy by finding justice for two good youths who have been legitimately wronged.

Synesius often found himself walking the same narrow path that this letter charts. Like Hypatia, Synesius struggled to balance the public activities and patronage roles expected of members of the later Roman elite with the demands of a philosophical life. Their situations differed because Synesius received frequent invitations to assume public office. Hypatia, whose gender made her ineligible to hold most civic posts, never dealt with this sort of expectation. At the same time, the ways in which Synesius tried to serve his city while living a philosophical life seem to be broadly consistent with the ways in which Hypatia served Alexandria.

This offers an intriguing possibility. While Hypatia's gender restricted the sorts of public service she could perform, her teaching about what sorts of public activities were consistent with a philosophical life must have explained the principles that guided her choices. Her students were overwhelmingly (and perhaps exclusively) elite males, and Hypatia certainly taught them how to determine what sorts of political activities were consistent with a philosophical life. She knew that her male students had far more formal opportunities than she did to use philosophy to improve their cities. She understood that part of her job as a teacher of philosophy involved explaining the principles that guided the public practice of philosophy. The texts that Synesius wrote in which he describes the challenge of being a publicly engaged philosopher then can serve as a rough statement of the philosophical principles that likely guided Hypatia's own public activities.

Philosophical Principles and Public Service

Synesius sets out the basic limits of a philosopher's public role in a letter written to the Constantinopolitan lawyer Pylamenes in 405.[46] The letter develops the idea that Synesius is the only philosopher in Libya, a conceit that Synesius also adopts elsewhere in his correspondence.[47] After praising the literary qualities of a letter that Pylamenes sent, Synesius invites him to ask the many governors and money lenders who regularly visit Cyrene to bring additional letters to him. Synesius describes his solitary pursuit of philosophy in Cyrene, a place where Synesius has no other philosophers with whom to interact. Synesius then asks Pylamenes to "pray together with me on the one hand that I can remain as I am, and on the other that you will leave behind the horrible public square, you who make such bad use of your nature."[48] Synesius urges Pylamenes to turn his thoughts away from the riches of the world and towards the things that make one truly happy. This is why, Synesius continues, I "enjoy being mocked that, while my relatives pursue imperial offices, I alone among them am a private citizen."[49] While they have their bodies guarded by soldiers, Synesius's soul "is guarded by virtues." This is essential, he claims, "because circumstances no longer permit a philosopher to concern himself with the affairs of state."[50]

This letter offers a classic statement of how a philosopher ought to function in late Roman society. Synesius asserts his philosophical purity, proclaims his disinterest in pursuing an administrative office, affirms his aversion to taking up a public career for the sake of wealth and honor, and counsels his friend to embrace a philosophical life instead of a life of the world. Synesius clearly appreciated the dangers of drifting into the murky territory once inhabited by Themistius and Maximus, and he understood the need to place the pursuit of truth above the rewards of a public career.

Despite this claim, Synesius frequently allowed himself to be pulled away from this life of pure contemplation. It was, he said in another letter from 405, the obligation of a philosopher to interrupt his philosophical contemplation if he was called to help with administration.[51] Late in his life, Synesius would answer such a call to become the Christian bishop of Ptolemais.[52] In a letter to his brother that recorded the terms under which Synesius agreed to serve as bishop, Synesius emphasizes that the people of Ptolemais have called him away from his books in order to take the job. Synesius writes that he plans to accept this summons, but only if serving as bishop does not require him to abandon philosophy. This condition has a peculiar meaning for Synesius. He understood that a bishop must preach to the common people, but he found things like the story of the Resurrection to be absurd. Synesius was, however, willing to repeat to his congregations whatever legends the church asked him to tell. This is the job of the bishop and "the philosophic mind admits the use of falsehood" as a teaching tool for lower minds. Synesius would do this only if he was permitted to "pursue philosophy at home while spreading legends outside."[53]

A letter written in 413, by contrast, shows Synesius coming perilously close to making the same sorts of claims that Themistius had in the past. This short note commends the service of a governor named Marcellinus and celebrates his role in beating back a barbarian attack on the city of Ptolemais. In it Synesius praises Marcellinus concisely while reminding him that Synesius's philosophical background prevents him from offering empty flattery. Instead of seeking a reward, Synesius spoke because Marcellinus's service was so exemplary and touched so many people that, as a philosopher, Synesius was compelled to speak on behalf of everyone.[54] Synesius clearly sensed that he had come close to crossing the line into flattery, and he understood immediately the need to preemptively defend himself against that charge.

In all of these cases, Synesius claimed that his public activities grew out of a philosophical commitment to his fellow citizens that he must have learned from Hypatia. At the same time, pure philosophical motives were not the only reasons he agreed to advocate for others. A group of four letters in which Synesius proudly trumpets a request he received from the Alexandrian city council to recommend one of its members to Libyan notables suggests that he also took pride in the demands that others made of his time.[55] Like the letter to Pylamenes, these letters reinforce Synesius's status as an enlightened liaison between urban, civilized areas of the empire like Alexandria and the marginal, uncultured land of Libya.[56] Synesius valued his philosophical pursuits, but he also very clearly enjoyed it when he could show off his unique position as a philosopher whose influence bridged two very different worlds.

There were, however, moments when the survival of the state truly depended upon Synesius's unique combination of wisdom and political connections. This seems to be the motivation behind Synesius's composition of *De Regno*, a work in which he urges the emperor Arcadius to embrace philosophy and turn away from a group of dangerous advisors.[57] This speech invokes the freedom of speech that philosophers commanded before laying out a set of instructions for how Arcadius should rule. This process begins by ruling one's own soul philosophically, but if a king achieves this, the benefits will then flow out to all under his control by encouraging his friends to embrace a good path and defeating all enemies.[58] Tyranny lurks, ready to ensnare a ruler who cannot govern his soul and cannot discern a true friend from a flattering enemy, but a king who can recognize friends and mind their counsel will always succeed.[59] Synesius then turns the speech in a different direction, warning the emperor that the barbarians who serve in the military around him deceive him, fog his mind, and lure him away from serious thought by encouraging luxury.[60] Synesius concludes that the threat to the state is dire, but the empire is still redeemable if Arcadius decides to become the beacon of virtue a true king must. He instructs the emperor to excuse the Germans serving in high offices, avoid luxury, and embrace philosophy.[61]

De Regno differed in tone and force from the philosophically adorned summaries of imperial talking-point memos for which Themistius received rewards in earlier decades. Synesius courted danger by speaking bluntly about the threat that Gothic leaders serving the emperor might rebel, but he did so from a sincere feeling that things needed to change dramatically or the empire would be at risk. He saw that the combined influence of courtiers who promoted luxury over substance and Gothic military leaders who pursued their own interests over those of the state could shatter the Roman political order.[62]

Synesius intervened as philosophy required by using the philosopher's freedom of expression to call the emperor away from tyranny and toward the rule of reason. As the subsequent rebellion of the Gothic commander Gaïnas showed, Synesius was both right to fear the Goths serving Arcadius and far too optimistic about the emperor's character.[63]

A different sort of crisis pressed Synesius into service when, in the summer of 411, Cyrene came under attack from barbarian raiders. Synesius sent a series of letters out to well-placed associates seeking urgent help. In a letter to the bureaucrat Troilus, Synesius compliments him for his embrace of philosophy and tells him about the war and famine that have descended on Cyrene. The place that gave birth to Synesius will "be honored [by Troilus] because of its citizen who is a philosopher, but he will pity it because of the gentleness of his nature."[64] This should, Synesius continues, induce Troilus to approach his boss, the praetorian prefect Anthemius, and convince him to rescue the city from these misfortunes. Synesius then offers a carefully blended mix of details about the terrible situation in Cyrenaica and philosophical injunctions describing the obligation of Troilus to convince Anthemius to act. A similar letter written at the same time to Anysius, the military governor of the region who had stepped down about a month prior to the attacks, requests that he persuade the emperor to offer performance bonuses to one specific military unit and to send more members of that unit to the region.[65] Unlike Troilus, Anysius entertained no pretentions of being a philosopher, and the appeal has no direct philosophical references, but here, too, Synesius trades off of his reputation as a philosopher to request imperial relief for his home region.

Philosophical action in a time of crisis sometimes involved more than writing letters to imperial officials. In 405, Synesius organized a rag-tag militia to defend Cyrene against raiders. In a letter to Olympius, his classmate at Hypatia's school, Synesius asks for help getting bows and arrows in case enemies besiege the city.[66] Although the letter does create an interesting rhetorical contrast between the luxurious gifts that Olympius might send and the weapons that Synesius desperately needs, its detailed descriptions of how the materials will be used suggests that the request was quite serious.[67] Synesius complains about the poor quality of Egyptian arrows and, fashioning himself a later version of Archimedes, he brags about a piece of artillery he has built to throw heavy stones from the turrets of fortifications.

If the letter to Olympius presents Synesius as Archimedes, another letter written that same year to his brother suggests that, like Socrates at the Battle of Potidaea or the Athenian teacher Dexippus following the sack of Athens in 267 CE, Synesius actually took the field in defense of his city. Synesius organized a force of local citizens that could fight barbarian raiders using hatchets, lances, scimitars, and even olive-wood clubs. The letter, which purports to be written the night before this force was to battle the barbarians, suggests that Synesius himself planned to fight and entrusted his children to his brother should he die.[68]

Synesius's military service, in the end, illustrates the true extent of a philosopher's obligation to his city. The philosopher did whatever it took to guide the city and its citizens along a more philosophical path. If he or she thought that the interests of philosophy required it, the philosopher did everything from helping a friend in a contentious lawsuit to taking up arms to defend his or her home. Although some philosophers cynically profited from these activities, true philosophers acted in this way because they thought that they must. They, almost alone among their fellow citizens, weighed their public actions not by what rewards they could receive or by what penalties they might suffer. Instead, they considered only how their interventions would have the greatest effect. Synesius suggests that public affairs often took him away from his life of contemplation and teaching, but this did not make such activity any less a part of the philosophical life. A philosopher who put his or her own desire for a tranquil life over the needs of his fellow citizens was no less selfish and unphilosophical than one who engaged in public activity out of a desire for money and office. In both cases, he privileged his own comfort over the proper application of philosophical virtues.

Hypatia certainly agreed with this sentiment. It could not have been particularly appealing for a female pagan philosopher to step into Alexandrian public life as the religious conflicts of the mid-380s began to heat up. It would have been even less appealing for Hypatia to work with her students to recreate some sort of cultural consensus that traditional culture could coexist with Christianity in Alexandria after the Serapeum riot. Undoubtedly, Hypatia would rather have lived a simple life of teaching and philosophical contemplation. At the same time, all sources agree that she became deeply engaged in the life of her city and remained so for decades. Synesius helps us to understand why she did this. Alexandria was not threatened by barbarians as Cyrenaica would be in 405, but it did face the real risk of social disintegration in the 390s. At the turn of the fifth century, Alexandria needed Hypatia to step forward to serve it just as Cyrenaica required Synesius to defend it. Hypatia's obligation as a philosopher was to move the city, its leaders, and its residents towards a more philosophical way of living. In a city that had just experienced a wave of violence led by philosophers, she especially needed to show Alexandrians how philosophy retained a central role in directing their affairs. While this sort of philosophical leadership seems less dangerous than leading a militia into battle with barbarians, we will see that both types of philosophically inspired public activity could be fatal.

7

Hypatia's Sisters

By the time that Hypatia's most famous student, Synesius, left her school in the mid-390s, Hypatia had assumed an active political role in one of the largest and most complicated cities on earth. Hypatia's gender prevented her from holding most civic offices and exercising formal power in Alexandria, but the informal expectations of how elite, educated women were supposed to behave did more to define the public role she assumed. Beneath all that Hypatia accomplished was the reality that, by publicly teaching and practicing philosophy, Hypatia was a woman operating in what remained a predominantly male environment. Hypatia always stood out in ways that attracted second looks, curious comments, unwanted amorous advances, or insensitive remarks from those around her. As a self-assured philosopher who (at least ostensibly) cared little about what ignorant people said about her, these things may not have particularly bothered Hypatia. Depending upon the situation, these incidents could either be obstacles that Hypatia needed to overcome or situations that she could skillfully turn in ways that enhanced her prestige. But this does not change the fact that Hypatia navigated a set of formal restrictions on her conduct, unwritten assumptions about her proper role, and regular annoyances unlike anything that her male counterparts faced.

Although we often imagine that Hypatia confronted these issues alone, female philosophers were not particularly rare in antiquity. As early as 1690, Gilles Ménage collected the names and identifying details for over sixty-five female philosophers.[1] Scholars have periodically returned to recapitulate and expand this list. It now includes figures ranging across time from Aspasia and Theano in the fifth century BCE through sixth-century CE figures like Theodora, the woman to whom Damascius dedicated his *Life of Isidore*.[2] While nearly all of these surveys devote considerable space to the career of Hypatia, her female contemporaries get much less attention. In some cases, they get none at all.[3] But their anonymity has little to do with their philosophical achievements.

Hypatia had four significant female contemporaries who were trained as philosophers, taught philosophy or mathematics, or played a public role like the one she assumed. Three of these, Pandrosion of Alexandria, Sosipatra of Pergamum, and the wife of Maximus of Ephesus, are older than Hypatia. The fourth woman, Asclepigenia of Athens, was the daughter of Hypatia's younger rival, the Athenian philosopher Plutarch. Each of these women, however, established a philosophical reputation that was described, recognized, and admired by her male contemporaries. None of her peers were quite as accomplished as Hypatia, but a closer look at the ways in which they navigated similar obstacles shows what was unique about Hypatia and what her gender meant to Hypatia's emergence as one of the empire's most prominent philosophical voices.

Pandrosion

The activities of the early fourth-century Alexandrian mathematician Pandrosion most closely resembled those of Hypatia. While Pandrosion may have had the highest profile of these four women during her lifetime, she left no significant imprint on the historical record. No narrative source mentions her, none of her writings survive, and nothing written by her students has been preserved.[4] Pandrosion is instead known only from the arguments made against her by Pappus in Book 3 of his *Collectio*.[5] In this section of the text, Pappus takes issue with a method of finding cube roots that Pandrosion pioneered. His criticism takes the form of an address to Pandrosion that is at times both pedantic and aggressive.[6] It begins with Pappus sarcastically defining for Pandrosion what the basic mathematical terms *problem* and *theorem* mean.[7] A problem, he writes, is a test of a proposition that can ultimately be possible or impossible. A theorem, however, must be demonstrated to be correct. Pappus then tells Pandrosion that anyone who claims to know mathematics should be censured if she confuses these things and sets up a mathematical investigation incorrectly.

This matters, Pappus continues, because "some people who claimed to have learned mathematics from you lately gave us an ignorant explanation of problems."[8] Pappus condescendingly offers to explain the proofs of these and related questions to Pandrosion, "for your benefit and that of other lovers of learning."[9] Pappus then proceeds through a series of problems related to him by students of Pandrosion. The first student is described as "someone who seems to be a great geometrician,"[10] but who nonetheless "set his problems ignorantly" when he sought to determine cube roots and their squares. When this student brought his work to Pappus and asked the mathematician to critique it, his ignorance moved Pappus to write a thorough repudiation of the method.

Pappus's repudiation is both comprehensive and convincing, but it is also completely unfair. Modern mathematicians have found that the approach attributed to Pandrosion's student works at least as well as that favored by Pappus.[11] It is possible that Pappus may truly have believed that Pandrosion was introducing a terrible mathematical practice that needed explicit correction, but it is more likely that this attack on Pandrosion and her prominent student reflects a genuine rivalry between Pandrosion and Pappus.

The second section of Book 3 further suggests that Pappus saw Pandrosion as a genuine rival worth engaging. It focuses on the problem of "exhibiting the arithmetic, geometric, and harmonic means in a semicircle." Pappus mocks "another certain person" who claimed that these could be exhibited simply by drawing four lines within the semicircle. Again, however, Pappus is being somewhat disingenuous. Pappus affirms that this method does discover the geometric and arithmetic means, but he discards it because the speaker does not explicitly say how one of the lines marks the harmonic mean.[12] Technically, this may have been true, but it was also self-evident that the method did actually mark the harmonic mean. The missing explanation that Pappus felt doomed Pandrosion's approach would have been essentially a superfluous gloss to an otherwise sound and thorough discussion. Here, too, a modern assessment of the method employed by Pandrosion's student confirms that it works as well as that with which Pappus sought to replace it.[13]

Ultimately, Pappus's critiques provide little direct information about Pandrosion and her activities. He does, however, offer some tantalizing glimpses into the world of this innovative and influential female mathematician. It is clear that Pandrosion was a contemporary of Pappus who was active in Alexandria in the early or middle part of the fourth century. If the methods that Pappus criticizes were truly new, Pandrosion may well have been a younger rival of Pappus and a contemporary of Hypatia's father, Theon. This means that the young Hypatia would certainly have known about Pandrosion's career and may even have known Pandrosion herself.

Pappus's text also shows that Pandrosion's teaching activities resembled those of Hypatia. All of the articles and pronouns that Pappus uses to describe Pandrosion's students are masculine. This suggests that, like Hypatia, Pandrosion taught mathematics to male students, probably in some sort of a public setting. Pappus's comment that one of her students is thought to be a great geometrician also indicates that Pandrosion and the members of her circle had begun to earn a reputation in Alexandria for laying out innovative mathematical approaches.

The blame that Pappus assigns to Pandrosion for the failures of her students also suggests that Pandrosion was somehow involved in the creation, review, or publication of the texts that Pappus had read. This points to a scenario like the one in which Synesius sent some of his philosophical works to Hypatia so that she could comment on them before he distributed them more widely.[14] It is also possible that the mathematical works of Pandrosion's students that Pappus saw may have resulted from an even closer intellectual collaboration between Pandrosion and the men in her circle. If this process resembled that through which students in fifth-century philosophical schools authored their first commentaries under the supervision of their teacher, the work on cube roots that Pappus critiqued may have been the equivalent of a thesis in which Pandrosion and her student worked together to apply her teaching to a new problem.[15] In either case, however, Pappus felt confident that he could convincingly tie to Pandrosion the things that he found to be problematic in the work of her students. This sort of attack indicates that Pandrosion had developed a reputation as a successful mentor of high-profile male students.

The scant information that Pappus provides does not allow us to say much more about Pandrosion. We know, however, that Pappus and others in the Alexandrian mathematical establishment appear to have ultimately stifled whatever innovative techniques Pandrosion and her students pioneered. Not only do no texts by Pandrosion currently survive, but none of the great Platonic mathematicians of the later fifth and early sixth centuries like Proclus and Marinus seem to know anything about her, her students, or their ideas. Later Byzantine and Arabic mathematicians also seem not to know about her. This suggests that her scholarly line ended at some point in fourth century, and that, when it did, her work and those of her students was eventually forgotten. Pappus prevailed over Pandrosion. This victory had the unfortunate effect of almost completely obscuring the legacy of the Alexandrian female intellectual whose career likely served as a model for the young Hypatia.

Sosipatra

Sosipatra presents the opposite problem from that posed by Pandrosion. Pandrosion was quite influential while she lived but quickly forgotten after her death, whereas Sosipatra has a historical legacy that far surpasses the impact that she had during life. In fact, more ancient narrative material survives about Sosipatra than about any other late antique female philosopher, including Hypatia.[16] This is again largely happenstance. Sosipatra belonged to the intellectual family of Eunapius of Sardis, an author who composed biographical sketches of his teachers, their teachers, and all of the other members of his intellectual family tree in his celebrated work *The Lives of the Sophists and Philosophers*.[17] This work survives in large part because the intellectual lineage to which Eunapius belonged ultimately shaped the Byzantine and Renaissance Platonic tradition. Later Platonists saw themselves as descendants of the men and women Eunapius describes, and, for this reason, they continued to read and copy the biographies that Eunapius wrote. Unfortunately, this understandable activity has sometimes distorted the contemporary impact of the figures Eunapius describes. Sosipatra undoubtedly benefitted the most from this.

The wife of Iamblichus's student Eustathius, Sosipatra belongs to Eunapius's intellectual family because she served as a secondary advisor to Eunapius's teacher Chrysanthius. She was born near Ephesus into a wealthy family.[18] According to Eunapius, at the age of five she was entrusted to the care of two Chaldeans who took her away, taught her, and initiated her into a host of religious mysteries.[19] When they returned her to her home, they gave Sosipatra garments for religious mysteries and secret books. They then disappeared.[20] This rather implausible story sets up the intuitive brilliance that Eunapius suggests Sosipatra displayed for the rest of her life. Eunapius writes that she had no teachers other than the mysterious Chaldeans, but she could readily recite "the works of the poets, philosophers, and orators. And those works that others comprehend only incompletely and dimly . . . she could explain with ease, serenely and painlessly."[21] When she reached her teens, she married Eustathius and correctly predicted that the marriage would last five years and produce three children.[22] Upon Eustathius's death, Sosipatra moved to her family's estate in Pergamum and attached herself to the teaching circle of Aedesius.

Sosipatra played a unique role in Aedesius's school. Eunapius makes it clear that she did not teach publicly and that her teaching was not open to every student of Aedesius. Instead, she "philosophized in her own home" and opened the space only to those who were members of the inner circle of Aedesius's school.[23] They were devoted to her and regularly sought her out for instruction because the teaching of Sosipatra was of such high quality that she even "rivaled" Aedesius. Her lessons then served as a crucial part of the philosophical training that he provided.[24]

Eunapius recounts two anecdotes that involve Sosipatra's relationship with Philometer, a kinsman. In the first story, Eunapius describes a magical spell that Philometer cast in an effort to induce Sosipatra to fall in love with him. Sosipatra detected this and, with the help of Maximus of Ephesus, she was able to turn it back.[25] In the second instance, Sosipatra was teaching the students of Aedesius in her home when she stopped in midsentence and remarked that she sensed that Philometer's carriage had overturned. It was later learned that the carriage had in fact toppled at that very moment.[26] Eunapius then concludes his portrait with a discussion of Sosipatra's three children. Two of them betrayed the legacy of their parents by becoming lawyers.[27] The third was the philosopher Antoninus, who moved to Egypt and spent most of his time at the temple of Serapis in the Alexandrian suburb of Canopus.[28]

There are a few elements of Eunapius's portrait of Sosipatra that have immediate relevance to Hypatia. Although Hypatia never married and Sosipatra did, the biographical traditions associated with both women contain memorable anecdotes that emphasize their ability to resist the charms of male suitors. Beyond this point, however, the similarities begin to break down. Both women were philosophers who taught male students, but their educational backgrounds, the source of their authority as teachers, and the nature of their teaching were all radically different. Hypatia was trained in a scholastic setting according to established mathematical, geometric, and philosophical curricula. Her educational pedigree strongly resembled that of other conventionally trained late Roman philosophers and mathematicians. Sosipatra, by contrast, was instructed in divine arts by teachers who, Eunapius suggests, may have been supernatural beings.[29] She had great knowledge of poetry, rhetoric and philosophy, but this knowledge was not acquired from any particular teacher. These pedigrees lent the two women different types of authority over students. As Synesius's letters to her show, Hypatia's expertise in these conventional disciplines fostered teacher-student relationships that mirrored those enjoyed by male teachers and their disciples.[30] Eunapius makes it clear that Sosipatra was capable of commenting on and explaining any of the ideas contained within even the most complicated philosophical text, but she did not do this in any regular or programmatic fashion. Sosipatra was respected for her teaching of the noncanonical but more spectacular areas of theology and religious mysteries.[31]

These features also helped to determine the nature of the philosophical schools in which each woman participated. Hypatia was the head of a philosophical circle and taught in a school that was open to all who wanted to come.[32] She served as the intellectual parent to her students and led their initiation into the higher mysteries of philosophy.[33] In other words, her teaching and the school in which it occurred were both framed in traditional ways that reflected the conventional basis of her authority as a teacher. For all of her intellectual and spiritual gifts, Sosipatra did not enjoy this type of relationship with those who studied under her. Unlike Hypatia, her teaching was done in her own home in a semipublic space to which access was usually restricted. It also covered "elective" subjects that were not part of the traditional curriculum and were only offered to selected members of the school of Aedesius.[34] Her teaching supplemented the training that formed the core of the intellectual patrimony that students took away from Aedesius. To use a modern analogy, Hypatia did the equivalent of admitting students, supervising their coursework, and advising their dissertations, while Sosipatra gave esoteric graduate seminars and served as an outside member of the doctoral committees headed by Aedesius.

Asclepigenia and the Wife of Maximus of Ephesus

We can say less about Asclepigenia and the wife of Maximus of Ephesus, two of Hypatia's other contemporaries, but the little that we know further develops our picture of the range of activities open to female philosophers. The Athenian Asclepigenia provides another example of a female philosopher who taught advanced philosophy to male students in a semiprivate space. The only mention of her appears in a short passage of Marinus's *Life of Proclus* that explains how Proclus manifested what Marinus terms the "theurgic virtue," the highest of the six philosophical virtues around which the text is organized.[35] Proclus, Marinus explains, had a "more divine foreknowledge of things to come . . . because he indulged himself in the compositions and the conversations and even the sacred and silent top spinnings of the Chaldeans."[36] He possessed these skills, Marinus continues, because, while studying under Syrianus, "he received these things and learned their significance and other application from Asclepigenia, the daughter of Plutarch. For the rites and entire theurgic teaching from the great Nestorius[37] were preserved by her alone because they were handed down to her by her father."[38]

Like Hypatia, Asclepigenia was the daughter of an accomplished teacher who personally supervised her education. Asclepigenia's teaching of Proclus, however, more closely resembles that done by Sosipatra for the students of Aedesius. Asclepigenia provided supplementary instruction in areas that were essential for a philosopher to function on the highest level. This teaching was not part of the regular curriculum but was instead only offered in special circumstances to a select subgroup of students. Syrianus, Proclus's main teacher, was initially unwilling (and ultimately unable) to provide training in these areas.[39] Proclus went to Asclepigenia because he needed to. The instruction he received, however, was first-rate, and the theurgic virtues that Asclepigenia helped Proclus to develop are held out as the absolute pinnacle of Proclus's philosophical accomplishments by his successors. Asclepigenia evidently had a wide and profound philosophical knowledge, but, like Sosipatra, she found herself teaching important materials that were outside of the standard Platonic curriculum. There is no evidence to say conclusively that her gender prevented her from doing the more conventional exegesis of texts that formed the backbone of a Platonic education, but it is also clear that her gender enabled her to do the sort of esoteric theurgical teaching that male counterparts like Syrianus sometimes avoided.[40]

If Asclepigenia can help us to better contextualize the teaching that Hypatia did, the wife of Maximus of Ephesus offers a useful analog to the public role that Hypatia found herself playing. Like Sosipatra, she is known only from Eunapius's *Lives of Sophists*, but, unlike her Pergamene peer, she is not the subject of a dedicated biography. In fact, she only appears in the text twice and her name is never even mentioned.[41] Eunapius introduces her only so that he can contrast her admirable actions and character with those of her husband, Maximus. Her first appearance comes at a point in the text when Maximus manipulated omens until they seemed to favor his decision to join Julian at court. At that moment, "all the people of Asia flocked in haste to Maximus" in order to seek favors from him. This was, of course, also the moment when Maximus's lust for influence and the adoration of the public began to draw him away from proper philosophical practice.[42]

According to Eunapius, Maximus's wife behaved differently. While Maximus held court with his new clients, "the women poured in by the side-door to see his wife, marveling at her happiness … and so profound was her knowledge of philosophy that she made Maximus seem not to know how to swim or even know his alphabet."[43] As we saw earlier, Maximus's decision to take on a public role under Julian caused the unraveling of his career and ultimately led to his execution. Though his wife was forced into a public position by his actions, Eunapius makes clear that her philosophical purity remained intact despite her husband's unphilosophical worldly ambitions. In this, she showed herself to be a much superior philosopher.

The second anecdote that Eunapius tells about Maximus's wife further reinforces the impression that she held fast to a philosophical way of life even after her husband had fallen away. After the deaths of the emperors Julian and Jovian and the failed usurpation of Julian's family member Procopius, the emperor Valens launched an investigation into the conduct and loyalties of Julian's most trusted associates. Maximus was fined an immense sum, sent back to Asia to collect it, and then tortured when he could not come up with the money. He instructed his wife to buy poison so that he could commit suicide. She did this and, when she brought it to him, "she insisted on drinking it first and immediately died . . . but Maximus did not drink."[44] Maximus eventually was saved from further tortures by a friendly government official, but he squandered this second chance by again taking on a set of inappropriate activities.[45] In Eunapius's account, Maximus's failings are highlighted by his wife's ability to blend philosophical learning and appropriate philosophical behavior. Although Maximus was more renowned, his wife proved herself more philosophical because she chose to die rather than suffer through a life in which philosophers were persecuted.

Maximus's wife shows us two important things about Hypatia's female philosophical contemporaries. First, her experiences reveal that Hypatia was not unique in receiving clients and using her influence to further the interests of others. This does not tell the whole story, however. While Hypatia met with male governors in public settings, the wife of Maximus conducted her patronage activity among women in a different space of her home from that in which her husband spoke with male petitioners. The two women played similar roles, but the scope of Hypatia's activity is far more impressive. Second, the way in which Maximus's wife died shows that the martyrdom of a female philosopher carried very powerful symbolic weight. The suicide of such a committed philosopher highlighted the dangerous political climate that emerged following the death of Julian and underlined the unjust persecution that philosophers suffered under Valens. Eunapius also, of course, used her heroism to illustrate Maximus's failings. His wife bravely died, whereas Maximus demurred and ultimately backed out of their suicide pact. In death, as in life, Eunapius reveals that Maximus's wife had proven herself to be the superior philosopher.

Hypatia Reconsidered

These four female teachers and philosophers provide us with a range of close but inexact matches for what Hypatia would do in her career. Pandrosion taught some of the same material as Hypatia in the same city in which Hypatia would later be active. Like Hypatia, she also instructed male students and apparently supervised high-level original work done by them. Pandrosion, however, does not seem to have achieved the level of influence that Hypatia did. Pandrosion must have done things like writing letters of reference for her students and their friends, but no evidence survives that allows one to see the true extent of her social authority. It is reasonable to assume, however, that Pandrosion had nothing like the political reach of Hypatia. Pappus's attacks on Pandrosion suggest that she was something of an insurgent whose ideas and students conflicted with the Alexandrian mathematical establishment. Because she was not even the most influential mathematician in Alexandria during her lifetime, it is hard to imagine governors and other dignitaries courting Pandrosion in the way that they did Hypatia. Hypatia, by contrast, seems to have been a creature of the Alexandrian establishment whose great skill convinced many Alexandrians that mathematics ought to be a subordinate component of Platonic philosophical training. While Pandrosion's innovations generated resistance, Hypatia seems to have genuinely succeeded in changing the intellectual dynamics of the city. Because of this, audiences with her had a symbolic impact that a similar meeting with Pandrosion never could.

The other three women offer less exact parallels for what Hypatia did. Like Hypatia, Asclepigenia and Sosipatra both taught advanced philosophy to male students. The conditions under which this teaching occurred, however, differed dramatically. Asclepigenia and Sosipatra taught in their own homes and depended upon a male philosopher with whom they had developed a relationship to provide them with students. Because they did not teach publicly, Asclepigenia and Sosipatra had no other way to attract pupils. Their ability to continue teaching depended upon the whims of male philosophers who headed the philosophical circles from which the students came. These were learned women, but they were not teachers who controlled the logistics of their teaching. Hypatia did. She was recognized as the true philosophical parent of male students and could tell them what to study and when to study it. Unlike Asclepigenia and Sosiptra, Hypatia also taught all of the texts within the standard philosophical curriculum in public to any students who wished to learn. This meant that she controlled the access that students had to her and superintended their entire progression through the curriculum. Hypatia's success then depended on the quality of her instruction rather than on her ability to maintain a cooperative relationship with a male philosopher. This certainly enabled Hypatia to have a much greater intellectual impact than talented peers like Sosipatra and Asclepigenia.

These other female philosophers suggest that Hypatia's great public prominence was perhaps the most unique feature of her career. The only one of these other women for whom we have any evidence of public activity is the wife of Maximus of Ephesus. The wife of Maximus apparently had female clients, and she used her influence at the court of Julian to help them in whatever way she could. She gained this access to the court through her husband, however, and she could exercise it only as long as he remained influential. Once Julian died and Maximus fell from favor, his wife's public activities also stopped. She had become no less of a philosopher, but she had lost all of the influence that Maximus's prominence had once opened to her.

Hypatia was a different case. The public role that she played and the influence that she had grew out of philosophical virtues that she exercised in her own right. Hypatia earned her public position through her learning and the public displays of her philosophical lifestyle. That position would only be lost only if she ceased to be seen as a philosopher whose life embodied her teaching. Unlike the wife of Maximus, who apparently only fielded requests from female petitioners, Hypatia also had male clients and associates, as well as a voice on policy matters that her older counterpart never did. Hypatia thus played a far more prominent and permanent public role than we can see attributed to any of her female philosophical peers.

Pandrosion, Sosipatra, Asclepigenia, and Maximus's wife show that women could do things very similar to what Hypatia did. But none of the men who wrote about them speak of the challenges a woman faced if she actually tried to do these things. These challenges would have been significant. The comments that Socrates and Damascius make about Hypatia's beauty suggest that her appearance was always noticed and commented upon, a fact that must have been annoying to Hypatia. Other comments suggest something a little more distressing. Socrates and Damascius, for example, both say that everyone in the cities respected Hypatia for her temperance and virtue, but they also make it clear that she had to demonstrate this virtue in ways that male contemporaries did not. While some male philosophers advertised chastity as a mark of their virtue, the ancient prejudice that women were more susceptible to sexual passion than men meant that celibacy became much more important to show when the teacher was a woman.[46] This explains the odd emphasis that male authors place on stories that demonstrate a female philosopher's ability to resist sexual temptation. As we have seen, memorable anecdotes illustrate, in graphic fashion, the ways in which Hypatia and Sosipatra were impervious to the pursuit of male suitors. This allows authors like Eunapius and Damascius to dispense with any notion that their subject's gender negatively impacted her ability to resist carnal temptation. It is also, not coincidentally, a tool that can preemptively dispel any suspicions about the sexual activities of women who spend much of their time alone with groups of young men.[47]

This tendency in our literary sources must certainly reflect the sorts of conversations that perpetually surrounded women like Hypatia and Sosipatra. They were single women who spent time in private with young, often unmarried, men. Even if they had a strong reputation for chastity and temperance, it is hard to imagine a world in which people did not gossip about their sexuality. The stories that our authors tell respond to the rumors that probably surrounded these women for every day of their professional lives.

Hypatia also faced more subtle forms of discrimination that men either did not remark on or did not even notice. When Hypatia wore a *tribon*, the traditional cloak of a philosopher, she advertised her philosophical achievements.[48] A man wearing this cloak called attention to his education and cultivation. When a woman wore it, however, the *tribon* called more attention to her gender than it did to her intellect. Indeed, Damascius even engages in a little bit of word play that makes light of the fact that Hypatia wore the *tribon*. His odd comment that Hypatia "wrapped herself in the philosopher's cloak" is followed in the text by the two words "the woman," and then by another clause in which Damascius mentions Hypatia going out in the middle of the city to teach.[49] This is an elegant little quip. Both the clause about Hypatia wearing a *tribon* and the one describing her teaching in the city contain feminine singular participles that make clear that Damascius is speaking about a woman. His addition of "the woman" between them is superfluous, but also quite deliberate. Damascius added these words so that he could emphasize the oddity of a woman putting on a philosopher's cloak to go into the middle of the city to teach. He does nothing of the sort to any man in his text.

This reflects the persistent attention to her gender that Hypatia faced throughout her career. She was always recognized as a FEMALE philosopher, and therefore she was always different from most other philosophers around her. No male author could have completely understood what her experience was like, and none appears to have tried.

If Pappus's digs against Pandrosion are any guide, Hypatia may have been seen as less skilled than her male contemporaries, and her students may consequently have been taken less seriously. It is likely that Hypatia acutely understood this prejudice. She may have labored under the impression that male opinions about her gender forced her to work constantly to convince men that the knowledge she had and influence she claimed was legitimate. But it is also possible that Hypatia did not particularly care what these men thought. She may have been completely secure in her position because she felt that she had developed the full complement of philosophical virtues and lived completely in accordance with them. Her philosophy would then have transcended the gender of her body and allowed her to function completely on the ungendered level of the soul. Even if this was the case, Hypatia needed to steel herself to ignore the endless rumors, slights, and annoyances that she faced. These things represented an additional obstacle to pure contemplation that her male colleagues did not experience and never needed to overcome.

We cannot know what Hypatia thought as she endured these things. We can say, though, that when Hypatia decided to teach in public and assume the philosopher's public advocacy role, she set out to do something that was extremely difficult and emotionally taxing. And, in a world before feminism, she did it alone. She was not trying to advance a movement or create opportunities for the next generation of women. No movement existed, and there was no real hope of her charting a path that other women could later follow. Hypatia pushed past the limits of what other female philosophers had done because this was what she wanted to do. She accepted the glances, whispers, and jokes of her male contemporaries, knowing full well that they were a special burden that she had to bear in order to live the life she wanted. There is a real heroism in this that is seldom appreciated.

8

Murder in the Street

By the 410s, Hypatia's commitment to philosophical public service had placed her at the center of a new, pragmatic Alexandrian status quo that emerged in the years following the Serapeum destruction. The city council and imperial governors retained control over the political affairs of the city, the Nicene bishop managed the largest Christian group in the city, and Hypatia's circle modeled the possibility of elite and ecclesiastical coexistence. We have seen how, in the later 390s and early 400s, Theophilus corresponded with Hypatia's students and went so far as to preside at the wedding of Synesius.[1] Theophilus eventually convinced Synesius to become a bishop, and even agreed to let him remain true to the philosophy Hypatia had taught while he presided over his congregation.

Peaceful coexistence and cooperation should not be mistaken for trust, however. This was an uneasy working relationship. Synesius, for example, was clear that he did not trust Theophilus to remain true to his guarantee of philosophical autonomy. In fact, Synesius wrote out the conditions under which he agreed to serve as bishop in a letter he addressed to his brother before he accepted ordination. This was an insurance policy to protect him against later accusations of heresy should Theophilus's attitude change.[2]

The bishop, the civic elites, and philosophers like Synesius were able to work together for as long as Theophilus lived. When Theophilus died in 412, however, the city again erupted in conflict. Theophilus had been grooming his nephew Cyril to succeed him, but Theophilus fell ill before Cyril had consolidated enough support to make the transition seamlessly.[3] Apparently incapacitated by the illness, Theophilus lingered on long enough for affairs in the church to begin to drift.[4] In the interim, Timothy, an archdeacon in the Alexandrian church, appears to have organized a challenge to Cyril. When Theophilus eventually succumbed, partisans of Cyril and Timothy mobilized and began fighting in the streets. The struggle went on for three days and concluded only when Abundantius, the military commander of imperial troops based in Egypt, backed Cyril.[5]

While the fighting concluded quickly and decisively, the aftermath was messy. The contest between Timothy and Cyril lasted just long enough for the Novatian Christian leaders in Alexandria to express support for Timothy.[6] This proved to be a serious mistake. Cyril was a tough, resolute leader who had neither the inclination nor the temperament to forgive people who dared to challenge him. Soon after he secured power, Cyril took measures to punish these outsiders who had meddled in his succession. He targeted the Novatians first. Cyril ordered his followers to close up their churches in Alexandria, confiscate all of the sacramental vessels they used in services, and strip their bishop, Theopemptus, of all of his property.[7]

Cyril's vindictive punishment of the Novatians hinted at a broader shift that Alexandrian political life would undergo in the next few years. Cyril understood that he was less secure in his position than Theophilus had been, and he resolved to respond to any challenges he faced with threats of violence. This put the Theophilan consensus through which elites and clergy would work together to try to limit unrest under tremendous strain. Even Synesius, who was only indirectly involved with this transition, seems wary of Cyril.[8]

Further strains appeared after a new round of violence broke out in the city in 414. This was caused by, of all things, a show put on by a group of dancers.[9] The governor, Orestes, published an imperial edict regulating dancing performances that had been very loudly and publicly applauded by a Christian teacher named Hierax. Hierax was known to be a strong public supporter of Cyril, and when he appeared at a dance performance in the theater the following Saturday, the largely Jewish crowd suspected that the bishop had sent him to stir up trouble. Orestes shared their suspicion and he ordered Hierax to be arrested and tortured publicly in the theater.

Perhaps because he suspected members of the Jewish community of supporting his rival Timothy in 412, Cyril saw the arrest of Hierax as a challenge to his power.[10] Cyril summoned Alexandria's Jewish leaders to a meeting and threatened to punish them personally if they did not stop the Jewish attacks on Christians. One can imagine that this both bewildered and terrified the leaders of the Jewish community. While Jews had called for the punishment of Hierax and applauded his torture, Orestes had actually ordered it carried out. Jewish leaders, whose followers had not attacked anyone, had neither the power nor the authority to restrain the governor from punishing Hierax. They must have immediately understood that Cyril was now trying to compel the Jewish community leaders to silence all public Jewish complaints about Hierax and other followers of Cyril.

If Theophilus had tried something like this, his reputation for ferocity and skill as a politician may well have intimidated his guests. But, in 414, Cyril did not seem as fearsome as Theophilus. Cyril was just a young bishop who had barely survived the coup of a Christian rival in 412 and who had just seen the governor back a Jewish complaint against one of his followers.[11] Cyril's threats looked like a badly concealed bluff—and the Alexandrian Jewish leadership was prepared to call it. When news of this meeting reached the wider Jewish community, the response was violent indignation. Far from silencing Jewish critics, Cyril's action instead incited them. Contemporary sources speak about Jews organizing a massacre of Christians in the city by calling out that the main church in Alexandria was on fire and then cutting down those Christians who rushed to put out the flames.[12] This particular detail seems unlikely, but there is no doubt that a Jewish-Christian riot of some sort erupted, and that, in the initial phase, Jewish fighters seem to have bested the Christians.

The next morning, Cyril assembled a large group of his own followers and counterattacked. His associates seized Jewish synagogues, stole the possessions of the Jews thought to be involved in the previous night's violence, and drove them from the city. While some contemporary Christian sources speak about this event leading to the complete expulsion of all Jews from Alexandria, such a thing was plainly impossible in a city that was at one point 20 percent Jewish.[13] But this was a significant show of force designed to send a message to anyone who doubted Cyril's strength.

The Jewish-Christian violence posed a different sort of threat to Orestes. His primary responsibility as governor was to keep the chaotic city of Alexandria under some semblance of control. His decision to regulate theatrical performances had backfired. Instead of calming the city, it had caused a riot. The punishment of Hierax had further inflamed the city, and the recent Jewish-Christian conflict produced a level of tension in Alexandria not matched since the Serapeum destruction. With the city fast slipping out of his control, Orestes sent a report of the recent developments to the court of the child emperor Theodosius II. Cyril also sent a report. While the two messages traveled to Constantinople, Cyril's congregation prevailed upon him to send emissaries to Orestes to try to reach some sort of reconciliation.

Orestes then made his second big mistake. He flatly turned down Cyril's request for negotiations. The reasons for his obstinacy are obscure. It is possible that Orestes believed that the imperial court would respond as it had done with the Serapeum violence by sending a strong signal that all violence must cease. It is equally possible that he misjudged the power of Cyril. Orestes's rejection of negotiations, however, redefined the situation. Up to this point, the conflict had been between proxies. Orestes had punished Hierax and supporters of Cyril had attacked Jews, but the bishop and the prefect had not yet been in direct conflict with one another. Orestes's refusal to discuss reconciliation with Cyril, however, created a situation where the two now faced off directly against each other. Neither could give ground without losing face.

Cyril responded first. He came before Orestes with the Gospels in his hand, "believing that respect for religion would induce [Orestes] to lay aside his resentment."[14] This subtle power play allowed Cyril to claim that his authority as a Christian leader surpassed the temporal power that Orestes wielded. It also offered Orestes a chance to gently back down in a way that saved face by reaffirming his Christian piety. Actions like these had allowed bishops in other cities to assert a wholly symbolic religious authority over political leaders while political leaders could claim to have made amends for their misdeeds.[15] Cyril probably hoped it would work in this case, too. Orestes, however, remained unmoved. Orestes had been baptized by the patriarch Atticus of Constantinople, and the conflicts that pitted bishops of Constantinople against those of Alexandria meant that Orestes had no interest in suggesting that an Alexandrian bishop enjoyed any type of authority over government officials.[16] Instead of backing down, Orestes dug in further.

Cyril then moved from the subtle assertion of his religious authority over Orestes to a more overt and confrontational challenge to the governor. In a clear escalation of the conflict, Cyril called 500 monks from the monasteries of Nitria to Alexandria. These monks were not like the peaceful Franciscans that we might now picture. They were instead a group of devoted followers of the Alexandrian bishop who would not hesitate to take to the streets. They had proven intensely loyal to their patriarch on many occasions, but their zealousness also meant that their actions were often difficult to predict. When they entered the city, the ascetics swarmed around Orestes's chariot and began to call him a pagan and an idolater. Clearly frightened, Orestes protested that he was a baptized Christian, but the monks were not at all interested in hearing this.

Cyril's summons of the monks of Nitria escalated his conflict with the prefect, but the bishop did not intend for the incident to become violent. The crowd of monks was supposed to awaken Orestes to the danger of confronting Cyril and bring him to the table to make a deal. This remained a negotiation, albeit one that was getting ever more contentious. Unfortunately for Cyril, some of the monks that he summoned from the desert did not understand the role that they were meant to play. One of them, a man named Ammonius, got carried away and threw a stone at Orestes's head. Surrounded by monks who were yelling at the governor, and seeing the blood streaming from his wound, the prefect's bodyguards fled in order to escape what they thought was an organized attempt by the monks to stone imperial agents to death. Orestes was saved only when a crowd of Alexandrians spirited him to safety.

Cyril certainly neither planned nor sanctioned a physical attack on the prefect. Inspired by his love of the bishop and his hatred of Cyril's enemies, Ammonius had acted on his own. At the same time, Ammonius's assault on Orestes fundamentally changed the conflict. Neither prefect nor bishop could now easily step back from it. Orestes could not leave a physical attack on his person unpunished. He ordered Ammonius arrested and had the monk tortured so severely that he died from its effects. He then sent a report of this incident of sedition to Constantinople.

This put Cyril in the difficult position of either agreeing that Ammonius deserved to die for his aggressive defense of his patriarch or celebrating Ammonius's actions. Both approaches had their dangers. Ammonius had clearly gone beyond any acceptable form of protest, a fact that Alexandria's own citizens acknowledged when they rescued the prefect from the crowd of monks. Cyril ignored this reality at his peril. At the same time, he had called the monks from the desert, and if he did not support them when they came under fire, he could not expect the monastic cavalry to come the next time he called.

Cyril ultimately decided to back the monks. He wrote a report to the emperor outlining his version of the events that led to Orestes's stoning and Ammonius's death. He then took to the pulpit to describe for his followers what Ammonius's death meant. The monk, Cyril proclaimed, was actually a martyr whose defense of Christian piety led to him being killed by a hostile governor. He was to be given a new name, Thaumasius, and his life and the actions that led to its end were to be celebrated by Alexandria's Christians.[17]

It is not clear how many people Cyril expected would accept this. Most members of his congregation certainly did not. They knew, Socrates Scholasticus tells us, that Ammonius "had suffered his punishment because he was rash, not because he would not deny Christ."[18] It seems Cyril understood this too. After his initial sermon proclaiming Ammonius a martyr, Cyril seems to have stopped mentioning the event. But Cyril's praise of Ammonius was not intended to convince the Alexandrian laity that they had been wrong to step in and save Orestes. It was instead a gesture of profound appreciation to the Nitrian monks, as well as an attempt to cement their continued support in what now looked like it would become a long and serious conflict with imperial authorities.

After these events, Orestes also realized that the conflict with Cyril required him to do things differently. The emperor and his closest advisors had now received at least one report explaining that Orestes's stubbornness had made a manageable situation worse. If things continued to spiral downward, they would have further reason to suspect Orestes's competence. Whatever his feelings about Cyril, Orestes knew that he needed to find a way to keep order in Alexandria if he wanted to have any further role in imperial administration. The average prefect in this period served for a little less than two years.[19] With a quick reconciliation with Cyril now looking unlikely, Orestes needed a way to calm the city and keep it controlled until his term ended. To do this, he decided to reach out to the Alexandrian councilors and other members of the civic elite. Because they would also be held responsible for any serious anti-imperial violence, these Alexandrian elites were at least as invested as Orestes in ensuring stability in the city.[20]

Orestes turned to Hypatia to build this coalition.[21] Hypatia seemed like the ultimate neutral arbiter. This was a moment when, Damascius writes, "the name of philosophy seemed most esteemed and worthy of honor to those who ran the affairs of the city," and Hypatia embodied the old Greek tradition of the publicly engaged, wise philosopher.[22] Her role was more than just symbolic. As a pagan who had not taken sides in the disagreement between Cyril and Timothy, she had no preexisting conflict with Cyril. While there is nothing to support the speculation that Hypatia once taught Cyril, she and her students had worked productively with Theophilus in the past.[23] The community of students she led exemplified the very sort of elite pagan-Christian cooperation that Orestes now sought in the city. She was a good symbolic and practical leader of Orestes's anti-Cyrillian coalition.

Hypatia and Orestes met regularly at his home following Ammonius's attack. After a time, they were joined by a religiously mixed group of Alexandrian elites.[24] They likely spent most of their time discussing how to manage tensions in the city in a way that minimized conflict. Not long after their meetings began, Orestes and many of the city's other leading Christians stopped attending services at which Cyril presided. This was perfectly reasonable after the recent attack on Orestes by Ammonius and Cyril's proclamation of Ammonius as a martyr, but it looked far more insidious to Cyril and his supporters. A pagan source tells us that Cyril soon grew jealous of the crowds who flocked to Hypatia's house and the influence she appeared to wield in the city.[25]

Cyril's supporters reacted with even more anger. The relationship between the prefect and the bishop had become so poisonous that Cyril's partisans suspected that Orestes was actively plotting against Cyril. A rumor began to spread that Hypatia had bewitched Orestes through some strange combination of Pythagorean music, astrolabes, and magic.[26] The evidence for this is dubious, but those who believed the rumor saw proof in the continued hostility between Cyril and Orestes, the fact that Orestes had stopped attending church, and the absence of many other leading Christians from services.[27] Hypatia had little to do with any of these things; they were natural result of elite anger at Cyril's celebration of Ammonius as a martyr. In this climate, however, Cyril's supporters could not blame the monks who had come into the city to advocate for the patriarch. They also could not openly blame the prefect himself, a charge that, if expressed too forcefully, could border on treason.[28] They instead fixated on Orestes's meetings with Hypatia as the one thing that corresponded with the break in relations between the patriarch and the prefect. In their minds, Hypatia had to be the reason that things had gotten so much worse.

It was a short leap from this point to the charge that the pagan philosopher Hypatia used magic to control the prefect. It had been a generation since the Serapeum, but Alexandrians certainly remembered hearing about the rituals that Olympus had used to galvanize the pagan Serapeum defenders.[29] Hypatia was not a theurgist like Olympus, but the nuances separating Hypatia's Platonism and that of Olympus would be lost on most ordinary Christians. They were not philosophers, and they did not care about the different schools of Platonists active in the early fifth century. If Olympus was a magician whose rites had caused disruption and violence in the city, then Hypatia could be one, too.[30]

This was a moment when two very different Alexandrias collided. In Hypatia's world of educated governors and civic elites, the distinctive philosophy that she had practiced and taught for the past thirty years pointed toward an enlightened social consensus that could allow traditional intellectual life and Christianity to coexist peacefully in the city. In that world, Hypatia was a force for stability. Most Alexandrians, however, did not belong to this civic elite and had little patience for the nuance of their conversations. They had no philosophical training, they wanted none, and they could not appreciate the importance of Hypatia's intellectual or political achievements. For the supporters of Cyril who belonged to this group, Hypatia did not seem like a force for stability in Alexandria. She looked like the primary obstacle preventing the reconciliation of Cyril and Orestes.

A group led by a man named Peter (who was either a reader or a presbyter in the church) decided to confront Hypatia in March 415.[31] The timing matters because March could be a difficult month for certain workers in Alexandria. The Mediterranean sailing season had not yet opened, and many of the men who worked the Mediterranean harbor had no steady work and no steady income.[32] This seasonal slowing was predictable, but it is equally true that people often do not adequately prepare for the shortages of money and food that a lull in seasonal work can cause. Those who were Alexandrian citizens had access to grain provided by the city, but those who had come from the countryside to work in the city had no such food support.[33] If they could not find work, they were left to depend on the kindness of friends or the charity of the bishop.[34] Other workers in the city, like the *parabalani* that the bishop hired to work as hospital attendants, also depended directly on the bishop for sustenance.[35] The number of people in Alexandria directly dependent upon Cyril that spring made it easy for Peter to recruit a group to go with him and find Hypatia.

It is unlikely that Peter and his band set out with the intention to kill Hypatia. The later Roman world was a violent place, but the mobs that confronted members of the later Roman elite rarely set out with murder on their minds. As was the case with Cyril's mobilization of the Nitrian monks against Orestes, most mobs were marshaled to intimidate and use the threat of violence to change the political dynamic in a city. Demonstrations like the one in the theater that started the conflict between Cyril and Orestes were common, conflicts between gangs of youths sometimes occurred, and one has to imagine that angry mobs called on people's residences as well. On rare occasions, these mobs grew angry enough that they attacked the property of prominent people.[36] In 375, a mob in Rome angered by a remark supposedly uttered during a food shortage by a former prefect of Rome's grain supply burned down his house.[37] Not coincidentally, the former prefect was in his country home and far away from danger when the mob appeared. The mob had vented their anger, a message had been sent, but the prefect had not been harmed.

Although Alexandria had a reputation for being a riotous place, Alexandrian mobs killed prominent people, on average, roughly once every fifty years between the reign of Constantine and that of Justinian.[38] The only times in the fourth and fifth centuries that mobs appear to have set out with murderous intent involved attacks on the bishop George in 361 and the bishop Proterius in 457.[39] Each of these bishops were deeply despised in the city, and their murders followed soon after the death of an unpopular emperor who had protected them. Neither variable was present in 415.

Peter and his band of supporters probably set out to frighten Hypatia into withdrawing from her public role advising Orestes. Perhaps they intended to have a noisy demonstration outside of the walls of her townhouse. Maybe they were even angry enough that they wanted to burn her house down. It is hard to imagine, however, that they went out intending to kill. It seems, though, that fortune intervened in a most calamitous way. The angry mob came upon Hypatia in public, either while she was teaching or as she was returning home in her carriage.[40] If she had been behind the walls of her house, they would have yelled, screamed, and tried to terrify her, but it is extremely unlikely that they would have broken in and seized her. In public, however, Hypatia was unprotected and easily surrounded by a crowd. The situation quickly got out of control. Hypatia was dragged through the street and taken to the Caesareum church along Alexandria's waterfront. The mob stripped her and tore her body apart using broken roof tiles, an easily available and surprisingly lethal weapon for urban combat.[41] One source tells us that they even cut out her eyes.[42] Hypatia's mangled remains were then taken to a place called the Cinaron, where they were burned.[43]

In killing Hypatia in so brutal a fashion, the mob was following an old Alexandrian script. Since at least the third century BCE, the bodies of the vilest criminals had been dragged through the city and cremated beyond the city limits as a symbolic purification of the city. The first known case of this type of behavior involved a Ptolemaic official named Agathocles in the third century BCE, but a Christian persecution in 248 CE and the lynching of Bishop George of Cappadocia in 361 provided more contemporary parallels.[44] The most recent victim of this, however, was the cult statue of Serapis. Following the destruction of the god's temple in 392, the statue was dismembered, the pieces dragged throughout the city, and the remains burned. This act of ritual civic cleansing defined the god's presence as pollution and offered the city a release from it. John of Nikiu suggests that, in the frenzy of their attack on her, Hypatia's murderers may have been recalling the fate of the Serapis statue.[45] If Peter and his partisans believed the rumors that Hypatia had been using magic to control the prefect, some of them may well have felt that they had succeeded in cleansing the city of pagan pollution when they burned Hypatia's body.

Almost no one else shared this belief. Hypatia's murder horrified people across the empire. Few outside of the narrow group of people involved in the killing accepted that the murder of Hypatia was the same thing as the execution of a dangerous criminal or the destruction of the statue of Serapis. To the wider world, Hypatia was neither a criminal nor a religious symbol. She was an accomplished philosopher whose research had made meaningful contributions to the intellectual life of the empire and whose public activities had shaped the political life of her city. For decades Hypatia had embodied the ancient ideal of the philosopher as a teacher of, model for, and councilor to her fellow citizens. The attack on Hypatia represented an assault on one of the cultural foundations on which the late ancient world rested.

The response was swift and fierce. Aside from Damascius, who wrote more than a century after the attack, no source claims that Cyril ordered the attack on Hypatia—but all agree that he was ultimately responsible for creating the climate that caused it. Socrates Scholasticus wrote of Hypatia's murder: "This affair brought no slight opprobrium upon Cyril and the whole Alexandrian church. Indeed nothing is farther from the spirit of Christianity than murders, fights, and similar things."[46] Other accounts echo Socrates's judgment.[47] These authors were not just concerned with the centuries-old custom of respecting the prerogatives of philosophers to freely offer advice in public. They also reflected a visceral abhorrence of the senseless violence of the attack. Even the emperor felt this. Probably prompted by an alarmed prefect and a frightened Alexandrian city council, Theodosius II's advisors began an investigation of the murder. Unlike the two previous inquiries into Cyril's conduct, this one brought real sanctions against the patriarch. The *parabalani*, the paid workers under Cyril's control, were legally transferred to the control of the prefect.[48] We are told that Cyril escaped even more serious penalties only by paying exorbitant bribes to one of Theodosius's officials.[49]

Hypatia's murder immediately resonated across Alexandria, but its echo reverberated within the city for more than a century. The culture in Hypatia's school that joined pagan and Christian philosophers in a common, nonconfessional, purely contemplative philosophical pursuit died with her. Hypatia had trained no heir and had no spouse or children who could take over for her. This left a crucial vacuum in Alexandria's intellectual life. Hypatia had overturned the dominance that mathematicians had enjoyed for centuries in Alexandria. In the three decades that she was active, Hypatia had begun to establish a distinctive type of philosophical instruction that was particularly well suited to the majority Christian city in which she taught. In her work and her life she embodied a philosophical system that was Platonic but not Iamblichan, and that placed a heavy emphasis on the obligation of the philosopher to remain publicly engaged in her city. Her example was a powerful one and her work was inspirational, but the roots of her school remained shallow in the 410s. It is always far easier for a great thinker to undermine an old intellectual consensus than it is for her to establish a new one. Hypatia had done the former on her own, but she, like most other great philosophers, needed capable and persuasive successors to carry on her work. She had none.

This meant that Alexandrian intellectual life began to drift in the decades following her murder. From the very limited information that we have about them, it seems that the Alexandrian teachers that Proclus encountered in the late 420s and early 430s may have taught the Plotinian-Porphyrian Platonism that Hypatia established. It is clear, however, that they were of middling quality and not terribly inspirational.[50] Unlike Hypatia, they could not compete with the growing influence of the Athenian school. Their limitations, in fact, pushed Proclus, the most gifted philosopher of the fifth century, to leave Alexandria and study instead in Athens. More Alexandrian students followed Proclus to Athens. As the 430s progressed, some of these students of Plutarch's Athenian school began returning to Alexandria in order to teach what they had learned in Athens. The Athenian philosophical colonies set up in Alexandria by Hierocles in the 430s, Hermeias in the 440s, Ammonius and Asclepiodotus in the 460s and 470s, and Isidore in the 480s ultimately crowded out any Hypatian-style teachers who remained.[51] It would not be until after the emperor Justinian's closing of the Athenian school in 529 that Alexandria would again become the leading center of a school of Platonic thought.[52] Hypatia's murder, then, marked the first time in nearly 700 years that the city did not house the Eastern Mediterranean's preeminent center for either mathematics or philosophy.

Hypatia's death had a profound and chilling effect on intercommunal relations in the city as well. Hypatia embodied a particular ideal of elite pagan intellectuals working with and supporting the political institutions of the Christian Roman Empire. Hypatia was not the only fourth-century figure to do this. Themistius was an even more prominent and powerful advocate for this sort of pagan philosophical engagement and cooperation with Christian authorities.[53] Hypatia, however, was the last pagan philosopher who would do this programmatically. Pagan philosophers continued to meet with governors, advocate for local causes, and otherwise remain engaged sporadically in their cities, but Hypatia's death also ushered in a new way of thinking about the Roman state.[54] After 415, philosophers and their students largely stopped telling stories of philosophers who worked with Christian authorities and instead began collecting tales of philosophers who resisted Christian persecution. In the decades to come, Alexandrian pagan intellectuals retold the story of Hypatia's murder as the first in a line of Christian persecutions they would suffer.[55] Instead of a symbol of the possibility of a pagan-Christian philosophical consensus, Hypatia became a pagan martyr for philosophy.

Traditions celebrating philosophical political resistance to Christian rulers grew up alongside these tales of martyrdom. Damascius celebrates pagan intellectuals who involved themselves in a number of fifth-century plots to assassinate Christian emperors. Few of these plots went anywhere, and only one, the revolt of Illus in 484, represented even a semi-serious threat to the ruling emperor.[56] At the same time, though, the thought of philosophers involving themselves in such seditious activities would have been inconceivable to Hypatia or her students. They felt strongly that the job of a philosopher was to reform an unphilosophical regime, not to overthrow it. Hypatia's murder by Christian fanatics and the failure of the state to severely punish those responsible for it fueled this new, intense suspicion of Christian-led institutions.

No one in March 415 could have imagined all of these outcomes for the city of Alexandria and the intellectual life of the empire. The power of Hypatia's mind and the force of her example gave the illusion that the intellectual program and political consensus that she had built rested on a solid footing. It did not. These things could endure only as long as Hypatia did. When Hypatia was suddenly snatched from the city, neither she nor those who valued what she had created had the chance to plan for the aftermath of her death. But Hypatia's death did more than weaken what she had created. It unleashed forces that destroyed both her intellectual and her political legacies. No pagan philosopher would again entertain Hypatia's idea that one of his students could work alongside an Alexandrian Christian bishop. He could never imagine a bishop presiding over the wedding of a member of his inner circle. Hypatia's murder had turned bishops from possible collaborators in maintaining the urban peace to the leaders of what Damascius would call "the opposing party." For the rest of antiquity, pagan philosophers would see the clergy as dangerous, jealous figures who were also utterly unphilosophical. Any pagan philosopher who dared to work with them was immediately tarred as a treacherous, greedy charlatan.[57]

This hostility to close cooperation with Christian authority also encouraged philosophical pagans to embrace even more strongly a Platonism that affirmed and enhanced pagan religious practices. If

Christian leaders were the enemy, then the non-Christian religious traditions celebrated and preserved by Iamblichan Platonists looked ever more appealing. It is going too far to say that Hypatia's murder created a sense of pagan identity among philosophers that did not exist before, but her brutal death certainly emphasized the gulf between pagan philosophers and the Christian masses. There would be little appeal left for the contemplative, confessionally neutral philosophy that Hypatia's Christian and pagan students could share.

All of this would have deeply disappointed Hypatia. She had worked her entire life to build a philosophical system that fit the particular city in which she lived. She had succeeded for almost thirty-five years. Hypatia had done so well, in fact, that no one, herself included, realized that she had held back a massive social and intellectual tide. It would have saddened her to learn how quickly the world she had built and superintended could disappear. But it would probably enrage her to learn that she has been famous for the past 1,600 years not because of the world she sustained, but because of the awful way in which she left it. The next two chapters will tell the story of how Hypatia's gruesome death came to define her legacy.

9

The Memory of Hypatia

The discordance between the type of person that Hypatia was and the brutal way in which she died explains the initial shock that many people felt at her murder. People across the empire came to see her death as a new and frightening break from the social conventions that had ensured the functioning of the empire for centuries. Hypatia had never been a public official, nor had she been an officeholder. She was a philosopher who engaged in public life in order to make her city and her fellow citizens better. Historically, such figures had been exempt from the sorts of displays of intimidation and violence that sometimes accompanied political gridlock in Roman cities. The metastasis of violence her death represented would have seemed as profoundly dangerous and destabilizing to people in Alexandria and Constantinople as the urban riots in the spring and summer of 1968 seemed to people in the United States. The horror of Hypatia's murder blended with the fear of what might come next to make people profoundly anxious.

As time passed, Alexandria quieted. Instead of heralding the explosion of even greater anarchy, Hypatia's death finally resolved the conflict between Orestes, Cyril, and the Alexandrian elites. All parties feared further escalation and appear to have stood down. Orestes seems to have finished his term in office and left Egypt; we hear nothing more about him. Cyril, for his part, would remain Alexandria's bishop until 444, during which time the city would remain free from major riots. This period of calm did not, however, make people forget Hypatia's death. Outside of Alexandria, the murder of a female philosopher and the role that Cyril had played in creating the climate that led to it fit too neatly into a larger narrative about the Alexandrian bishop to be forgotten. This was particularly true because the peace that Cyril had brought to Alexandria did not extend to the wider empire. Cyril's rivalry with bishop Nestorius of Constantinople, the empire-wide Christological division that this ultimately provoked, and Cyril's use of force and intimidation to emerge victorious ensured that the memory of Hypatia's murder stayed alive.

Hypatia in Ecclesiastical Histories and Chronicles

Cyril's central role in the theological conflicts of the mid-fifth century perversely ensured that Hypatia's murder featured prominently in the histories covering that period. This happened because the most skilled and influential Greek historians of the mid-fifth century wrote church histories. Socrates Scholasticus, the most successful of these ecclesiastical historians, wrote a narrative that blended political and military events with a discussion of affairs in the church. Socrates did this because "when public affairs are disturbed so too are those of the church, as if from a sort of sympathy."[1] The murder of Hypatia was a perfect incident on which Socrates could focus to make this point. In Socrates's telling, Hypatia was a pillar of the Roman political and social establishment who was killed because of a conflict in the church. This incident showed, in stark relief, the direct connection between trouble in the church and trouble in the world.

Socrates mentions Hypatia in the final book of his *Ecclesiastical History* as part of a larger discussion about the connection between the attitudes of individual bishops toward the minority Novatian Christian community and the political situation in their home cities.[2] The first fifteen chapters of the seventh book lay out nothing less than a tale of three cities in which ecclesiastical affairs provide the basic rhythm to which secular events move.[3] Socrates begins with Constantinople and outlines the surprisingly calm and orderly government of the city following the death of the emperor Arcadius. He implicitly credits this to the character of Atticus, the bishop of Constantinople, a bishop whose friendly relationships with Novatians ensured the peace of the church while encouraging stability and prosperity within Constantinople. Socrates then turns to Alexandria and Rome, the second and third cities in his triad. In Socrates's view, neither city found itself as fortunate as the Eastern capital in its choice of ecclesiastical leadership. Each of them saw the turmoil in its churches mirrored in its political life.

Socrates's narrative jumps from city to city, but its basic progression is clear. In Constantinople, a period that could have been chaotic and dangerous was instead smooth and calm because the city's bishop behaved moderately towards Novatians. In Rome, Socrates describes a very different situation. Its bishop, Innocent I, took away the churches of the Novatians in the city. Socrates then describes the sack of Rome by Alaric in 410, an event that he says occurred because Alaric was compelled by God to devastate the city.[4] Intriguingly, the Roman narrative is jammed in the middle of Socrates's account of affairs in Alexandria.[5] Socrates begins his discussion of Alexandrian events by talking about the initial struggle through which Cyril took control of the bishopric and the punishment he inflicted on the Novatians. He then jumps to Innocent's actions in Rome and the sack of the city that resulted from them. When he returns to Alexandria, Socrates picks up with the conflict between Cyril and Orestes. This structure is deliberate and pushes Socrates's readers to understand that Alexandria's troubles in 414 and 415 are connected to Cyril's actions against the Novatians in the same way that Alaric's sack of Rome grew out of Innocent's persecution of that group.

The murder of Hypatia climaxes Socrates's entire tale of three cities. Like any skilled writer, Socrates invested significant effort in making such a critical part of his history work thematically.[6] Socrates sketches his Hypatia very precisely. In the first sentences of the chapter, he offers a mini-panegyric of Hypatia. The daughter of Theon, Hypatia was the most gifted philosopher of her age. Her virtue and purity of mind gave her the authority to regularly address assemblies of men. Her frequent interactions with men were not a concern, Socrates explains, because of her great virtue and dignity. At the halfway point in the chapter, Socrates abruptly shifts the narrative. He writes:, "The political rivalry of that time armed itself against her."[7] The second half of the chapter then describes the horror and brutality of Hypatia's murder. Socrates describes the passions that enflamed the mob in a way that contrasts clearly with Hypatia's own moderation. He similarly recounts the stripping and violation of her body in a way that contrasts it with the dignity that she enjoyed in life. The entire discussion culminates in Socrates's statement that "nothing can be further from the spirit of Christianity" than actions like this.

Nothing that Socrates says about Hypatia is demonstrably untrue. He wrote at a time when many people were still alive who had known Hypatia.[8] Between the publication of Synesius's letters and the circulation of Hypatia's own writings, people could verify what Socrates said about her.[9] At the same time, it is clear that, one generation after the end of Hypatia's life, her death had already defined her. Socrates does not manufacture any information about her life, but he also has no interest in giving a full and well-rounded account of Hypatia's career either. All of the details that Socrates provides about Hypatia stand in rhetorical opposition to the attributes of the Christian mob that killed her. Hypatia, then, had become a character in Socrates's text whose profile did nothing more and nothing less than what the story required. She appeared in the text simply because she could be made to die in the most resonant and shocking way possible.

Socrates was not the only church historian of his generation to use the figure of Hypatia to attack Cyril and his partisans. Around the same time that Socrates wrote, the non-Nicene historian Philostorgius composed a church history that included a chapter about Hypatia.[10] In it, he describes Hypatia as a gifted protégé of her father, Theon, who taught philosophy, geometry, and astronomy to many people. He then described how "she was torn to pieces by those who were presbyters in the Homousian (i.e., Nicene) faction."[11] There are clear similarities between how Socrates and Philostorgius use the character of Hypatia. Whereas Socrates used her murder to discredit Cyril, Philostorgius deployed it to discredit Nicene Christians more generally. Unfortunately, because Philostorgius's text survives only in an epitome probably composed by a Nicene bishop in ninth-century Constantinople, we cannot now understand whether his version of Hypatia was more nuanced than that of Socrates.[12] One suspects, however, that the Hypatia of Philostorgius was also sketched in a way designed to highlight the unreasoning brutality of the Christians who killed her.

Hypatia's character became even less distinctive in the church histories and Christian chronicles of the sixth century. Sometime in the 540s or early 550s, Socrates Scholasticus's account of Hypatia's death was included in the Latin *Historia Tripartita*, a project superintended by the Italian aristocrat Cassiodorus that combined and translated the texts of the three most famous Greek church histories of the mid-fifth century. Socrates's story of Hypatia's murder then came to define Hypatia in the Latin West.[13] At roughly the same moment, the

Antiochene and Constantinopolitan chronicler John Malalas noted that the Alexandrians, "after being given free reign by their bishop," seized and burned "Hypatia, the famous philosopher, who had a great reputation and was an old woman."[14] Like Philostorgius, Malalas survives only in a later epitome, but the epitome nevertheless offers enough to see that Malalas follows the same blueprint that Socrates does. His Hypatia is sparsely sketched in such a way that her wisdom and virtue stands in stark contrast to the uncontrolled fury of the Alexandrian mob that killed her and the bishop that enabled them to do so.

The sixth-century historian and lexicographer Hesychius of Miletus also appears to have drawn upon this tradition that sketched the rationality of Hypatia against the violent ignorance of the Alexandrian mob.[15] In his *Onomatologus*, a work that profiled the men and women Hesychius considered to be the most important Greek thinkers of the classical and post-classical world, he offered a short profile of Hypatia. Many of the profiles in the *Onomatologus* offer basic biographical details about the thinker that are then flushed out with pithy quotations selected to show a little bit about his or her character. Hesychius's Hypatia, like the Hypatia in Socrates, appears to exist in the text simply so that her death can be noted. Hesychius begins by describing Hypatia as "the daughter of the geometrician and Alexandrian philosopher Theon, she was herself a philosopher and was very well known." He then describes how "she was torn to pieces and her body was abused and scattered across the city." She suffered this "on account of jealousy and her superior wisdom and, most of all, her knowledge about astronomy."[16]

Hypatia and the History of Philosophy

Hesychius's account is interesting because it seems to have taken no account of another, much more nuanced account of Hypatia's life and practical philosophy that appeared in the philosopher Damascius's *Life of Isidore* shortly before Hesychius wrote. Damascius assembled this assessment of the career and character of his philosophical father Isidore between 517 and 526 in response to a request from Theodora, a female member of his school.[17] Working with Damascius's *Life of Isidore* can be tricky. The original text is lost. Less than 50 percent of it now survives in scattered fragments found primarily in either the

Bibliotheke (or *Library*) composed by the Constantinopolitan patriarch Photius in the ninth century, or in excerpts repurposed to form entries in the *Suda*, a tenth-century Greek lexicon.[18] We are fortunate that the summary comes from Photius, however, because the *Bibliotheke* contains a large collection of texts, some of which still survive intact. Those surviving texts prove that the summaries that Photius provides do, in the main, follow the narrative progression of the original texts. We can then confidently use Photius's summary of Damascius's *Life of Isidore* as a skeleton for reconstructing the way in which Damascius's argument developed. This makes it possible to place back in Damascius's text some of the pieces of the *Suda* in which the phrases or ideas overlap with Photius's summaries.[19]

The reconstructed *Life of Isidore* reveals how Damascius undertook the difficult task of defining Isidore as the embodiment of philosophical virtue. Isidore wrote no commentaries, he did not particularly like reading the commentaries written by others, and he had a difficult time relating to his students and fellow citizens.[20] Damascius also could not point to any real institutional contributions made by Isidore. His career was defined less by building and running a school than by running away from institutional or political situations that he found detrimental to his philosophical practice.[21] Damascius, however, believed that Isidore embodied the ideal combination of inspired philosophical understanding and uncompromising philosophical practice.[22] He decided that he could best convince his readers of this by comparing Isidore's achievements with those of his most recent contemporaries.

Although most other late antique biographies of this type were organized around discrete accounts of the lives of a group of individuals, Damascius's *Life of Isidore* instead discusses specific historical moments in which Greek intellectuals displayed their virtues and vices. Some figures appear in only one discussion, while others, like Damascius's contemporaries Marinus and Asclepiodotus, are profiled and then reappear multiple times throughout the text. Damascius did this quite deliberately. All of these discussions have a direct bearing on how one is supposed to understand the unique combination of intellectual and practical virtues that Isidore possessed. This approach also enables Damascius to speak about the relative virtues and deficiencies of Isidore, his predecessors, and his contemporaries in a way that acknowledges Isidore's obvious limitations while also highlighting his superiority to all philosophers of his day.[23]

Hypatia died more than a century before Damascius wrote, but he discusses her at length in two different parts of the text. Hypatia first appears in a section that outlines philosophical resistance to and victimization by Christian authorities. The section begins by describing a lawyer named Leontius who appears to have abandoned the gods in order to serve Christian officials. Instead of the wealth and honors he expected, Leontius instead "totally corrupted his soul."[24] The next profile offers a counterpoint to Leontius. It focuses on Olympus, his spiritual leadership during the Serapeum defense in 392, and the steadfast faith in the old gods that he maintained throughout his life.[25]

Hypatia appears in the text after Olympus. Damascius introduces her as the daughter of the mathematician Theon. He explains that Hypatia mastered mathematics but was naturally drawn to other elements of philosophy as well. Damascius respected Hypatia, and he describes her as "skilled and dialectical in speech, wise and politic in behavior" and "a gifted teacher, who reached the peak of moral virtue and was just and prudent."[26] He underlines her virtue by telling the story of how Hypatia "cured" her love-struck student of his unphilosophical feelings for her. Damascius then indicates that her character ensured that "the entire city naturally loved her and held her in high esteem, while the powers-that-be paid their respects first to her."[27] Damascius completes his portrait by describing Hypatia's murder. He explains that Cyril, "the one who presided over the opposing sect," saw a crowd of people gathered around Hypatia's house and asked why she was receiving such attention. Cyril heard that "honors were being paid to the philosopher Hypatia and that this was her house. When he heard this, envy so gnawed at his soul that he soon began to plot her murder."[28] Damascius then describes the crowd of men seizing Hypatia when she left her house, their brutal attack on her, and the "pollution and disgrace" that fell on the entire city because of it.

The *Life of Isidore* describes Hypatia here because her murder made her a philosophical martyr, but Damascius's presentation of Hypatia is more developed and nuanced than those of Socrates, Philostorgius, and the later authors who imitated them. Unlike the church historians, Damascius is not primarily concerned with highlighting the villainy of Cyril and his followers; this was a given for his audience of pagan philosophers. Damascius is interested instead in showing how Hypatia lived and thrived amid a climate where such villainy existed. Writing in the last years before the emperor Justinian closed the Athenian

Neoplatonic school, Damascius wanted to emphasize how Hypatia continued to teach publicly and live her life at "the peak of practical virtue" despite the jealousy of Cyril and the hostility of Christian mobs. For Damascius, Hypatia's martyrdom provides a tragic but heroic certification that, unlike Leontius, she remained true to her philosophical practice for her entire life. And, unlike Olympus, Hypatia paid for this devotion with her life.

While this justly famous profile of Hypatia is Damascius's most extensive discussion of her, it is not the only time she appears in his text. Indeed, she is one of the few philosophers to whom Damascius explicitly compares Isidore. When Damascius returns to Hypatia, he comments that "Isidore and Hypatia were very different, not only as a man differs from a woman, but as a true philosopher differs from a mathematician."[29] This comparison is easy to misunderstand. At first glance, this looks to be a gratuitous insult intended to diminish the importance of Hypatia. Damascius was a great admirer of Iamblichus and certainly must have felt that Hypatia's reliance on a Platonism framed by Porphyry and Plotinus stunted her philosophical knowledge.[30] Damascius clearly felt that Isidore was the superior philosopher, and he says so. At the same time, this comparison must be read within the context of Damascius's larger work. Hypatia had earlier been established by Damascius as a philosophical martyr who remained true to the practice of philosophy even in the face of mortal danger. Damascius says nothing here that contradicts this positive impression. His comment is less an attack on Hypatia than it is an attempt to better explain the achievements of Isidore. If Hypatia was seriously flawed, it would not say much about Isidore if he surpassed her. What Damascius does instead is evoke the prominence, authority, and personal sacrifice of Hypatia that he has already established in order to better illustrate the superior qualities that Isidore possessed. For this comparison to work effectively, Damascius must elevate Isidore above Hypatia without diminishing her real and admired virtues.

Hypatia in Byzantium

Damascius's portrait of Hypatia defined her legacy for future historians of philosophy, but, because of the complicated nature of Damascius's text, later readers sometimes misunderstood what his profile of Hypatia was designed to do. Indeed, it may not have taken long for this to happen. In the tenth century, the *Suda* included a long entry on Hypatia that combined summaries of the two accounts of Hypatia's life drawn from two different sources. The collator of the *Suda* did not make any attempt to blend the two accounts, however. The first eleven lines of the *Suda* profile derive from one source and the rest comes from Damascius.

The ultimate origin of those first eleven lines presents an interesting question. Much of that material came from Hesychius, but whoever wrote it also included some material from Damascius that he or she clearly misunderstood. The entry follows Hesychius in describing Hypatia as a well-known Alexandrian philosopher who was the daughter of Theon. It includes the very odd statement that "she was the wife of the philosopher Isidore" before running through a list of her publications. It then describes how "she was torn to pieces and her body was abused and scattered across the city." She suffered this "on account of jealousy and her superior wisdom and, most of all, her knowledge about astronomy." The notice concludes by saying that some people say this was done "by Cyril," while others say it was because "the Alexandrians are rash and prone to strife by their very nature," as one can see in the murder of their bishops George and Proterius.[31]

The core of this material comes from Hesychius, but the list of publications, the discussion of the deaths of the bishops George and Proterius, and the odd statement about Hypatia's marriage all have no parallels in any of the other fragments of Hesychius's *Onomatologus*. He does not seem to have discussed topics like this in the text. These points of information, then, must come from some other source. It is, however, unlikely that the *Suda* compiler blended Hesychius with these other things. The *Suda* compiler seems untroubled by the fact that the first eleven lines of the entry repeat a number of points made in the Damascius material that forms the rest of the entry. This suggests that he copied from the two sources in a way that left their contents discrete from one another.

This is important, because the oddest detail in this entry, the comment that Hypatia was the wife of Isidore, must derive from a misunderstanding of Damascius that originated with the author of the earlier source copied by the *Suda*. Not only is the story of Hypatia's marriage both clearly untrue and chronologically impossible, but it is also directly contradicted a few lines later when, drawing from the *Life of Isidore* instead of this other source, the *Suda* compiler writes that "she remained a virgin."[32] This mistake is, however, easily explained as a misunderstanding of the comparison that Damascius makes between Isidore and Hypatia in which he says that the differences between Hypatia's geometry and Isidore's philosophy are as great as those that separate a man and a woman. This confusion is not as strange as it sounds. The Greek word *gynē* can mean both "wife" and "woman." At some point between the appearance of the *Life of Isidore* in the sixth century and that of the *Suda* in the tenth, someone misunderstood which meaning of *gynē* Damascius intended.[33] This does show, however, that Damascius's profile soon became the main source used by later intellectual historians and biographers writing about Hypatia. It also means that Damascius's profile was almost as quickly misunderstood.

As one moves into the middle Byzantine period, the two profiles of Hypatia created by Socrates and Damascius form the basis of two distinctive ways that she was remembered. For Byzantine chroniclers and ecclesiastical historians in later centuries, the view of Hypatia as a victim of violence remains prominent. As time progressed, however, the role of Cyril in creating the conditions that led to her murder is increasingly downplayed.[34] Some Byzantine authors, like the early ninth-century chronicler Theophanes, neglect to mention that Cyril was in any way connected to her murder.[35] Much of this had to do with the eventual legacy of Cyril, a bishop who was canonized and came to represent one of the touchstones of orthodoxy in Byzantium. He could no longer be the sort of villain Socrates set out to make him. Ultimately, though, later authors cared more about the basic information that Socrates and his contemporaries provided than they did about the intricate narrative context Socrates constructed to give it meaning. While Socrates himself had distilled elements of the real-life Hypatia into a literary character whose death had a very specific sort of meaning, later authors simplified her even more into a victim of mob violence.

A different, more Damascian idea of Hypatia also endured. In the ninth century, the patriarch Photius included both Damascius's *Life of Isidore* and Socrates's *Ecclesiastical History* in his *Bibliotheke*.[36] He quickly summarized Socrates's text in a few lines, but he was much more taken by Damascius. He returned two times to Damascius's *Isidore* in the *Bibliotheke* and the only mentions that he makes of Hypatia in this immense epitome of Greek literature come from Damascius.[37] Photius also does not mention Hypatia's murder despite having read about it in both sources. To him, Hypatia merited inclusion as an intellectual alone.

This memory of a Hypatia defined by her intellectual accomplishments rather than her murder lived on until the last centuries of Byzantium. This is why, in the mid-fourteenth century, Nicephorus Gregoras could describe Eudokia Palaiologina as so "unrivaled in the beauty of her appearance, formidable in speaking, dainty in her bearing" and "learned in the liberal arts ... that she was called another Theano the Pythagorean or Hypatia by those of us who are wise."[38] While an author like Gregoras understood Hypatia to be a prototypical wise and temperate female philosopher, she seems to have been little more than a name to him. If Gregoras knew of Damascius's portrait of her, he certainly did not appreciate the intricate way in which Damascius sketched her.

Hypatia in the Egyptian Historical Tradition

One ancient author stands alone in his treatment of Hypatia. The *Chronicle* composed by John, the bishop of Nikiu in Egypt, at the very end of the seventh century CE folds the murder of Hypatia into a history of the world extending from Adam until the Muslim conquest of Egypt. Until it reaches the seventh century, this text is largely derivative and heavily dependent upon the text of the chronicler John Malalas and, for the Theodosian dynasty, that of Socrates Scholasticus.[39] The text does diverge from these originals at some points, and when it does so, John almost invariably drew upon materials that circulated in Egyptian oral, liturgical, and literary traditions. These supplements cover a host of subjects, but most of them relate directly to the authority that Egyptian bishops claimed. John's discussion of the Serapeum destruction, for example, includes an oral tradition from Nikiu that foretold Theophilus's success in attacking paganism.[40] His accounts of the persecution of anti-Chalcedonian Christians under Justinian draw heavily upon stories of the heroic resistance offered by bishop Severus of Antioch that are also found in Egyptian liturgical contexts.[41] Perhaps the most notable example is John's account of the invasion of Egypt by the Achaemenid Persian king Cambyses, a discussion that draws upon a fictionalized Coptic account of the invasion that dates to the later Roman period.[42]

John's account of the murder of Hypatia represents one of the most interesting points at which this Egyptian material is added. Although

John used many of the details found in Socrates Scholasticus to establish the background to Hypatia's murder, his account presents Cyril in a
very different light.[43] Gone is every trace of Socrates's tale of three cities
and any implication that Cyril had done anything wrong in the lead-up
to Hypatia's murder. Instead, John shifted responsibility for the events
away from Cyril and onto Hypatia. He needed to make Hypatia's killing seem like a heroic triumph for Cyril. The only way that he could do
this was to transform Hypatia into a villain.

John does this by making Hypatia, not Cyril, responsible for all
of the disorder in Alexandria. His account begins by explaining that
Hypatia appeared in Alexandria during the reign of Theodosius II. "A
female philosopher, a pagan," he writes, "she was devoted at all times
to magic, astrolabes, and instruments of music and she beguiled many
people through her Satanic wiles."[44] Among her victims, John continues, was Orestes who, under her influence, stopped going to church
and stood by while a group of Jews stationed armed men around the
city in order to "wickedly massacre the Christians."[45] The surviving
Alexandrian Christians then organized a raid in which they "marched
in wrath to the synagogues of the Jews and took possession of them,
and purified them and turned them into churches.[46] After the Jewish
"assassins" were expelled from the city, the crowd "proceeded to seek
for the pagan woman who had beguiled the people of the city and the
prefect through her enchantments."[47] They found Hypatia, brought her
to the cathedral, tore off her clothing, and "dragged her through the
streets of the city until she died. And they carried her to a place named
Cinaron and they burned her body."[48] All the people then "surrounded
the patriarch Cyril and named him 'the new Theophilus,' for he had
destroyed the last remains of idolatry in the city."[49]

John skillfully repackaged the details of Socrates's narrative in a
way that makes Hypatia rather than Cyril the primary driver of these
events. This required him to do some remarkable things. First, he
needed to compress the timeline of events so that the Jewish-Christian
riot of 414 (in which Hypatia had no involvement) and the murder of
Hypatia in the spring of 415 seem to take place in quick succession. This
enables John to claim that the sorcery of Hypatia caused both events.[50]

John also needed to explain to his readers how the brutal murder
of anyone, even a purported magician like Hypatia, could be a heroic
act. To do this, John equates the attack on Hypatia with the actions
that Theophilus took against the Serapeum a generation earlier. This,

too, is done skillfully. The actions that John ascribes to Cyril's partisans mirror the course of events that led to Theophilus's transformation of the Serapeum. The anti-Christian violence that preceded these two events also looks similar. In both cases, non-Christian mobs resorted to guerilla tactics to seize and kill innocent Christians. In response, both Cyril and Theophilus ordered the seizure of non-Christian religious buildings, their "purification" and replacement with churches or shrines dedicated to Christian martyrs,[51] and the expulsion from Alexandria of the pagans and Jews who led the violence. The two bishops then turned their attention to the pagan entities at the center of the conflict. Theophilus targeted the Serapeum in 392, and Cyril went after Hypatia in 415, but the responses are described in strikingly similar terms. John's description of the murder of Hypatia parallels the ritual purification of the city that accompanied the destruction of the cultic statue of Serapis. Like the Serapis statue, Hypatia was seized, dismembered, and paraded through the streets of the city before her remains were burned. The comparison between these events concludes with the statement that these actions made Cyril "a new Theophilus."

An Egyptian Christian reading John's account at the turn of the eighth century may well have been convinced that the murder of Hypatia was a great triumph for Cyril, but it does not seem that other Egyptian authors found her death particularly noteworthy. While much of the specifically Egyptian content found elsewhere in John of Nikiu's *Chronicle* mirrors material found in later Egyptian Christian texts, no mention of Hypatia ever appears in subsequent Coptic texts that discuss Cyril. In the long run, John's version of this event remains confined to his text, a text that now survives only in a single manuscript containing an incomplete Ethiopic translation. It was completely unknown to Byzantine authors and was discovered by later Europeans only when the Ethiopic text was translated in 1879.[52]

In late antiquity, Hypatia's story quickly became intertwined with those of Cyril and the Alexandrian church. On one level, this is odd. Hypatia had very few actual dealings with either Cyril or the church he led. Had she died in an ordinary way, Cyril would hardly have figured into the story of her life at all. But Hypatia did not die in an ordinary way. Her gruesome murder shocked her contemporaries in a way that would not be easily forgotten. It came at the beginning of a period of profound social and political disruption that dramatically altered the Roman world. Cyril's aggressive opposition to the theology of the

Constantinopolitan bishop Nestorius permanently split the Roman Christian church from its Persian cousin in the 430s. Then, in 451, the actions of supporters of Cyril's successor, Dioscorus, led to another split in the church within the empire that remains unresolved to this day.[53] Temples continued to fall. Pagan philosophical teachers also became an endangered species, with the last of these dinosaurs passing away sometime in the late 560s.[54] The world in which Hypatia lived seemed a distant memory to later authors.

This explains why so many late antique authors saw Hypatia's murder as a historical turning point. They remembered the horrific story of Hypatia's death and felt that it heralded the emergence of historical trends that would dramatically change life in the empire over the next few decades. When they wrote about Hypatia, late antique and Byzantine authors did so with an eye toward the future that began when her life ended. That future looked different to each author. For John of Nikiu, Hypatia's murder began a triumphant time in which paganism had finally been vanquished. For Damascius, this moment began a reign of terror that showed no sign of ever ceasing. But as Hypatia became a literary weather vane that gave first warning of whatever coming storm an author wanted to describe, her actual story began to get lost. As we will see in the next chapter, modern authors often did not treat her any more fairly.

10

A Modern Symbol

The first author to make Hypatia the focus of a lengthy study written in a modern European language was the Irish philosopher and free-thinker John Toland (1670–1722).[1] Toland made a name for himself in 1696 when he published a book called *Christianity not Mysterious*. Toland was prosecuted for arguing in the book that the Bible recounts no miracles that could not be understood rationally, and he was condemned by the Irish Parliament to be burned at the stake. He avoided this fate by staying in England. Irish authorities then burned copies of his book publicly instead. This event set off in Toland an ever-increasing hostility to ecclesiastical institutions in general, and to those of the Catholic Church in particular. Toland wrote prolifically for the next quarter century, and by the time he turned to Hypatia near the end of his life, his works had become quite hostile to the Catholic Church and other hierarchical institutions.

Toland placed his treatise on Hypatia in a collection of four essays called the *Tetradymus*.[2] In it, he proposed to use Hypatia's murder to contrast her virtue with the viciousness of the Alexandrian Christian leadership. While this was Toland's larger aim, the work begins with a far different tone. Hypatia's career, Toland claims, demonstrates that "women have no less reason to value themselves," because "there existed a lady of such rare accomplishments."[3] The next few pages offer Hypatia as an object lesson for what female intellectuals can achieve if they are allowed to do so. Toland describes her education in the "most abstruse sciences" and criticizes people for thinking that these things require "too much Labour and Application for the delicate Constitution of Women."[4] Not only did Hypatia's learning justifiably make her the head of the Platonic school in Alexandria but, Toland continues, this offers a lesson for his own time. The few women of his day who had taken a doctorate are highly praised but not ever given any academic positions or titles.[5] Hypatia's life reveals what similar women could achieve if society gave them the chance to do so.

Toland's discussion soon shifts from pointing out how the example of Hypatia makes contemporary restrictions on intelligent women look ridiculous, but he never entirely lets the matter of her gender drop. When discussing Damascius's comparison of Hypatia and Isidore, Toland writes that Damascius's use of gender as a natural point of comparison makes little sense. Saying that a female intellectual is inferior to a man because of her gender is "as if we in England for example did reckon King James superior to Queen Elizabeth because the first ... was a man and the last a woman."[6]

The body of Toland's essay reconstructs Hypatia's life and work using the same ancient sources that were surveyed in Chapter 9.[7] His portrait is more compelling and sympathetic than those found in most ancient authors, though occasionally it also dwells a little too long on her beauty and the effect that this had on men.[8] The last few pages of the book take a different turn, however. It is here, when the account moves from Hypatia's life to her death, that Toland's anti-clericalism becomes pronounced. Toland attacks Cyril for so inflaming the Alexandrian clergy that only "the Blood of Hypatia, shed in the most inhuman Manner, could glut" their fury.[9] In Toland's view, this led to a "deluge of ignorance, superstition, and tyranny" that marked the beginning of "persecutions ... to suppress any efforts that might be used for the restoring of Virtue and Learning."[10]

Toland's treatise had an immediate impact that would help to shape the way that Hypatia was remembered by many of the most important thinkers of the eighteenth and early nineteenth centuries. His forceful attacks on Cyril and the Alexandrian clergy were quickly answered in 1721 by the Englishman Thomas Lewis, who addressed Toland's claims in a pamphlet titled *The History of Hypatia, a Most Impudent School-Mistress of Alexandria*.[11] Although Lewis frames this work as a response to Toland's entire *Tetradymus*, the thrust of his argument is directed against Hypatia. Lewis argues that Hypatia was no one special, but instead merely an educated woman whose learning did not exceed that of many other women of the day.[12] She is famous not for her learning but because the "Puritan" Socrates and the "heathen" Damascius used her death to unfairly attack the reputation of Cyril, an activity that Toland has now cynically repeated.

Lewis's attack was predictable, but it was more inflammatory than substantial. In 1728, however, a "Dissertation sur Hypacie" appeared in volume 5 of the French periodical *Continuation des Mémoires de litterature et d'histoire*, edited by Pierre-Nicholas Desmolets.[13] The author, identified only as M. G., undertook this project, he says, in response to a request to know more about Hypatia sent to him by a Mademoiselle B.[14] The "Dissertation sur Hypacie" begins, as promised, with a discussion of Hypatia's achievements. The author acknowledges that many educated women had been active as philosophers in the ancient world, and mocks as absurd the notion expressed by some in the 1700s that learning made "some women ridiculous."[15] Despite this, Hypatia was not a Christian, and, the author claims, one must agree that "all those who acquire [learning] without Jesus Christ are a little less esteemed."[16]

This seemingly minor point looms quite large as the "Dissertation" proceeds. Much of the body of the work follows Toland in using ancient sources to outline Hypatia's career, but the author does this in a philologically sophisticated manner that points out both logical inconsistencies and poorly researched arguments in Toland's work. This carefully orchestrated argument emerges slowly. A few scattered criticisms of Toland for misreading sources appear in the first few pages of the "Dissertation," but these are just glancing blows designed to make the reader begin to question the reliability of Toland's analysis. The truly devastating critique of Toland develops through a series of deconstructions of the accounts of Hypatia's murder given by Socrates, Philostorgius, and Damascius. Socrates, he argues, was consistently critical of Cyril across his history and offers no evidence for Cyril's responsibility for Hypatia's death. Philostorgius does not even mention Cyril at all. And Damascius was easily discredited because he was a pagan.[17] M. G. then addresses the arguments of Toland explicitly. Despite all of the problems with these sources, Toland "does not add anything" to their flawed narratives. He also has no credibility. A man like this "who dares to attack God himself has no scruple to slander the saints. It is glorious that Cyril never had for himself adversaries so heretical and impious."[18]

The treatise does not end with this attack on Toland, however. The final page explains why the murder of Hypatia had such significance in the 1720s. Toland's use of Hypatia as a tool to attack the legacy of Cyril, a saint in the Catholic Church, threatened to set off religious violence at a time when such things risked becoming the source of wars between nations.[19] This "Dissertation," which was ostensibly devoted to the life and deeds of a female philosopher, had mutated into a defense of Cyril and a critique of early eighteenth-century religious factionalism.

This makes the letter from Mademoiselle B. that immediately follows the "Dissertation" so interesting.[20] She compliments the author on an erudite and tasteful treatise that honored Hypatia. This makes him "quite different in this from the rest of men and the learned of our day, who do not wish to agree that there are wise women. . . . They pretend that science does not go along with a sex of which the organs, so they say, are too weak to resist serious study."[21] The rest of the letter continues in this vein. Mademoiselle B. eviscerates the logic that women must be somehow incapable of study or of participating in learned conversations, she mocks the illogical idea that their organs are somehow weaker, and she points out that, if women were indeed inferior, this would mean that God had made an imperfect creation. She then concludes, "This is why it is wrong to dispense women from science. . . . It is a reflection that I have made long ago. You have given me the place to share this with you. I wish for the public good that you have, on my behalf, a chance to instruct the public about this subject."[22]

This short but gloriously passive-aggressive letter from the woman who commissioned the "Dissertation sur Hypacie" willfully misrepresents what the text accomplished. This learned woman wanted the text to use the life and deeds of Hypatia to make an argument that female intellectuals were just as capable as men. When she instead got a philologically powerful and rhetorically sophisticated anti-Toland polemic, she simply refused to acknowledge the text for what it was. By congratulating the author for proving points on which he spent little time and ignoring the arguments he developed at much greater length, Mademoiselle B tried to remake the text into what she hoped it would be. She was, in short, attempting to transform Hypatia from a victim of religious intolerance into an exemplar who demonstrated the true potential of female intellectuals.

Unfortunately, her efforts went nowhere. Although the "Dissertation sur Hypacie" prompted a response in the next volume of the *Continuation des Mémoires de litterature et d'histoire*, and would continue to generate reactions for the next five decades, no one seems to engage with the Hypatia of Mademoiselle B.[23] Her hopes for what Hypatia's life could mean to both men and women went unrealized. Instead, as the eighteenth century progressed, male authors increasingly subordinated the details of Hypatia's life to discussions about the implications of her death. She again became a symbol, a beautiful empty vessel whose virtue and learning existed only to be destroyed in a way that invited an author to assign blame. Following Toland, French intellectuals like Voltaire and English authors like Edward Gibbon placed the blame for her murder squarely on Cyril and, either implicitly or explicitly, used this event to attack the Catholic Church.[24] Catholic authors (and even some French Protestants) followed the author of the anonymous "Dissertation sur Hypacie" and responded equally vigorously that Cyril was not responsible, and that the fault lay instead with either the Alexandrian mob or with Peter the Lector.[25] As the arguments about Cyril's responsibility got more heated, Hypatia again began to fade into the background.

Nothing is more indicative of this trend than the entry on Hypatia that appeared in 1772 in Voltaire's *Dictionnaire philosophique*.[26] The first half of the entry asks the reader to consider the horror if Madame Dacier, a beautiful specialist in Homer whose 1699 translation of the *Iliad* gave many French men of letters their first exposure to the text, was killed in Notre Dame Cathedral by the archbishop of Paris because she refused to say that a poem written by a monk was superior to Homer.[27] This, Voltaire writes, "is precisely the history of Hypatia. She taught Homer and Plato in Alexandria at the time of Theodosius II. Saint Cyril incited the Christian populace against her." Voltaire has nothing more to say about Hypatia herself. The rest of the lengthy entry discusses the scholarly controversy about whether or not Cyril was responsible for her death. Voltaire even uses the entry to mock one critic in particular who wrote a two-volume rebuttal of an article in Diderot's *Encyclopédie* that touched on Hypatia. Voltaire concludes with the callous comment that "when one finds a beautiful woman completely naked, it is not for the purpose of massacring her."[28] Fifty years after Toland, the shape and fate of Hypatia's body had again completely overshadowed the depth and power of her mind.

This tendency became even more pronounced at the dawn of the Victorian era. Hypatia remained a common topic of scholarly and elite literary conversation throughout the late eighteenth and early nineteenth centuries, but she jumped into popular culture in the middle decades of the nineteenth century. Her first significant appearance as a literary character in a work of fiction came in Diodata Saluzzo Roero's 1827 poem *Ipazia ovvero delle filosofie*, a two-volume "novel in verse" that transforms Hypatia into a Christian and climaxes with her murder in a church beneath a cross.[29] Though the poet does criticize Toland's portrait of Hypatia as ill-founded in her preface, she acknowledges that her goal in writing the poem is to speak about larger questions of social change rather than the historical reality of Hypatia's life.[30]

Diodata Saluzzo Roero's "novel in verse" pointed toward the growing tendency among nineteenth-century authors to care less about the historical details of Hypatia's life and more about how her story could be adapted to interest contemporary readers. No nineteenth-century author did this more successfully than the English reverend and professor Charles Kingsley. Kingsley believed strongly that religion, social justice, and political freedom were intimately linked, but he was not passionate only about these admirable ideas. Kingsley also had a strong belief in a sort of "manful Christianity" that infused physical strength with Christian ideas that do "not exalt the feminine virtues to the exclusion of the masculine."[31] This manful Christianity required one to disregard both what Kingsley saw as the effete "Anythingarianism" of contemporary thinkers like Ralph Waldo Emerson and the effeminacy of Catholic ideas of celibacy.[32] Kingsley blended this notion with a strong and unapologetic idea of European superiority that saw in "Teutonic" peoples a vital force that both re-enervated the ancient world and created the supposedly superior European culture of Kingsley's time.

Kingsley's novel *Hypatia: Or, New Foes with an Old Face* showcases all of these ideas within a literary world shaped quite deliberately by Orientalist and racist notions.[33] His Alexandria represents a historical dead end where the "effete remains" of ancient philosophy barely hung on as the "intrigues and villainies of the Byzantine court" swirled.[34] Kingsley populates the novel with a motley crew of monks, clergy, philosophers, Goths, Jews, and servants (whom he often takes pains to identify by their dark skin),[35] but Hypatia serves as the novel's key character. His Hypatia is a twenty-five-year–old, light-skinned, blonde-haired Greek woman with a noble bearing and deep philosophical knowledge. Despite her age, she heads a circle that, at various points in the novel, includes a Jew named Raphael, a former (and future) Egyptian monk named Philammon, and, for one meeting, both the exotic dancer Pelagia and a band of Goths. The familiar characters of

Cyril, Peter the Reader, Orestes, and Synesius appear, as do a random selection of figures from the early fifth-century Roman West including, implausibly, Saint Augustine.

Kingsley's *Hypatia* differs from all of the previous treatments of Hypatia's life by making the story bigger than Hypatia and Cyril. Hypatia is admirable but flawed, a devotee of an imperfect philosophical and religious system who is unable to appreciate the true, Christian wisdom crafted by contemporaries like Augustine. Cyril is also flawed, but in ways that are more subtle and nuanced than one sees in, say, the work of Toland. Kingsley's Cyril does not create the climate of violence that leads to Hypatia's murder but instead navigates it expertly. Responsibility for Hypatia's death then falls not on any one person or character but on a larger historical process that, in Kingsley's view, condemned Hypatia and destroyed the final vestiges of classical Hellenism that she dutifully preserved. Her city lost the chance to be revitalized when the Goths departed and Raphael, a Jewish former student of Hypatia who converted to Augustinian philosophy and Christianity, sailed away. Without their "manly Christianity," Alexandria and the rest of the Christian East fell into decadence and, ultimately, a fatal decline.

Kingsley ends the work with a call to his nineteenth-century audience to heed the lessons of the fifth century. He has, he claims, shown them their "own likenesses in toga and tunic, instead of coat and bonnet." He then warns them that "the same devil who tempted these old Egyptians tempts you. The same God who would have saved these old Egyptians if they had willed, will save you, if you will. Their sins are yours, their errors yours, their doom yours, their deliverance yours."[36] Victorian Englishmen and women needed to carefully and urgently choose either to fall into the same decadence as Hypatia's Alexandria or to embrace the vibrant, vital, and socially aware Christianity that Kingsley championed.

Kingsley's *Hypatia* was a huge success. Victorians, including the queen herself, loved the work and kept it in print for the rest of the century. Kingsley's novel sold well in England and was soon translated into a range of European languages.[37] It was also quickly adapted for the stage. The first adaptation, written by Elizabeth Bowers, was performed in Philadelphia in 1859, with the author herself playing Hypatia.[38] In 1893, a much more high-profile adaptation called simply *Hypatia* opened in London. Although this largely followed Kingsley's story, it toned down much of the anti-Semitism found in Kingsley's original.[39] Kingsley's work also inspired visual artists who sought to capture scenes or characters from the book. These include Charles William Mitchell's 1885 painting depicting a nude Hypatia standing before an altar in a church (see Figure 10.1) and Julia Margaret Cameron's 1867 photograph of the model Marie Spartali dressed to represent a young Hypatia (see Figure 10.2).[40]

Kingsley's novel showed the commercial and artistic potential of radical reinterpretations of Hypatia's story that strayed far from its

FIGURE 10.1. *Hypatia* by Charles William Mitchell.
Credit line: Wikimedia commons.

FIGURE 10.2. Julia Margaret Cameron's photo of Marie Spartali dressed to represent Hypatia.

Credit line: Wikimedia commons.

historical roots. By the middle of the twentieth century, authors, graphic novelists, and filmmakers had come to take tremendous liberties with her legacy. For some authors, Hypatia would remain primarily a symbol for the survival of philosophical rationalism. This was, for example, the identity that defined her in Mario Luzi's *Ipazia*, a work that says this about her death: "In this way, the dream of Hellenic Reason ended/ In this way, on the floor of Christ."[41] Even more pronounced was the death of Hypatia in Arnulf Zitelmann's German novel *Hypatia*. He describes her as a pagan sage who intended to create a Platonic state somewhere beyond the Pillars of Hercules, traveled the Mediterranean, and ended up murdered by a Christian mob after she gave an oration against Cyril in the Alexandrian Forum. Zitelmann saw her murder not only as the end of the ancient world, but also as an event that marked Hypatia as the first victim of the misogynist witch hunts that would plague future centuries.[42]

Zitelmann was neither the first nor the most memorable twentieth-century author to see in Hypatia's death a moment that transformed the opportunities available to women. As early as 1908, Carlo Pascal included Hypatia in a set of popularized biographies that included, among other subjects, Seneca and Giuseppe Garibaldi. Nearly half of his fifty-three page discussion of Hypatia focuses on her place in a long succession of female intellectuals. Pascal saw her death as the result of an "insolent and superstitious anti-female tendency" that destroyed the freedom to achieve that ancient women had enjoyed.[43] This particular way of understanding Hypatia's legacy became increasingly pronounced as the twentieth century progressed. Indeed, by the late 1980s, Hypatia's name had become attached to two academic journals devoted to feminist studies, *Hypatia: Feminist Studies* (begun in Athens in 1984) and *Hypatia: A Journal of Feminist Philosophy* (begun in 1986).

More fantastic literary representations of Hypatia also appeared in the late twentieth century. In 1989, Ursule Molinaro told a story of Hypatia's life in poetic prose. The work begins with Hypatia's murder, a murder that reflected an age in which "a new brand of Christians, politicians of faith" outlawed independent thought, "especially when thought by women." These Christians "offered a new model of depleasurized submission as they converted the great & lusty earthmother goddess into a chaste mother of a martyred god."[44] Molinaro's Hypatia did not belong to this Christian world. She was, instead, a woman who began taking lovers at a young age and continued to do so even after she married the philosopher Isidore. When her father saw in Hypatia's horoscope that she would be killed, he asked her to leave Alexandria. She refused, perhaps "sensing the end of an era, beyond which she had no desire to live."[45] She belonged in a world that allowed her "to be learned," "to share her learning," and to "become known because of her thoughts," and that permitted "the known thinking woman to have lovers, besides having a philosophical philosopher husband."[46] Christian gossip about Hypatia and her lover Orestes killed her, and Hypatia died "staring wide-eyed across a sea of bodies that were pausing briefly, getting ready to charge into the new Christian era in which she had no desire to live."[47]

Molinaro crafted her Hypatia to embody a fictional past that supported the intellectual and sexual values that Molinaro idealized. This had only a little to do with the historical Hypatia, but Molinaro's heroine at least bore some resemblance to the philosopher. The later twentieth and early twenty-first centuries saw even more fantastic literary license taken with Hypatia's legacy. She appears as, among other things, the inspiration for a community of philosophical satyrs in Umberto Eco's *Baudolino* and the presider at a 1921 Italian intellectual salon in the Hugo Pratt's graphic novel *Corto Maltese: Favola di Venezia*.[48] Even more imaginative is her place in the *Heirs of Alexandria* fantasy series.[49] The authors of this series construct an alternate universe in which John Chrysostom converted Hypatia to Christianity, she saved the Alexandrian Library from destruction, and then she helped to create a Christian world divided along north-south lines in which Rome and Spain depend upon the knowledge that she preserved.

None of these contemporary treatments of Hypatia had the popular impact of Alejandro Amenábar's 2009 film *Agora*. Starring Rachel Weisz as Hypatia, *Agora* uses her life to reconstruct the conflicts between religious extremism, intellectual accomplishment, and the public roles played by women. None of these themes are new (indeed, all of them were discussed in detail by Toland in 1720), but *Agora* frames them in a way that is particularly suited to the concerns of the early twenty-first century. Although most other modern adaptations of Hypatia's life focus on her achievements as a philosopher, Amenábar instead portrays Hypatia as the first astronomer to understand that we live in a heliocentric solar system in which the planets have an elliptical orbit. Less Plato than Copernicus, *Agora*'s Hypatia claims tangible scientific discoveries that seem much more important than philosophical enlightenment in the tech-driven 2000s.

Agora also spends much more time than any previous fictional adaptation of Hypatia's life developing the idea that extremism in Alexandria directly threatened women's opportunity to be publicly active. Previous artists had mentioned this shift, but none had done so with quite the power of Amenábar.[50] Amenábar also tells his story in a way that never neglects issues connected to Hypatia's gender. Our first glimpse into her teaching circle shows it to be a religiously mixed environment in which the ties between master and student are close enough that the (then pagan) Orestes feels free to express his love for Hypatia, first in private and then publicly in the Alexandrian theater. Hypatia responds by bringing a bloody menstrual rag to him during class, an adaptation of the powerful story Damascius once told about her. Even more distressingly, the film shows Hypatia being sexually assaulted by one of her father's slaves who had recently converted to Christianity, an assault that ends with her assailant breaking down in tears before Hypatia manumits him. Hypatia's gender also plays a crucial role in setting up the final conflict that will result in Hypatia's death. Amenábar artfully balances his narration of the growing tension between Orestes and Cyril with scenes portraying the maturation of the respectful friendship that Orestes eventually enjoys with Hypatia. These two stories come together when Cyril summons Orestes to a liturgical service and reads to him a passage from the Bible that prohibits a Christian from having a female teacher. Faced with a choice between his Christianity and his close relationship with Hypatia, Orestes consults with Synesius. Synesius tells Orestes that his Christianity must come first, and that his consultations with Hypatia must end immediately. Orestes reluctantly agrees to this just before the movie climaxes with Hypatia's murder.

Agora uses the figure of Hypatia to tell an eloquent (albeit historically dubious) story tracing the destruction of ancient Alexandrian intellectual culture and the growing limits being placed on female intellectuals. Its most powerful images are those depicting the violent intolerance of Christian monks and clergy. This has, of course, been a topic addressed in every treatment of Hypatia's life since the fifth century, but Amenábar depicts these religious extremists in a way that particularly resonates in a post-9/11 world. Dressed in ragged black clothing with covered heads and faces and long beards, *Agora's* monks and clergy look more like members of the Taliban than the Christian ascetics we imagine today. Their actions similarly correspond to actions taken by twenty-first-century religious extremists. Amenábar's Christian monks destroy ancient statues, restrict the public activity of women, and perpetrate massacres of religious minorities. These echoes of modern extremist movements allow contemporary audiences to imagine the fifth century by drawing upon their own twenty-first century images of violent religious movements.

From Toland's *Hypatia* in 1720 through Amenábar's *Agora* in 2009, the twin specters of religious extremism and social decline haunt every modern treatment of Hypatia. Her death has become a modern touchstone that symbolizes the destruction of something admirable, good, and irreplaceable, while the extremists who kill her are, invariably, people whose violence and beliefs place them on the wrong side of history. To people in the early modern and modern worlds, Hypatia's tale always portends social decline and a descent into ignorance. This not only fails to notice the history of the centuries that followed her death, but, more importantly, it also devalues the significance of her life.

Reconsidering a Legend

When the legend becomes fact, print the legend.

—*The Man Who Shot Liberty Valance*

The classic western *The Man Who Shot Liberty Valance* uses the conflict between the notorious outlaw Liberty Valance and the transplanted Eastern lawyer Ransom Stoddard to show how the violent norms of the Old West died and those of the modern state quickly replaced them. Stoddard, who represents the rule of law, is propelled to the US Senate and ultimately to the Colorado governor's mansion by the fame he gained for shooting Liberty Valance in a gunfight. Stoddard knew the entire time, however, that the real killer of Liberty Valance was Tom Doniphon (played by John Wayne). Doniphon, an old-style western gunfighter who was once the most respected man in the territory, had no place in the new Colorado. He died decades later, completely forgotten and penniless. When Senator Stoddard came to the funeral and told the entire story to the town newspaper following Doniphon's death, the editor refused to print it. The legend of Ransom Stoddard and the new Colorado it birthed meant too much to be discarded.

The legend of Hypatia has been told for 1,600 years. Hypatia's death, like that of Liberty Valance, has come to represent the end of an era, but no one quite agrees on what sort of era it concluded. For some authors, Hypatia's death marked the end of paganism and the final triumph of Christianity. For others, the ancient age of reason died with her and was replaced by long centuries of superstition. For still others, her murder concluded a time in which women enjoyed intellectual opportunities and political influence that they would not see again until modern times. But, in nearly every telling, a larger historical period died alongside Hypatia. This means that there are many Hypatias and many different characterizations of the period her death supposedly concluded.

Before her senseless murder became a temporal boundary, Hypatia was a real person living in a complicated and changing later Roman world. Fortunately, we can still tell the basic story of her life and the years in which she lived. Hypatia was born in 355 into an empire that was majority pagan, filled with pagan temples, and governed by imperial officials who were only beginning to appreciate the disruptive potential of angry Christian bishops and monks. She grew up in a wealthy household headed by a prominent teacher. She was educated in a curriculum that was filled with traditional religious content, and she would perhaps have been surprised to learn that, at some point in her childhood, her home city had become majority Christian.[1] In 361, when Hypatia was just beginning her formal education, the emperor Julian publicly announced his devotion to the old gods. Public sacrifice again became legal, temples were rebuilt, and the power that Christian bishops had been slowly accumulating was much reduced as Julian cut imperial support for the church and invited all exiled bishops back to their home cities.[2]

It took more than a generation for the new religious order established by Julian to be completely undone. The Christian majority in Alexandria grew during these years, as did the Christian population of the empire at large, but religious dynamics within individual cities changed much more slowly. Most forms of sacrifice remained legal, and temples everywhere remained open into the 380s. The practical reality of Roman religious life often lagged behind even these gradual changes in the law. Images of the gods and signs of human devotion to them remained visible everywhere in Alexandria during this time. Indeed, to many older men and women the line between "paganism" and "Christianity" often seemed rather incomprehensible. Like the emperor Julian, many people felt it perfectly acceptable to believe that both Christ and Serapis were divinities—and to worship both.

This was the world in which Hypatia grew into an adult and began her academic career. Hypatia moved through the schools of grammar and (probably) rhetoric in the 360s, studied mathematics and philosophy in the 370s and, in the early 380s, refined the arguments that she would use to she remake Alexandrian intellectual life. By 385, Hypatia had become Alexandria's most prominent intellectual, and she was quickly growing into the public role that would define the second half of her career.

Hypatia accomplished all of this in spite of the world in which she lived. Contrary to what some modern writers about Hypatia suppose, hers was not a world in which women enjoyed anything approaching equality.[3] It was, however, a world that permitted determined and talented women just enough freedom to carve out the kind of career that Hypatia did. This world required Hypatia to make significant sacrifices in exchange for her prominence. While Hypatia likely chose to remain a virgin and never marry for philosophical reasons, her decision to serve as the head of her own school of philosophy required her to make this choice a very public one. Not only did Hypatia share her sexual history with the world, but she allowed (and maybe even encouraged) the circulation of stories that highlighted her celibacy. She also endured other intrusions that male colleagues did not. Whenever Hypatia wore the traditional philosopher's cloak, her gender was noted with a mixture of curiosity and amusement. When she spoke in public, it is likely that she had to either speak more loudly or more frequently before men listened. Late fourth-century Alexandrian society did not expressly prohibit Hypatia from becoming a prominent, publicly engaged intellectual, but it did not make it easy for her either.

The Serapeum destruction in 392 made it impossible for Alexandrians to ignore the fourth century's slow but steady religious changes. While large numbers of Alexandrians still felt that religious identity mattered far less than other social markers, people like Olympus and Theophilus understood that the religious developments of the fourth century had opened profound divisions between pagans and Christians that they could exploit. Most Alexandrians did not yet divide the world between those who worshipped the old gods and those who did not, but they could be taught to do so.[4] Theophilus's mocking parades of pagan religious objects, Olympus's violent response to it, and the Christian destruction of the temple of Serapis were, at their core, incidents designed to show pagans and Christians that religious differences mattered profoundly. The Serapeum destruction did not dramatically change the religious realities of the Roman world, but it did force people to recognize that their world had already changed in ways that they had failed to appreciate.

No city can function for long when two large groups within it regularly confront each other violently. This is what made the second half of Hypatia's life so important. When the Alexandrian elites stopped fighting one another after the Serapeum amnesty in 392, Hypatia was there to pick up the pieces. She did not share the idea that people with different confessional backgrounds must be at odds with one another. Instead, she taught a philosophy that encouraged her students to love one another regardless of their religious background. The highest goal of this philosophy was contemplative union with God, but this was a goal that Hypatia felt Christians and non-Christians attending her school could pursue together. These ideas created a harmonious and religiously heterogeneous scholarly community, but Hypatia's impact extended beyond the tens of students whose philosophical training she supervised. Her teaching also encouraged students to use their training to reform the world around them. They were to push their fellow citizens to live their lives and govern their cities philosophically. Some of her students did this by discussing philosophy privately with their friends, others did it through civic office holding, and Synesius combined these things with, eventually, his service as a Christian bishop.

On the surface, Hypatia's success in creating a philosophical community to which Christians and pagans could comfortably belong looked like a return to the mid-fourth century world in which she grew up. Indeed, conditions within Alexandria permitted one to think that the city could still be governed according to the models of elite, nonconfessional consensus that had maintained order for most of the fourth century. Believing this was, however, indulging in an illusion. Following the Serapeum destruction, Theophilus had created a powerful coalition of supporters drawn from the Alexandrian Nicene church, the monasteries in the desert around Alexandria, and officials in the imperial court. His victory over the pagan rebels at the Serapeum had given him unmatched anti-pagan credentials. He had no need to engage in more religious provocations. He instead spent most of the next two decades reinforcing the coalition that he had built. Theophilus continued to cultivate his relationships with imperial officials while simultaneously building monasteries in and around Alexandria that brought large populations of monks into the city and its suburbs.[5] This work ensured that the Alexandrian bishop was far more powerful when Theophilus died in 412 than he had been when he first assumed office.

Theophilus's power, however, had developed out of sight and without ever being fully expressed. The governors, philosophers, and city councilors of Alexandria can be forgiven for again not recognizing the slow and steady process through which their world was changing.

Even if Hypatia understood what Theophilus had accomplished over those two decades, she would not have changed her behavior. Unless a state becomes irrevocably corrupt, the philosopher must remain engaged in its political life. Hypatia's public activity then did not in any way represent an endorsement of the political and religious climate of her city. But Hypatia's counsel remained greatly valued during the 390s and 400s. Not only did she exercise influence over governors and judges, but Synesius's close ties to Theophilus suggest that Hypatia may also have had at least a working relationship with the bishop. Hypatia functioned well in a city that, for two decades, proved receptive to the ideas of its most prominent philosopher.

It was only after Theophilus's departure that the true power of his coalition of supporters became evident. In the chaos that followed his death, members of the clergy, monks, and imperial officials first split into competing camps and then worked against each other as Cyril tried to consolidate power. By 414, Cyril had assumed control over the church as well as the lay and ascetic supporters that Theophilus had cultivated. He had not, however, been successful in building a strong relationship with the governor Orestes. In the later fourth century, this would have been a serious check on his authority. Theophilus, for example, could not have destroyed the Serapeum without imperial support. The ground had again shifted, however. Because of Theophilus's successful construction of a strong network of supporters in and around the city, Cyril had more powerful and more dedicated resources in 415 than his uncle did in 392. Cyril certainly did not want a conflict with Orestes or the Alexandrian city council, but he felt confident that he had the resources to prevail if one came.

Just as the philosopher Olympus failed to understand that pagans lacked the numbers and clout to violently confront Theophilus in 392, so too did Orestes, Hypatia, and the leading citizens of Alexandria misjudge the ability of the imperial administrative system to restrain Cyril. They did not see the depth and power of his support, and when they forced a confrontation with Cyril, they could not imagine that they would lose. But they were living in a world whose rules had become outdated. Neither Orestes nor Hypatia realized the danger in forcing

Cyril to unleash the real but often uncontrollable power of his ascetic and lay supporters in the city. When Cyril did call upon these supporters, he knew that a demonstration by them would have to be terrifying enough to force Orestes and Hypatia to capitulate. Cyril did not order the mob to become murderous, but it was also probably not a complete surprise to him when it did. Hypatia was the unfortunate casualty.

This is why Hypatia died, but these events say nothing about why her death had such meaning. For Hypatia's contemporaries, her death marked the frightful opening of a half-century during which Alexandrian bishops could credibly threaten (and occasionally even deploy) terrifying force if they felt that their interests were endangered. In this way, Hypatia's murder foreshadowed moments like the display of raw power that Cyril's successor Dioscorus used to commandeer the Robber Council of Ephesus in 449. Hypatia's death was, in a sense, the moment that the calamitous fifth century dawned on the Alexandrian church. It utterly terrified observers who were used to a different, less assertive form of Christian power.

It is just as important, however, to recognize what Hypatia's death did not mean. Her murder did not represent either the end of paganism or the closing of an age of reason. Despite repeated imperial efforts to suppress paganism, traditional religious practices survived (and, in some places, even thrived) well past the Islamic conquests of much of the Roman East in the seventh century. Indeed, the regular appearance of pagan communities in late sixth-, seventh-, and even tenth-century sources suggest that Hypatia's death meant very little to the religious dynamics of the later Roman world.[6]

The same is true for intellectual pursuits. Hypatia's murder did indeed doom the particular Plotinian Platonism that she taught, but it did not end philosophical teaching in Alexandria. In fact, quite the opposite occurred. Fifth- and sixth-century Alexandrian Platonists were some of the most prolific and influential teachers antiquity would ever see. Philosophers like Hierocles, Ammonius, John Philoponus, Simplicius, and Olympiodorus kept astronomical observations, taught mathematics, and authored many long and erudite commentaries on the works of Plato and Aristotle. After the emperor Justinian closed the Athenian Platonic school in 529, Alexandria would become the unquestioned and unrivaled center for philosophical studies in the Mediterranean. It would remain so for nearly another full century.[7] Even though Hypatia's death had destroyed one distinctive intellectual approach, serious mathematical and philosophical investigations continued without interruption in the Roman world.

Hypatia's death also did not represent the dawning of an age of misogyny or an end to equal opportunities for female intellectuals. It is true that no other female intellectuals followed the same path as Hypatia, but this was not because Hypatia lived in a more enlightened age. It was because no one quite like Hypatia would again appear in the ancient world. Hypatia had become prominent through tremendous personal talent, sheer force of will, and a determination to live philosophically despite the gossip, crude jokes, and slights of male contemporaries. Hypatia was unique not because she had more chances than the female intellectuals who came after her. She was instead uniquely willing to accept the harsh sacrifices her career demanded of her.

Ultimately, we must appreciate Hypatia for the person that she was, not the literary character that she became. She was a brilliant and fiercely determined woman whose talent and skill rebalanced Alexandria's intellectual culture and guided the city's political life. Hypatia's accomplishments were real and significant. While her death was indeed dramatic, we do her a tremendous disservice if we allow it to overshadow her life. We can be true to her memory only if we recognize the life she led as well as the death she suffered.

Notes

1. Socrates Scholasticus, *HE* 7.7.

2. This is suggested by John of Nikiu, *Chronicle* 84.87–103; Socrates Scholasticus, *HE* 7.15; and, perhaps obliquely, Damascius, *Isid.* 43E. For discussion of these texts and their interaction, see Chapter 9.

3. For discussion, see Chapter 6.

4. John of Nikiu, *Chronicle* 84.88. John says that Hypatia was "devoted at all times to magic, astrolabes and instruments of music, and she beguiled many people through Satanic wiles. And the governor of the city [Orestes] honoured her exceedingly; for she had beguiled him through her magic."

5. The date of 415 is based on Socrates Scholasticus and accepted by most modern scholars (e.g., M. Dzielska, *Hypatia of Alexandria*, trans. F. Lyra [Cambridge, MA, 1995], 93; C. Haas, *Alexandria in Late Antiquity* [Baltimore, 1997], 307–16). It has recently been argued (by Ari Belenkiy, "An Astronomical Murder?," *Astronomy and Geophysics* 51.2 [2010], 9–13) that the date of her murder was instead in March 416, and that her death was caused by an argument about the date of Easter in 417. As A. Cameron ("Hypatia: Life, Death, and Works," in *Wandering Poets and Other Essays on Late Greek Literature and Philosophy* [Oxford, 2016], 185–203, at 190) has shown, though, there is absolutely no evidence that Hypatia was ever interested in calculating the date of Easter or interacting with Christian officials concerned about this.

6. See, for example, the detailed discussion in B. Shaw, *Sacred Violence and Sectarian Hatred in the Age of Augustine* (Cambridge, 2011), 235ff.

7. The few larger late antique Alexandrian houses that have been excavated are oriented around a central courtyard rather than the street. For plans and reconstructions, see J. McKenzie, *The Architecture of Alexandria and Egypt, 300 BC–700 AD* (New Haven, 2007), 217–20, as well as figures 372–74.

8. Socrates, *HE* 7.15.

9. Philostorgius (*HE* 8.9) uses this as an indication of the venality of all Nicene Christians. Socrates (*HE* 7.15) says that "this brought no small opprobrium onto Cyril and the Alexandrian church." Writing in the later sixth century, John Malalas (*Chronicle* 13.39) criticizes Cyril for giving the people of his city free reign to attack Hypatia. These sources and their contexts are discussed in greater detail in Chapter 9.

10. Hypatia's legacy in later literature is treated in detail in Chapter 10.

11. As of July 2015, Hypatia had over 635,000 Google search results, well behind Plato (over 90,000,000), Socrates (25,000,000), Aristotle (22,000,000), and Pythagoras (9,100,000) but far ahead of Neoplatonists like Plotinus (458,000), Porphyry of Tyre (65,000), Iamblichus (224,000), Proclus (408,000), and Damascius (97,500).

12. Cyril has 523,000 results.

13. This is discussed in detail in Chapter 9.

Chapter 1

1. Parts of this chapter expand upon and update an earlier discussion of Alexandrian life first published in E. Watts, *City and School in Late Antique Athens and Alexandria* (Berkeley, 2006), Chapter 6.

2. It is estimated that during the high season a grain barge entered the Nile canal leading to the city every twelve seconds. See C. Galvão-Sobrinho, *Doctrine and Power: Theological Controversy and Christian Leadership in the Later Roman Empire* (Berkeley, 2013), 58.

3. Alexandria was the site through which most of the exports of Egypt were shipped to the rest of the Roman world. Although it accounted for a much lower volume of trade, the opening of a canal linking the Red Sea to the Nile also made Alexandria a natural transit point for the shipment of goods from locations on the Indian Ocean. See P. M. Fraser, *Ptolemaic Alexandria* (Oxford, 1970), 800–801.

4. Strabo, *Geography* 17.1.7.

5. P. M. Fraser, "A Syriac *Notitia Urbis Alexandrinae*," *JEA* 37 (1951), 103–8. For discussion of this list and its basic credibility, see E. Watts, *Riot in Alexandria* (Berkeley, 2010), 13 n. 57.

6. On the Caesareum, see McKenzie, *Architecture of Alexandria*, 77–78. For descriptions of the temple itself see Strabo, 17.1.10; Pliny, *NH* 36.14.69; as well as the discussion of H. Hanlein-Schäfer, *Veneratio Augusti, eine Studie zu den Templen des ersten römischen Kaisers* (Rome, 1985), 203–4.

7. For discussion see Haas, *Alexandria in Late Antiquity*, 280–95.

8. Such is the view of Ammianus Marcellinus (22.16.12), who ranks it second in the world to the Capitolium in Rome.

9. This statue was reported created by the sculptor Bryaxis (Clement, *Protr.* 4.48.1–3).

10. For a detailed discussion of the Serapeum site, see J. McKenzie, S. Gibson, and A. T. Reyes, "Reconstructing the Serapeum in Alexandria from the Archeological Evidence," *JRS* 94 (2004), 73–121; and McKenzie, *Architecture of Alexandria*, 198–203.

11. An exceptional and concise description of the founding of these institutions is found in Fraser, *Ptolemaic Alexandria*, 305–35.

12. For the cultural significance of the Museum in the Ptolemaic period, see A. Erskine, "Culture and Power in Ptolemaic Egypt: The Museum and Library of Alexandria," *Greece and Rome* 42 (1995), 38–48.

13. Such is the (probably correct) supposition of Fraser, *Ptolemaic Alexandria*, 314.

14. Strabo, 17.1.8. A second-century BCE Delian inscription dedicated to Chrysermus, a member of a prominent Alexandrian family, calls him the "*Epistates* of the *Mouseion*" (*Ins. Dél.* 1525). For this, see Fraser, *Ptolemaic Alexandria*, 316.

15. Fraser, *Ptolemaic Alexandria*, 318.

16. Strabo, 17.1.8

17. McKenzie, *Architecture of Alexandria*, 184.

18. N. Lewis, *"Literati* in the Service of Roman Emperors: Politics before Culture,"* in *Coins, Culture and History in the Ancient World: Numismatic and Other Studies in Honor of Bluma L. Trell*, ed. L. Casson and M. Price (Detroit, 1981), 149–66.

19. D. Delia, "From Romance to Rhetoric: The Alexandrian Library in Classical and Islamic Traditions," *American Historical Review* 97 (1992), 1449–67.

20. Tzetzes (*Prolegomena de comoedia Aristophanis* 2.10) remarks that there were 400,000 rolls containing a number of different works, and 90,000 rolls containing only one work.

21. Aulus Gellius, *Noc. Att.* 7.17.3; Seneca, *De Tranq.* 9.5; and Cassius Dio, 43.38.2.

22. Plutarch, *Antony* 58. The significance of this gift and the question of whether it actually occurred are discussed by Fraser, *Ptolemaic Alexandria*, 335; and Delia, "From Romance to Rhetoric," 1462.

23. For the Caesareum, see Philo, *Legatio* 151. The Claudianum is mentioned in Suetonius, *Claudius* 42.2. For comment on this, see Delia, "From Romance to Rhetoric," 1458 n. 37; McKenzie, *Architecture of Alexandria*, 184.

24. Fraser, *Ptolemaic Alexandria*, 323.

25. For the daughter library, see Epiphanius, *De Mens. Et Pond.* 11. Tzetzes (19–20) also mentions a second library that he calls "the Outer Library."

26. Ammianus, 22.16.12. This is either a count of all of the individual books in each author's composition (so Homer's *Iliad* counts as twenty-four works, not one) or a wild exaggeration.

27. Lewis, *"Literati* in the Service of Roman Emperors,"* 157.

28. A stone statue base that was originally dedicated to the rhetor Aelius Demetrios, a member of the Museum, was reused in the reign of Diocletian. For this, see E. Breccia, *Catalogue générale des antiquité égyptiennes du Musée d'Alexandrie (nos. 1–568): Inscrizione greche e latine* (Cairo, 1911), n. 146; and Delia, "From Romance to Rhetoric," 1455. His Museum connection was reaffirmed by C. P. Jones, "A Friend of Galen," *Classical Quarterly* 17 (1967), 311–12.

29. Aurelian's forces completely destroyed the Bruchion quarter in which the Museum was situated. The later sack of the city in the reign of Diocletian would have completed what was begun twenty-five years before. For this, see A. J. Butler, *The Arab Conquest of Egypt* (2nd ed. by P. M. Fraser) (Oxford, 1978), 411. Eusebius wrongly attributes the destruction of the quarter to Claudius Gothicus, an emperor who never personally campaigned in Egypt (7.32.7–12).

30. The existence of a physical space known as the Museum in Alexandria is attested by Zacharias Scholasticus in the later fifth century (*Ammonius*, ln. 367).

31. *CTh* 16.10–1. For discussion of this anti-pagan legislation and its context, see Chapter 4.

32. For Horapollon's conversion, see Damascius, *Isid.* 120B. For his Museum membership, see J. Maspero, "Horapollon et la fin du paganisme Égyptien," *BIFAO* 11 (1914), 163–95.

33. For an extensive comparison between the two cities in late antiquity, see Watts, *City and School*.

34. I. Morris, *Why the West Rules—For Now* (New York, 2010), 632.

35. The Alexandrian population has been estimated to be around 500,000 people during the Roman imperial period, and perhaps slightly less by the fifth century. For

a survey of the various numbers suggested over time, see D. Delia, "The Population of Roman Alexandria," *TAPA* 118 (1988), 275–92. For a sense of the congestion of the city, see C. Haas, "John Moschus and Late Antique Alexandria," in *Alexandrie Medievale* 2, ed. C. Decobert (Cairo, 2002), 47–59, at 51–52; and McKenzie, *Architecture of Alexandria*, 218.

36. For the Lycian and Phrygian communities see Haas, *Alexandria in Late Antiquity*, 49; and *IGRR* 1.1078, *SEG* 8.359, *OGIS* 658.

37. Strabo, 17.1.6; Q. Curtius, 4.33; Tacitus, 4.83–84; Clement, *Protrepticus* 4.42. For discussion see Haas, *Alexandria in Late Antiquity*, 49.

38. C. Laes, *Children in the Roman Empire* (Cambridge, 2011), 65–66.

39. B. Rawson, *Children and Childhood in Roman Italy* (Oxford, 2003), 103.

40. For diseases in the Roman world, see W. Scheidel, *Death on the Nile: Disease and the Demography of Roman Egypt* (Leiden, 2001); and Scheidel, "Demography, Disease, and Death," in *The Cambridge Companion to Ancient Rome*, ed. P. Erdkamp (Cambridge, 2013), 45–59.

41. N. Morley, *Metropolis and Hinterland: The City of Rome and the Italian Economy, 200 B.C.–A.D. 200* (Cambridge, 1996), 39–54; W. Scheidel, "Germs for Rome," in *Rome the Cosmopolis*, ed. C. Edwards and G. Woolf (Cambridge, 2003), 158–76, at 175–76; and Scheidel, "Human Mobility in Roman Italy, I: The Free Population," *JRS* 94 (2004): 1–26, at 15–19.

42. For migrants in the city, see *P. Giss.* 40.2; *POxy* 1643 (AD 298); Cassius Dio, 78.23.2; and the discussion of C. Galvão-Sobrinho, *Doctrine and Power*, 57, 215 n. 83.

43. Haas, *Alexandria in Late Antiquity*, 42.

44. Haas, *Alexandria in Late Antiquity*, 42, see also n. 75.

45. Haas, personal communication.

46. J. Keenan, " 'Die Binnenwanderung' in Byzantine Egypt," *GRBS* 51 (2011): 57–82; Galvão-Sobrinho, *Doctrine and Power*, 57.

47. Haas, "John Moschus," 52. This view is confirmed by *P. Lond.* 3.1164f28 and the excavations undertaken at Kom el-Dikka (M. Rodziewicz, *Les habitations romaines tardives d'Alexandrie à la lumière des fouilles polonaises à Kom el-Dikka, Alexandrie III* [Warsaw, 1984], 330). See, too, the Louvre OA3317, an ivory showing the Alexandrian skyline.

48. This is part of the important Kom el-Dikka excavation. For discussion, see Haas, *Alexandria*, 49; McKenzie, *Architecture of Alexandria*, 218.

49. John Moschus, *Prat. Spir.* 207. On this passage see the discussion of Haas, "John Moschus," 52.

50. It had just over 2,000 houses, while the other four quarters all had over 5,000.

51. Underlining this point is the fact that devotees of traditional religion had no name for themselves in the period and did not conceive of themselves as any sort of unified confession (a point proven quite effectively by I. Sandwell, *Religious Identity in Late Antiquity: Greeks, Jews, and Christians in Antioch* [Cambridge, 2007]).

52. This brief discussion owes much to the account of Haas, *Alexandria in Late Antiquity*, 57–59. Sailors: *CTh* 13.5.32, Philostorgius, *HE* 2.2; Shopkeepers: Leontius, *Life of John the Almsgiver*, 16; Gravediggers: Epiphanius, *Haer.* 76.1.6–7.

53. *IG* XIV.198, an honorific inscription erected by the association of Alexandrian *naukleroi*, shows this collective spirit. The public duties of the *collegia* are discussed in *CTh.* 14.27.2. For both, see Haas, *Alexandria in Late Antiquity*, 59.

54. This was apparently particularly true of longshoremen (Philostorgius, 2.2a). For discussion, see C Galvão-Sobrinho, *Doctrine and Power*, 54–59.

55. For the cultural ties that bound members of the late Roman aristocracy, see Watts, *City and School*, 1–23; P. Brown, *Power and Persuasion in Late Antiquity* (Madison, WI, 1992), 35–36.

56. P. Garnsey, "Roman Patronage," in *From the Tetrarchs to the Theodosians*, ed. S. McGill, C. Sogno, and E. Watts (Cambridge, 2010), 33–54.

57. Eunapius, for example, found it admirable but rather remarkable that the philosopher Aedesius was able to talk comfortably with vegetable sellers, weavers, and carpenters (*VS* 482).

Chapter 2

1. For the date of her birth, see Dzielska, *Hypatia of Alexandria*, 68; R. Penella, *Greek Philosophers and Sophists* (Leeds, 1990), 126–28; R. Penella, "When Was Hypatia Born?," *Historia* 33 (1984), 126–28. In this, they are following John Malalas (14.12), who says that Hypatia was an older woman at the time of her death in 415.

2. On Himerius, see T. D. Barnes, "Himerius and the Fourth Century," *Classical Philology* 82 (1987), 22. On Themistius's marriage, see Themistius, *Or.* 21.244b, as well as the discussion in E. Watts, *The Final Pagan Generation* (Berkeley, 2015), 75.

3. This is perhaps best described in Himerius, *Or.* 8.

4. The Alexandrian woman Aedesia was a relative of the philosopher Syrianus and the wife of the Platonist Hermeias. When Hermeias died prematurely, we are told that she chose the teachers of her sons Ammonius and Heliodorus (Damascius, *Isid.* 56, 57B). For discussion, see Watts, *City and School*, 207–9.

5. The most thorough discussion of education of all types in the Roman world is that of R. Cribiore, *Gymnastics of the Mind: Greek Education in Hellenistic and Roman Egypt* (Princeton, 2001).

6. For these students, see Cribiore, *Gymnastics of the Mind*, 75.

7. K. Bradley, "Wet-Nursing at Rome: A Study in Social Relations," in *The Family in Ancient Rome: New Perspectives*, ed. B. Rawson (London, 1986), 201–29; S. Crespo Ortiz de Zarate, *Nutrices en el Imperio Romano*, 2 vols. (Valladolid, 2005–2006). For their role in speech training, see Quintilian, *Inst.* 1.1.4–5. For the use of stories, see Strabo, *Geog.* 1.2.8; Tacitus, *Dial. Or.* 29.

8. On grammatical training, see R. A. Kaster, *Guardians of Language: The Grammarian and Society in Late Antiquity* (Berkeley, 1988), 12–14.

9. The shift from a tonal accent to a stress accent is placed in roughly the second century CE. The difficulties that students had with this shift in accentuation are clear from the way student exercises handled the problem. On it, see R. Cribiore, *Writing, Teachers, and Students in Graeco-Roman Egypt* (Atlanta, 1996), numbers 292 and 340.

10. Kaster, *Guardians of Language*, 12–14.

11. For an especially thorough discussion of the *progymnasmata*, see Cribiore, *Gymnastics of the Mind*, 221–30.

12. One student, Euphemius, enrolled under Libanius at age eleven (Libanius, *Ep.* 634=Cribiore 16; for the age of eleven, see R. Cribiore, *The School of Libanius in Late Antique Antioch* [Princeton, 2007], 240). Eunapius joined a school of rhetoric at age sixteen (*VS* 485), perhaps a bit later than usual. Libanius made this jump at age fourteen.

13. Cribiore, *School of Libanius*, 31, discusses part-time study split between the two schools. Eusebius and Thalassius, assistant teachers in the sophist Libanius's school,

seem to have taught the *progymnasmata* to entering students. For a description of their role, see *Epp.* 905–9 and 922–26 as well as *Oration* 31. For discussion, see A. Norman, *Libanius: Autobiography and Selected Letters*, Vol. 2 (Cambridge, MA, 1990), 454–61; Cribiore, *School of Libanius*, 33–37.

14. For this limit, see *CTh* 14.9.1.

15. This was the basic pattern. For the probable variations of approach from school to school, see R. Lamberton, "The Schools of Platonic Philosophy of the Roman Empire: The Evidence of the Biographies," in *Education in Greek and Roman Antiquity*, ed. Y. L. Too (Leiden, 2001), 442–45, 455.

16. The various prolegomena to philosophy helped students to understand the architecture of the philosophical curriculum and how the individual texts within it fit together. For these discussions, see, J. Mansfeld, *Prolegomena: Questions to Be Settled before the Study of an Author or Text* (Leiden, 1994), and, less directly, J. Mansfeld, *Prolegomena mathematica: From Apollonius of Perga to late Neoplatonism* (Leiden, 1998).

17. E. Watts, "Doctrine, Anecdote, and Action: Reconsidering the Social History of the Last Platonists (c. 430–c. 550 CE)," *Classical Philology* 106 (2011), 226–44.

18. P. Heather, "New Men for New Constantines?" in *New Constantines: The Rhythm of Imperial Renewal in Byzantium, 4th–13th Centuries*, ed. P. Magdalino (Aldershot, 1994), 11–34.

19. *CTh* 14.9.1.

20. This is shown by a law of 425 (*CTh* 14.9.3) that required there to be five sophists and ten grammarians for Greek, three orators and ten grammarians of Latin, two law professors, and only one philosopher employed at public expense in Constantinople. A similar emphasis upon Greek and Latin grammar and rhetoric is found in the emperor Gratian's law about teaching in Trier (*CTh* 13.3.11).

21. For an example of a student taking a "gap year" to study philosophy before going to law school, see Zacharias Scholasticus, *Vit. Sev.* 46–47.

22. For a sense of the costs associated with this sort of endeavor, see Cribiore, *School of Libanius*, 185–90.

23. Kaster, *Guardians of Language*, 26–27; P. Petit, *Les Étudiants de Libanius* (Paris 1957), 62–65. Note, however, the cautions of Cribiore, *School of Libanius*, 177.

24. For issues associated with contested wills, see Watts, *Final Pagan Generation*, 99–101; Libanius, *Epp.* 115, 192.

25. Libanius, *Ep.* 379 describes the case of a student who left his care before completing his course in order to get married.

26. *PLRE* I.675–6 (Fabia Anconia Paulina 4). The poem survives as *CIL* VI.1779=Dessau 1259 and is inscribed on a four-sided stele. It seems to have circulated publicly in the 380s because Jerome (*Ep.* 23.2) engages with its language. For this, see M. Kahlos, *Vettius Agorius Praetextatus: A Senatorial Life in Between* (Rome, 2002), 160–62.

27. On Eudocia's poetry, see B. Stowers, "Eudocia: The Making of a Homeric Christian," PhD diss., University of Cincinnati, 2008; and, on her epic poems in particular, A. Cameron, "The Empress and the Poet," in *Wandering Poets and Other Essays*, 37–80, at 73–78.

28. Cribiore, *Gymnastics of the Mind*, 84.

29. Cribiore, *Gymnastics of the Mind*, 75, 98. For a woman conversant with literary culture, see *P. Brem.* 59, which contains a joke that echoes a passage of Lucian.

30. These are the Egyptian grammarian Hermione and the North African Volusia Tertullina. For discussion, see Cribiore, *Gymnastics of the Mind*, 79; D. Montserrat, "Heron 'Bearer of *philosophia*' and Hermione *grammatike*," *JEA* 83 (1997), 223–26; S. Agusta-Boularot and M. Bousbaa, "Une inscription inedité de Cherchell (Algérie): *Volusia Tertullina grammat(ica)*," *L'Africa Romana* 11 (1994), 164–73.

31. B. Shaw, "'With Whom I Lived:' Measuring Roman Marriage," *Ancient Society* 32 (2002), 195–242; Laes, *Children in the Roman Empire*, 44–47.

32. For men resuming the study of rhetoric later in life, see Libanius's correspondent Firminus (*PLRE* I Firminus 3) and, in particular, Libanius, *Ep.* 1048.

33. This is discussed further in Chapter 7.

34. Philostorgius, *HE* 8.9 says that she was comprehensively trained in τὰ μαθήματα, a term that, in Philostorgius's work, can mean anything from mathematics to philosophy to systematic theology (e.g., *HE* 7.4b for Greek philosophy; 9.13 for theology; 3.15 ln. 12 for logic; 3.15 ln. 64 for a generalized system of knowledge). Given Philostorgius's subsequent reference to astral observations in the passage, however, a broadly drawn reference to math and all its related applications seems the best way to understand this term. For the expansion of Hypatia's philosophical interests and the marking of Theon as her instructor, see Damascius, *Isid.* fr. 43A.

35. These were commentaries on Hermogenes's περὶ ἰδεῶν and the περὶ στάσεων. For the texts, see H. Rabe, *Syriani in Hermogenem commentaria*, 2 vols. (Leipzig, 1892–1893).

36. For late antique philosophers teaching grammar, see Eunapius, *VS* 502 (Chrysanthius); Zacharias Scholasticus, *Vit. Sev.* 15 (Horapollon); Simplcius, *de Caelo* 119.7 (John Philoponus).

37. For these mutual relationships across different educational levels, see the discussion of Cribiore, *School of Libanius*, 32–34. A more precise parallel may be the collection of pagan teachers offering grammatical, rhetorical, mathematical, and philosophical instruction in Alexandria in the 470s and 480s, a network described in both Zacharias Scholastcius's *Life of Severus* and Damascius's *Life of Isidore*. On this group and their relationships with one another, see Watts, *City and School*, 217–18; P. Athanassiadi, *Damascius: The Philosophical History* (Athens, 1999), 20ff.

38. This is a point made in a personal conversation by Raffaella Cribiore, to whom I am grateful for the suggestion.

39. We have no sense, for example, that any of the other female philosophers of the period had extensive formal rhetorical training, though it would not be at all surprising if they did.

40. For the connection between mathematics and philosophy, see the more detailed discussion below.

41. *Proc.* 9; D. O'Meara, *Pythagoras Revived: Mathematics and Philosophy in Late Antiquity* (Oxford, 1989), 97–99; and J. Pépin, *Théologie cosmique et théologie chrétienne* (Paris, 1964), 380–86.

42. J. Duffy, "Byzantine Medicine in the Sixth and Seventh Centuries: Aspects of Teaching and Practice," *DOP* 38 (1984), 21–27, at 21–22.

43. It is likely that the *Collectio* is made up of a group of writings by Pappus. Some of these were published (or publishable), and others seem to be little more than drafts or extended notes. For discussion of the *Collectio*, see Mansfeld, *Prolegomena mathematica*, 6–21; A. Jones, *Pappus of Alexandria: Book 7 of the Collection*, Vol. 1 (New York, 1986), 3–9. Mansfeld (*Prolegomena mathematica*, 7) argues against the idea of random drafts, on the basis of the headings of some of the individual books within it. For

the definitive modern study of Pappus, see S. Cuomo, *Pappus of Alexandria and the Mathematics of Late Antiquity* (Cambridge, 2000).

44. On the idea of the *Collectio* as a compendium that treats a range of subjects, see Mansfeld, *Prolegomena mathematica*, 7.

45. For discussion, see Jones, *Pappus*, 3–4.

46. This text of Apollonius has been lost and its identity is unclear. For a possible identification, see J. L. Heiberg, *Apollonii Pergaei quae Graece exstant cum commentariis antiquis*, Vol. 2 (Leipzig, 1893), 124, though Jones (*Pappus*, 4) dismisses this.

47. For the notion of a canon here, see Mansfeld, *Prolegomena mathematica*, 11–14.

48. For the connection between the "Little Astronomy" of Pappus and the "Big Astronomy" of Ptolemy, see Mansfeld, *Prolegomena mathematica*, 16–88. For Ptolemy's *Almagest* as "Big Astronomy" (τὸν Μέγαν ἀστρονόμον ἤτοι Σύνταξιν), see *Suda* Π 3033.

49. Cassiodorus, *Inst.* 2.7.2, 155–23, and the comments of Mansfeld, *Prolegomena mathematica*, 17–18.

50. This Plutarch is, of course, distinct from the second-century biographer, Plutarch of Chaeronea.

51. *Proc.* 12.

52. That this work came primarily from the mind of Syrianus was first suggested by K. Praechter, "Die griechischen Aristoteleskommentatoren," *BZ* 18 (1909), 516–38, at 524.

53. L. G. Westerink, "Deux commentaires sur Nicomaque: Asclépius et Jean Philopon," *REG* 77 (1964), 526–35, at 530; L. Tarán, *Asclepius of Tralles, Commentary to Nicomachus' Introduction to Arithmetic* (Philadelphia, 1969), 10–13.

54. This dating is based upon R. Sorabji, "John Philoponus," in *Philoponus and the Rejection of Aristotelian Science*, ed. R. Sorabji (London, 1987), 1–40. The only commentary from this period that has a date is the *Physics* commentary, which John states was finished on May 10, 517 (*in Phys.* 703.16).

55. *Suda* Υ 166. For discussion see Cameron, "Hypatia," 190–91.

56. Cameron, "Hypatia," 191.

57. Cameron, "Hypatia," 191.

58. This was first noticed by A. Rome, "Le troisième livre sur l'Almagest par Théon et Hypatie," *Annales de la Société Scientifique de Bruxelles* 46 (1926), 1–14. For additional discussion, see M. Deakin, *Hypatia of Alexandria: Mathematician and Martyr* (Amherst, NY, 2007), 91–94.

59. For discussion of the difficulty of a project like this, see Cameron, "Hypatia," 191–93.

60. T. L. Heath, *Euclid: The Thirteen Books of the Elements* (Cambridge, 1909), 54–58.

61. For a discussion of "Ptolemism" and Hypatia's possible connection to it, see A. Bernard, "Theon of Alexandria and Hypatia," in *The Cambridge History of Philosophy in Late Antiquity*, Vol. 1, ed. L. Gerson (Cambridge, 2010), 417–36.

62. O'Meara, *Pythagoras Revived*, 10–23. On Nicomachus and Numenius, see also J. Dillon, *The Middle Platonists, 80 B.C. to A. D. 220*, 2nd ed. (Ithaca, NY: 1996), 352–61 (Nicomachus) and 361–80 (Numenius).

63. On this dissension, see E. Watts, "Creating the Academy: Historical Discourse and the Shape of Community in the Old Academy," *JHS* 127 (2007): 106–22; J. Dillon, *The Heirs of Plato: A Study of the Old Academy* (Oxford, 2003), 205ff.

64. For the relationship between their ideas, see O'Meara, *Pythagoras Revived*, 16.

65. O'Meara, *Pythagoras Revived*, 19–22. This idea is laid out in *Int. Ar.* 1.2.1; 2.18.14. For discussion, see too Dillon, *Middle Platonists*, 353–54.

66. *Plot.* 3.

67. Watts, *City and School*, 155–61.

68. Dillon, *Middle Platonists*, 381–82. The Numenius connection is suggested by the charge made against Plotinus that his ideas were reheated versions of Numenius (*Plot.* 18).

69. For discussion of this, see Mansfeld, *Prolegomena mathematica*, 99–119; Bernard, "Theon and Hypatia," 430–31.

70. Pappus, *Collectio* 350 (Hultsch). See Cuomo, *Pappus of Alexandria*, 76–80; Mansfeld, *Prolegomena mathematica*, 104; and Bernard, "Theon and Hypatia," 430.

71. Pappus, *Collectio* 350.20ff. Pappus claims that these philosophers affirm that the First God is the Demiurge, a view that Plotinus and all Neoplatonists of his intellectual line do not hold. For discussion, see Cuomo, *Pappus of Alexandria*, 81.

72. For this identification, see Mansfeld, *Prolegomena mathematica*, 105.

73. Mansfeld, *Prolegomena mathematica*, 117.

74. Cuomo, *Pappus of Alexandria*, 83–84; Mansfeld, *Prolegomena mathematica*, 104. Bernard ("Theon and Hypatia," 431), however, suggests that these allusions to the *Timaeus* "hardly represent much more than commonplaces." Given the larger context, Cuomo's and Mansfeld's assessments of Pappus's Platonic knowledge seem more plausible.

75. Cuomo, *Pappus of Alexandria*, 86.

76. *Suda* Π 265.

77. *Suda* Π 265 explicitly describes Pappus and Theon as contemporary philosophers.

78. Indeed, although later sources (and most modern scholars) tend to ignore his philosophical background, earlier authors like Socrates Scholasticus (*HE* 7.12) and the *Suda* (Θ 205, Π 265) describe him as a philosopher, a description echoed by Malalas as well.

79. Or possibly the Dog Star, if the text is amended slightly. *Suda* Θ 205.

80. Bernard, "Theon and Hypatia," 428, on the basis of Theon's discussion of some key passages of Ptolemy's *Almagest*.

81. This seems especially likely because Theon seems more comfortable engaging the philosophy of Aristotle than that of Plato (Bernard, "Theon and Hypatia," 427).

82. For a discussion of this passage, see H. Harich-Schwarzbauer, *Hypatia: Die spätantiken Quellen; Eingeleitet, kommentiert, und interpretiert* (Bern, 2011), 252–4.

Chapter 3

1. O. Neugebauer (*A History of Mathematical Astronomy* [Philadelphia, 1975], 873) rightly contends that Theon's book *On the Small Astrolabe* appeared around 400 CE. For an alternative view, see Alan Cameron and J. Long, *Barbarians and Politics at the Court of Arcadius* (Berkeley, 1993), 54–55.

2. The letters of Hypatia's student Synesius show that Theon remained a presence at the school as late as the mid-390s, but Synesius apparently neither took any classes from him nor thought that such a thing was possible. It was long argued that Synesius did not even know Theon, but this has been called into question by D. Roques ("La

Famille d'Hypatie," *REG* 108 [1995], 128–49), who equates Theon with the Theoteknos mentioned in Synesius, *Ep.* 16.

3. Watts, *City and School*, 68, on the basis of Eunapius, *VS* 474. Prohaeresius's arrangement parallels one that Philostratus describes at *VS* 606.

4. *Proc.* 12. For discussion, see Watts, *City and School*, 96–98.

5. For Libanius's last years, see Watts, *Final Pagan Generation*, 192–209.

6. While an illness is certainly a possibility, there is no evidence that Theon was sick. Additionally, Libanius, whose teaching career ended only a few years after Theon apparently ceded control of his school to Hypatia, maintained his public position even when his health was failing. This suggests that ill health did not necessarily force a professor into retirement in the late fourth century.

7. For financial obligations of women property holders, see J. Evans Grubbs, *Women and the Law in the Roman Empire* (London, 2002), 74–80. Note as well the provisions of *CJ* 10.42.9, a law of Diocletian and Maximian that would have been in force during Hypatia's life.

8. As a Museum member, Theon likely already had an exemption from curial service, but he could lose this exemption if he stepped down before age sixty. Constantine set the curial retirement age at sixty in a law of 324 (*POxy* 889 and *PSI* 685). For discussion, see T. Parkin, *Old Age in the Roman World* (Baltimore, 2003), 134–53.

9. The fifth-century scale of physical, ethical, social, purifying, theoretical, and theurgic virtues contrasted with the traditional idea of Plato (developed in *Republic* IV.427E ff.) that the four classifiable virtues of *sophia*, *andreia*, *sophronsunē*, and *dikaiosunē* exist in different parts of the soul. For discussion, see H. Blumenthal, "Marinus' *Life of Proclus*: Neoplatonist Biography," *Byzantion* 54 (1984), 471–93, at 476–77. Synesius, *Ep.* 140 outlines a hierarchy of virtues modeled on Porphyry, *Sententiae* 32 and offers a possible model for the system that Hypatia understood.

10. *Proc.* 2.

11. Synesius describes a scale of virtues that separates those concerned with the tangible world and those concerned with higher levels of reality in *Ep.* 140. For discussion, see J. Bregman, *Synesius of Cyrene, Philosopher Bishop* (Berkeley, 1982), 26–28.

12. *Proc.* 9.

13. *Suda* Θ 205.

14. Synesius, *Ep.* 129. This was addressed to Pylamenes and requests texts by Alexander and the poet Nicostraus. For Alexander's use in the Platonic tradition, see, for example, Simplicius, *in Phys.* 707, 33; 1170, 13; 1176, 32; John Philoponus, *in An. Pr.* 126.21; Olympiodorus, *in Meteor.* 263, 21.

15. Synesius, *Ep.* 143. Note as well the discussion of Dzielska, *Hypatia*, 55.

16. Synesius, *Ep.* 139 references the *Life of Plotinus* (*Plot.* 2). The connection between the *Life of Plotinus* and Porphyry's edition of Plotinus's written works is made explicit at *Plot.*, 24–26. For discussion of this purpose, see M. Edwards, *Neoplatonic Saints: The Lives of Plotinus and Proclus by their Students* (Liverpool, 2000), xxxiv-xxxvi.

17. A process described by Aaron Johnson (*Religion and Identity in Porphyry of Tyre: The Limits of Hellenism in Late Antiquity* [Cambridge, 2013], 60) as translating the concept from "an ontological frame of meaning into a theological one."

18. Johnson, *Religion and Identity*, 63.

19. This is clear from the *Against Nemertius*, in which entities responsible for creating and ordering the cosmos, serving as savior of all, and acting providentially are all named simply God. See, e.g., *C. Nemert.* frs. 276, 279–82. See, too, Johnson, *Religion and Identity*, 63–64.

20. This was later criticized by Damascius in *On First Principles*, 1.86.

21. For Porphyry's notions of salvation and their distinction from the teachings of Iamblichus see now M. B. Simmons, *Universal Salvation in Late Antiquity: Porphyry of Tyre and the Pagan-Christian Debate*, (Oxford, 2015), 134–58 and Johnson, *Religion and Identity*, 123.

22. Plotinus, *Enneads* 1.8.14 (soul becoming bound to matter); 4.8.5–6 (contemplation as true existence).

23. The best description is that of Iamblichus, *De Myst.* 2.11.98, 3.7.114–18.117, 25.158–59. Among the many contemporary scholars who have written about theurgy are P. Athanassiadi, "The Chaldean Oracles: Theology and Theurgy," in *Pagan Monotheism in Late Antiquity*, ed. P. Athanassiadi and M. Frede (Oxford, 1999), 149–84; and G. Shaw, "Theurgy: Rituals of Unification in the Neoplatonism of Iamblichus," *Traditio* 41 (1985), 1–28.

24. For this idea, see Athanassiadi, "The Chaldean Oracles," 165f.

25. The most notable exponent of this position was Proclus. For his views and the contrasting perspective of Damascius, see Athanassiadi, "The Chaldean Oracles," 175. For other views of how the Chaldean texts could be interpreted, see I. Tanaseanu-Döbler, "Synesios und die Theurgie," in *Synesios von Kyrene: Politik-Literatur-Philosophie*, ed. H. Seng and L. M. Hoffmann (Turnhout, 2012), 201–30.

26. See Damascius, *Isid.* Ath. 85A; and Athanassiadi, "The Chaldean Oracles," 181.

27. Eunapius (*VS* 475) actually attributes the emperor Julian's conversion to Iamblichan Platonism to stories of miracles performed by a disciple of one of Iamblichus's students.

28. Socrates, *HE* 7.15.

29. The idea of a "Golden Chain" linking Plato to Plotinus, Porphyry, Iamblichus, and the later Athenian Platonists is discussed widely in late antiquity (e.g., Damascius, *Isid.* 73A, 98E; the seventh book of Hierocles of Alexandria's *On Providence*, summarized at Photius, *Bib.* 214.171a5). See, too, G. Fowden, "The Pagan Holy Man in Late Antique Society," *JHS* 102 (1982): 33–59, at 34.

30. For the situation in Athens in the later fifth and early sixth centuries, see Watts, *City and School*, 100–142.

31. Themistius (*Or.*20.234–36) describes the teaching of his father as part of an ecumenical system that drew upon Plato, Socrates, and Epicurus, but one in which Aristotle was always central. This may give some sense of Themistius's own priorities.

32. For Ptolemy and his system, see Bernard, "Theon and Hypatia," 423–24. As my analysis of Socrates, Synesius, and Damascius suggests, I do not agree with Bernard's assertion that Ptolemy's system squares with "a respectable part of the testimonies" about Hypatia's teaching. Contemporary sources frame her interests as much more Platonic than Ptolemist. Following Damascius in particular, I am much more inclined to see her teaching as a break with, rather than a continuation of, that of Theon and Pappus.

33. Zacharias Scholasticus, *Life of Isaiah*, 8.

34. Alan Cameron, "Iamblichus at Athens," *Athenaeum* 45 (1967): 143–53. The notion, advocated by H. D. Saffrey and L. G. Westerink (*Théologie Platonicienne* [Paris, 1968], xlii–xliii), that Priscus, a disciple of Iamblichus, was at least partially responsible for the introduction of Iamblichan teachings into Athens seems to conflate Eunapius's account of Priscus' life in Greece (*VS* 482) with a description of the horrors of Alaric's raid on Athens. Eunapius never specifies that Priscus took up residence in Athens, and, consequently, it is impossible to assume that he did so.

35. The first Iamblichan teacher that one can securely place around Alexandria was the idiosyncratic teacher Antoninus, who gave lessons outside the Serapeum in the suburb of Canopus but refused to teach or practice theurgy (Eunapius, *VS* 471–72). The first teacher to practice theurgy in a way that seems Iamblichan is Olympus, a figure not attested until the early 390s (*Isid.* 42F). They are discussed further in Chapter 4.

36. This is perhaps best evidenced by Porphyry's *Letter to Anebo* and Iamblichus's lengthy response to it, now called *De Mysteriis*. For this interaction, see now H. D. Saffrey and A. Segonds, *Jamblique: Réponse à Porphyre (De Mysteriis); Collection des universités de France, Série grecque, 496* (Paris, 2013), with the teacher-student relationship between Porphyry and Iamblichus explored in detail in Chapter 2. Note, too, the review of J. Dillon in *Bryn Mawr Classical Review* 2013.11.41. It is worth noting that the *Letter to Anebo* is ostensibly addressed to an Egyptian priest and Iamblichus's *De Mysteriis* is written under the Egyptian pseudonym Abammon, but, as Saffrey and Segonds prove in Chapter 3 of their edition of the text, there is really no doubt that the exchange was between Porphyry and Iamblichus. No actual connection to Egypt can be presumed.

37. On this point, see J. M. Rist, "Hypatia," *Phoenix* 19 (1965), 214–25; and E. Évrard, "A quel titre Hypatie enseigna-t-elle la philosophie?," *REG* 90 (1977), 69–74.

38. This is especially true of his attitudes towards theurgy. I. Tanaseanu-Döbler, *Konversion zur Philosophie in der Spätantike: Kaiser Julian und Synesios von Kyrene* (Stuttgart, 2005), 253–74; and S. Vollenweider, "Ein Mittleres zwischen Vater und Sohn: Zur Bedeutung des Neuplatonikers Porphyrios für die Hymnen des Synesios," in *Synesios von Kyrene*, 183–200.

39. On this see, Alan Cameron, *Barbarians and Politics*, 50–51. For the Christian usages of these texts, see M. Tardieu, "La Gnose Valentinienne et les Oracles Chaldaïques," in *The Rediscovery of Gnosticism*, Vol. 1, ed. B. Layton (Leiden, 1980), 194–237. For a detailed discussion of Chaldean elements in Synesius's *Hymns* in particular, see Bregman, *Synesius*, 29–36; 63, 83. For discussion of this Chaldean influence, see Vollenweider, "Ein Mittleres zwischen Vater und Sohn," 191; and Tanaseanu-Döbler, "Synesios und die Theurgie," 201–30—though the few parallels she sees between the dream divination treatise of Synesius and Iamblichus are not, in my view, substantial enough to prove that Synesius had direct knowledge of Iamblichus.

40. The fragments of Porphyry's commentary on the *Chaldean Oracles* show him discussing things like the identity of the First Principle and its place in the intelligible Triad (e.g., *De chal. orac.* Fr. 368, Smith). For his attitudes against theurgy and sacrifice, see the fragments of his treatise *On the Return of the Soul* (*Regr. anim.* Fr. 287, 294, Smith). For discussion, see Johnson, *Religion and Identity*, 266–70.

41. For this reading, see, too, Harich-Schwarzbauer, *Hypatia*, 195.

42. For an assessment of Socrates's knowledge of Platonism, see Harich-Schwarzbauer, *Hypatia*, 173–78.

43. Socrates, *HE* 5.16.

44. For discussion of the students of Hypatia and their possible confessional identifications, see Dzielska, *Hypatia*, 28–39.

45. Alexandria was known to have Novatian, Meletian, Arian, and Nicene Orthodox Christian communities at the time that Hypatia was teaching. For factionalism among Christians in the city, see Haas, *Alexandria in Late Antiquity*, 245–77.

46. For the difficulty in setting boundaries between Christian and non-Christian activities in the later fourth century, see C. Shepardson, *Controlling Contested*

Places: Late Antique Antioch and the Spatial Politics of Religious Controversy (Berkeley, 2014), Chapter 3.

47. Johnson, *Religion and Identity*, 123.

48. Bregman, *Syensius of Cyrene*, 23.

49. There were, of course, potential theological issues with Nicene Christianity if this philosophical approach to the divine was taken to its natural limit. A theology that privileges the One in the way that the Porphyrian system does moves quite close to Arianism. For discussion of this, see Bregman, *Synesius of Cyrene*, 80.

50. This is a common sentiment in Chrysostom's works. See, for example, *Ad Theodorum Lapsum* 1.9, 1.13; *Contra Eutropium* 1.1.

51. *Hymn* 1.52–99. For discussion see Bregman, *Synesius of Cyrene*, 29–39.

52. *Hymn* 1.72–75.

53. *Hymn* 4.6–8.

54. *Hymn* 4.9–11.

55. For discussion of Synesius's ideas and their connection to those of Porphyry, see Bregman, *Synesius of Cyrene*, 81–83. Synesius has followed a generally Porphyrian conception, although here he compresses the procession of the divine mind back into the One. For this view attributed to Porphyry, see Damascius, *Dubitationes et solutions de primis principiis*, Vol. 1.86.9–87.1 (Paris, 1889): Πορφύριον ἐροῦμεν τὴν μίαν τῶν πάντων ἀρχὴν εἶναι τὸν πατέρα τῆς νοητῆς τριάδος.

56. Bregman, *Synesius of Cyrene*, 78–85. The notion of Synesius's supposed conversion is developed extensively by T. Schmitt, *Die Bekehrung des Synesios von Kyrene: Politik und Philosophie, Hof und Provinz als Handlungsräume eines Aristokraten bis zu seiner Wahl zum Metropoliten von Ptolemaïs* (Munich-Leipzig, 2001). Against the idea of Synesius undergoing a religious conversion, however, see the excellent discussion of Tanaseanu-Döbler, *Konversion zur Philosophie*, 155–286.

57. For example, in *Epp.* 137–46, the mini-dossier of letters addressed to Herculian. For discussion, see Chapter 4.

Chapter 4

1. Porphyry (*Plot.* 3.7–15) makes clear that Ammonius Saccas, the teacher of Plotinus, taught in Alexandria but was not embraced by the intellectual establishment of the city. For discussion, see Watts, *City and School*, 155–56.

2. For this idea in the fourth century, see *Expositio totius mundi et gentium*, 52.4–10; Libanius, *Or.* 1.11–12; Synesius, *Epp.* 56 and 136.

3. For this point, see E. Watts, "Athens, Educational Reform and Philosophy," in *Athens in Late Antiquity*, ed. I. Tanaseanu-Döbler and S. Anghel (forthcoming).

4. Libanius, *Or.* 1.19.

5. Olympiodorus of Thebes, Fr. 28; Gregory Nazianzen, *Or.* 43.16.

6. For hazing in Athens, see, for example, Gregory Nazianzen, *Or.* 43.17.

7. Synesius, *Ep.* 56.7–10.

8. Synesius, *Ep.* 56.11–14.

9. On the death of Longinus, see *Historia Augusta, Aurelian* 27, 30; Zosimus, 1.56. Eunapius (*VS* 482) says that the philosopher Priscus taught in Greece in the later fourth century, and Libanius (*Ep.* 1076) suggests that Priscus met with a colleague of his in

Athens in 393. There is no evidence indicating that Priscus actually set up a school in Athens, however. On this, see Alan Cameron, "Iamblichus at Athens," 143–53.

10. Zosimus, 4.18.

11. Proclus, *In Rep.* II.324.12–325.10. For the Iamblichan connection to such practices, see Iamblichus, *On the Pythagorean Life*, 14.

12. Their relationship is ambiguously described by ancient sources. Marinus, *Proc.* 12 and 28, as well as Proclus, *In Rep.* II.64.6, seems to suggest Nestorius was Plutarch's grandfather. On the basis of Damascius (*Isid.* 64, a fragment not included in the earlier edition of Zintzen), P. Athanassiadi (*Philosophical History*, 173 n. 149) has suggested that Plutarch was Nestorius's son.

13. For a collection of the sources related to his career, see D. Taormina, *Plutarcho di Atene* (Rome, 1989), 107–44.

14. For his public prominence, see Watts, *City and School*, 92–96.

15. Watts, *City and School*, 84–87.

16. *IG* II/III² 3818. For the attribution of this inscription to Plutarch the scholarch, see Watts, *City and School*, 93 n. 72.

17. *Proc.* 10.

18. *Ep.* 136.7–8.

19. This is a clear reference to the recent Gothic sack of the city. For the Gothic sack by Alaric, see Eunapius, *VS* 476; Zosimus 5.5–6; A. Frantz, *The Athenian Agora XXIV: Late Antiquity 267–700* (Princeton, 1988), 49–56; A. Robertson Brown, "Banditry or Catastrophe? History, Archaeology, and Barbarian Raids on Roman Greece," in *Romans, Barbarians, and the Transformation of the Roman World*, ed. R. Mathisen and D. Shanzer (Aldershot, 2011), 79–96, at 90–92.

20. *Ep.* 136.16–22.

21. For Plutarch and Syrianus as the "pair of Plutarchans," see Watts, *City and School*, 138; G. Fowden, "The Athenian Agora and the Progress of Christianity," *JRA* 3 (1990), 494–500, at 500. Alan Cameron ("Hypatia," 189–90) has proposed a different identification, though his argument is based on the same information discussed in these earlier treatments.

22. On this term's ambiguity at the turn of the fifth century CE, see Watts, *City and School*, 94–95.

23. For Antoninus, see Eunapius, *VS* 470–72; Watts, *City and School*, 188–90. For Sosipatra, see Chapter 7.

24. Eunapius, *VS* 472. For this sort of interaction at the shrine, see D. Frankfurter, "The Consequences of Hellenism in Late Antique Egypt: Religious Worlds and Actors," *Archiv für Religionsgeschichte* 2 (2000), 162–94.

25. *VS* 471.

26. Damascius, *Isid.* 42F. Damascius's hearty endorsement of Olympus's teaching contrasts with his description of Hypatia as a mere "mathematician" in a way that suggests that Olympus, like Damascius, incorporated Iamblichan elements in his instruction.

27. Watts, *City and School*, 190, on the basis of Damascius, *Isid.* 42H.

28. Upon taking full control of the empire in 361, the pagan emperor Julian reversed all of the anti-pagan policies of his cousin Constantius II. Anti-pagan restrictions like those implemented by Constantius II did not return until the 380s. For discussion of this period and the developments in it, see Watts, *Final Pagan Generation*, 136–37, 181–88.

29. *CTh* 16.10.8.

30. *CTh* 16.10.9 is the Eastern law. The Western actions of the emperor Gratian can be reconstructed from *CTh* 16.10.20.1 and Symmachus's *Third Relatio*. For discussion, see Alan Cameron, *The Last Pagans of Rome* (Oxford, 2012), 39–51.

31. On Cynegius's campaigns, see Brown, *Power and Persuasion*, 107; J. F. Matthews, *Western Aristocracies and Imperial Court, A.D. 364–425* (Oxford, 1975), 140–42; and G. Fowden, "Bishops and Temples in the Eastern Roman Empire, AD 320–435," *JTS* 29 (1979), 53–78.

32. Libanius, *Or.* 1.255 (Antioch), *Or.* 30.44 (Edessa); Brown, *Power and Persuasion*, 108–9; N. McLynn, *Ambrose of Milan: Church and Court in a Christian Capital* (Berkeley, 1994), 298–309; M. Gaddis, *There Is No Crime for Those Who Have Christ* (Berkeley, 2005), 194–99 (Callinicum).

33. For the massive footprint of traditional religion in the Roman world in 300, see Watts, *Final Pagan Generation*, 18–35.

34. For overviews of the career of Theophilus, see Haas, *Alexandria in Late Antiquity*, 159–68; N. Russell, *Theophilus of Alexandria* (London, 2007), 3–45; and S. Davis, *The Early Coptic Papacy: The Egyptian Church and its Leadership in Late Antiquity* (Cairo, 2004), 63–70.

35. For the exiles of Athanasius and their later commemoration, see Watts, *Riot in Alexandria*, 163–89.

36. On the specific questions of Theophilus's involvement in the destruction of Alexandrian pagan temples, see the important discussion of J. Hahn, *Gewalt und religiöser Konflikt: Studien zu den Auseinandersetzungen zwischen Christen, Heiden, und Juden im Osten des Römischen Reiches (von Konstantin bis Theodosius II.)* (Berlin, 2004), 81–105.

37. Rufinus, *HE* 11.22 calls their reaction to events in 392 "not just their usual noisy protests."

38. These are *CTh* 16.10.10–11, dated to February and June of 391.

39. For the dating of the event to 392, see Hahn, *Gewalt und religiöser Konflikt*, 82–84; Hahn, "The Conversion of the Cult Statues: The Destruction of the Serapeum 392 AD and the Transformation of Alexandria into the 'Christ Loving' City," in *From Temple to Church: Destruction and Renewal of Local Cultic Topography in Late Antiquity*, ed. J. Hahn, S. Emmel, and U. Gotter (Leiden, 2008), 335–63, at 340.

40. Rufinus, *HE* 11.22. Sozomen suggests that this may have been a ruined temple of Dionysius (*HE* 7.15). Socrates Scholasticus (*HE* 5.16) suggests it may have been a Mithraeum.

41. Socrates, *HE* 5.16. For Theophilus as a provocateur here, see Hahn, *Gewalt und religiöser Konflikt*, 91–92.

42. Rufinus, *HE* 11.22 (trans. Amidon).

43. For the intellectual leadership of this group, see Watts, *City and School*, 190–91; and Hahn, *Gewalt und religiöser Konflikt*, 92–93.

44. Rufinus, *HE* 11.22; Socrates, *HE* 5.16. The Christian rhetorician Gessius seems to have been one of these prisoners, and after the rioters vacated the temple, he was found brutally murdered on its grounds (Palladas, *Anth Pal.* 7.686,1–6, a text that argues rather strongly against the recent idea of redating the corpus of Palladas to the 320s; Haas, *Alexandria*, 163). Hahn (*Gewalt und religiöser Konflikt*, 86–87) rightly draws attention to the fact that Rufinus's description of Christian captives being forced to sacrifice evokes earlier martyrdom narratives, and is therefore suspect.

45. Damascius, *Isid.* 42B.

46. Damascius, *Isid.* 42F.

47. Rufinus, *HE* 11.22 (trans. Amidon). J. Hahn (*Gewalt und religiöser Konflikt,* 87–88) thinks it improbable that these were the real terms under which the hill was evacuated.

48. Hahn, *Gewalt und religiöser Konflikt,* 99.

49. Damascius, *Isid.* 42G-H.

50. Socrates, *HE* 5.16.

51. Hahn (*Gewalt und religiöser Konflikt,*100) suggests this on the basis in part of *Anth. Gr.* 9.175. Cf. Alan Cameron, "Palladas and Christian Polemic," *JRS* 55 (1965): 17–30, esp. 27. If accepted, the recent arguments of K. Wilkinson ("Palladas and the Age of Constantine," *JRS* 99 [2009], 26–60) dating Palladas to the early fourth century would negate this point. See, however, Alan Cameron's important article ("Palladas: New Poems, New Date?," in *Wandering Poets and Other Essays,* 91–112) for an argument against abandoning the traditional date of Palladas.

52. This is *CTh* 16.10.12, a law that was too comprehensive to be truly enforceable. It likely was designed to provide a legal pretext to act against individual pagans in specific circumstances rather than to serve as a blanket prohibition that would be enforced at all times against all pagans.

53. John of Nikiu, 78.46 (trans. Charles); cf. Rufinus, *HE* 11.27–28; *Storia della Chiesa,* II.14.10–16.2; Sozomen, *HE* 7.15. On the martyrium and church, note the important discussion of the archaeological evidence by McKenzie, Gibson, and Reyes, "Reconstructing the Serapeum," 107–10; and the treatment of McKenzie, *Architecture of Alexandria,* 246.

54. Eunapius describes Theophilus "importing so-called monks into the sacred places" (*VS* 472), and then later mentions that he did this too at Canopus. This seems to suggest that Theophilus created two monasteries, one at the Alexandrian Serapeum complex and the other in Canopus.

55. Tychaion: Palladas, *Anth. Pal.* 9.180–83 (again noting the objections raised by Cameron to the redating of Palladas's poems to the 320s); Haas, *Alexandria,* 167; Hahn, *Gewalt und religiöser Konflikt,* 95. On the Tychaion more generally, see the important studies of C. Gibson, "Alexander in the Tychaion: Ps.-Libanius on the Statues," *GRBS* 47 (2007): 431–54; and "The Alexandrian Tychaion and the date of Ps.-Nicolaus *Progymnasmata,*" *CQ* 59 (2009), 608–23. Images: Rufinus, *HE* 11.29.

56. Although Rufinus (*HE* 11.27) and Eunapius (*VS* 472) both say that the temple and its associated buildings were completely leveled, Evagrius Scholasticus (*HE* 2.5) and the *Life of Peter the Iberian* (72) suggest that some parts of the old Serapeum site could still be used in the mid-fifth century.

57. Vinzent, "'Oxbridge' in der ausgehenden Spätantike," 71–72; Bregman, *Synesius,* 60. For Theophilus officiating at Synesius's wedding, see Synesius, *Ep.* 105.69–70.

Chapter 5

1. Damascius, *Isid.* 43A. For discussion of this passage, see Harich-Schwartzbauer, *Hypatia,* 254–59. The notion that the *tribon* had some connection to Cynics seems unlikely, given the use of this garment in mainstream settings like fourth-century Athenian schools of rhetoric.

2. This was Horapollon (PLRE 2: Fl. Horapollon 2). His positions are defined in *P. Cairo* 3.67295, published in Maspero, "Horapollon et la fin du paganisme égyptien," 163–95, at 163 ln. 1; 166 ln. 15.

3. For the remains of this complex at Kom el-Dikka, see G. Majcherek, "The Late Roman Auditoria: An Archeological Overview," in *Alexandria Auditoria of Kôm el-Dikka and Late Antique Education*, ed. T. Derda, T. Markiewicz, and E. Wipszycka (Warsaw, 2007), 11–50.

4. The chronology of the Kom el-Dikka site is difficult to reconstruct with any precision. For discussion, see Majcherek, "The Late Roman Auditoria," 29–38.

5. This has been posited by Vinzent, "Oxbridge in der ausgehenden Spätantike," 63–69.

6. For example, Damascius, *Isid.* 56. The term Τὴν δημοσίαν σίτησιν cannot mean anything other than a person who collects a public salary (e.g., *CJ* 1.11.10). On this, too, see Watts, *City and School*, 194–95. Against the idea of her being a public teacher, see Dzielska, *Hypatia*, 56–58.

7. For discussions of locations in which teaching took place see Cribiore, *Gymnastics of the Mind*, 21–34; and Cribiore, "Spaces for Teaching in Late Antiquity," in *Alexandria Auditoria of Kôm el-Dikka and Late Antique Education*, ed. T. Derda, T. Markiewicz, and E. Wipszycka (Warsaw, 2007), 143–50, at 144–47.

8. For this complex, see Chapter 1, above.

9. If Epicrates and Aelian are to be believed, discussions held in the Academy grove were open to all (Epicrates, fr. 11), while Plato led other seminars in his home, to which he welcomed only the most devoted of his followers (Aelian, *VH* 3.19). For Plotinus allowing strangers to attend his lectures, see Porphyry, *Plot.* 1. For Athenian teachers restricting access to their classes and teaching in their own homes, see Eunapius, *VS* 483.

10. Cribiore, *School of Libanius*, 112–14.

11. Marinus, *Proc.* 11.

12. Epicrates, fr. 11. For discussion, see Watts, "Creating the Academy," 108–9.

13. For this idea, see M. Baltes, "Plato's School, The Academy," *Hermathena* 155 (1993), 5–26, at 8, 18.

14. On the *Theages*, see R. Tarrant, "Socratic Synousia: A Post-Platonic Myth?," *Journal of the History of Philosophy* 43 (2005), 131–55.

15. Philostratus, *VS* 526–27. For discussion, see Watts, *City and School*, 29–30.

16. For example, Damascius, *Isid.* 72E, 108; Marinus, *Proc.* 8–9. For discussion, see Watts, *Riot in Alexandria*, 60–62.

17. This formulation comes for the *Life of Proclus* 38, but it parallels a structure also found in the *Life of Plotinus* 7.1–3.

18. *Plot.* 7.

19. This notion goes back at least as far as some early Pythagorean traditions, such as the spurious letter of Lysis, referenced by Porphyry, *Vit. Pyth.* 55 (p. 62, Des Places), Iamblichus, *Vit. Pyth.* 17.75–78; Synesius, *Ep.* 143.

20. Porphyry, *Plot.* 3.

21. D. Maldonado, "The Letter Collection of Synesius of Cyrene," in *Late Antique Letter Collections: A Critical Introduction and Reference Guide*, ed. C. Sogno, B. Storin, and E. Watts (Berkeley, 2016).

22. These 156 letters may only be a fraction of what once was included in the collection. For the possibility of a larger collection, see D. Roques, *Synésios de Cyrène, Tome II Correspondance* (Paris, 2003), cxxx-cxxxi.

23. On these bonds, see the discussion of Dzielska, *Hypatia*, 58–59.

24. A particularly good discussion of this tendency is L. Van Hoof, "The Letters of Libanius," in *Late Antique Epistolography*, 2016.

25. On this, see Sogno, Storin, and Watts, "Collected Epistolography in Late Antiquity," in *Late Antique Epistolography*, 2016.

26. Maldonado, "The Letter Collection of Synesius."

27. This is *Ep.* 15. For the nature of the hydroscope itself, see the extensive discussion in Roques, *Synésios*, 115 n. 4. For the possibility that Synesius sought this instrument in order to mix his own medicines, see the discussion of Deakin, *Hypatia of Alexandria*, 104–5. Dzielska (*Hypatia*, 78) proposes that the instrument was to be used in divination, but this seems unlikely. Harich-Schwarzbauer (*Hypatia*, 71–75) questions whether Synesius here describes an actual illness and suggests that the letter not be understood as a late composition. Given the intimate connection with the other letters in this group, it seems more likely that this letter belongs to the period near the end of his life when Synesius lost his family.

28. Hypatia presumably could find the instrument for him without such a detailed description.

29. On this process of editing letters later for publication, see Van Hoof, "Letters of Libanius," 2016.

30. Αὐτήν τέ σε καὶ διὰ σοῦ τοὺς μακαριωτάτους ἑταίρους ἀσπάζομαι, δέσποινα σεβασμία (*Ep.* 10.1–2). For the term *hetairoi* as one that marks the inner circle of a school in fourth century authors like Eunapius, see Watts, *City and School*, 51–53.

31. *Ep.* 16.1–3. The translation is my own, based on the text of Garzyra.

32. *Ep.* 16.9–13.

33. *Ep.* 16.16–18.

34. D. Roques, "La Famille d'Hypatie," 128–49, identifies Theoteknos with Hypatia's father, Theon. For discussion, see also Harich-Schwartzbauer, *Hypatia*, 79–80.

35. The reference is to *Crito* 54d. On this, see Roques, *Synésios*, 66 n. 3.

36. For the date of 404 see Roques, *Synésios*, 423 n. 1, and *Études*, 40–42.

37. See the discussion in Chapter 3, above, and the analysis of Vollenweider, "Ein Mittleres zwischen Vater und Sohn," 191.

38. For a detailed commentary on the text of *Ep.* 154, see Harich-Schwartzbauer, *Hypatia*, 96–128. Note as well the thorough discussion of Tanaseanu-Döbler, *Konversion zur Philosophie*, 229–52.

39. *Ep.* 154.91–95.

40. *Ep.* 154.95–99.

41. *Ep.* 1.1–5.

42. *Ep.* 1. 8–9.

43. On their coherence, see Maldonado, "The Letter Collection of Synesius"; and Roques, *Synésios*, cxxi.

44. *Ep.* 137.8–9.

45. For this date see Roques, *Etudes*, 87–103.

46. *Ep.* 140.7–10.

47. The ideas about philosophical love are certainly ones that Synesius legitimately held, but the letter itself responds somewhat playfully to a letter that Herculian sent to Synesius in which he complained about Synesius not corresponding regularly. In this way, it can be read as a companion to *Letters* 138 and 139, letters in which Synesius blames Herculian for the same offense.

48. *Ep.* 143.1–2. Like the agreements made by Plotinus and the other members of the inner circle of Ammonius Saccas to keep their master's teaching a secret, and those which bound Pythagorean initiates to silence, Hypatia's students also felt that access

to the most important elements of her philosophy needed to be restricted. For the Pythagorean roots, see the discussion of Dzielska, *Hypatia*, 60.

49. Synesius, *Ep.* 140.

50. Socrates, *HE* 7.15.3. For this passage read against the fifth-century Theodosian context in which it was written, see Harich-Schwartzbauer, *Hypatia*, 201–2.

51. Damascius, *Isid.* 43A.

52. Music was one of the four core mathematical disciplines and played an important role in the Pythagorean system.

53. *Isid.* 43 C. For this passage, note also the discussion of Harich-Schwartzbauer, *Hypatia*, 268–70.

54. For the Damascius passage, see too the discussion of Dzielska, *Hypatia*, 51, as well as the parallels she adduces to Plato, *Symposium* 218e and Plotinus, *Enneads* 1.6.8.

55. There have been many, many recent studies of female virginity in Christianity. Some key starting points for this topic are P. Brown, *The Body and Society: Men, Women, and Sexual Renunciation in Early Christianity* (Boston, 1988), 8–9, 260–63; E. Castelli, "Virginity and Its Meaning for Women's Sexuality in Early Christianity," *Journal of Feminist Studies in Religion* 2 (1986), 61–88; K. Cooper, *The Virgin and the Bride: Idealized Womanhood in Late Antiquity* (Cambridge, MA, 1999).

56. For example, Matthew 19.10–12, 22.30. For a particularly precise discussion of this idea, see also Theodoret, *Religious History*, Prologue.

57. Damascius, *Isid.* 97B.

58. Marinus, *Proc.* 36.

59. For discussion, see G. Clark, *Monica: An Ordinary Saint* (Oxford, 2015), Chapter 4.

60. *Isid.* 46E.

61. The Platonic succession in Alexandria that passed from at least Hermeias to Ammonius to, eventually, Olympiodorus, Elias, and David represents an example of the former. The Platonic school in Athens founded by Plutarch and headed by Syrianus, Proclus, Marinus, Isidore, Hegias, and Damascius is the rare example of the latter case. In the Athenian case, however, the family of Plutarch remained involved in the operation of the school until the death of Hegias (who was Plutarch's descendant). For both cases, see Watts, *City and School*, 79–142 (Athens) and 204–61 (Alexandria).

62. Fowden, "Pagan Holy Man," 36–37; E. Watts, "Damascius' Isidore: A Perfectly Imperfect Philosophical Exemplar," *Byzantina et Slavica Cracoviensia* 7 (2014), 159–68.

63. Best commentator ever: *Isid.* 57C; morally corrupt: *Isid.* 118B.

64. *Isid.* 111.

Chapter 6

1. A point made, for example, by Themistius, *Or.* 1.1a; Julian, *Letter to Themistius*, 254b. For discussion of this position claimed by philosophers, see Brown, *Power and Persuasion*, 62f. For the larger context of this idea of philosophical free speech, see the intriguing insights in the lectures of M. Foucault delivered at the Collège de France in the spring of 1984, as well as the analysis of Foucault's discussions in them by J. Franēk, "Philosophical Parrhesia as Aesthetics of Existence," *Continental Philosophy Review* 39 (2006), 113–34.

2. For the Pythagorean martyrs, see Iamblichus, *Vit. Pyth.*, Ch. 35. On Thraesa Paetus, see, for example, Cassius Dio, 62.15.2; 62.26.4 and Tacitus, *Annals* 14.12; 16.34–5.

3. This idea has clear Pythagorean and Platonic roots. For Pythagoreans playing this role, see Iamblichus, *Vit. Pyth.* 31. Note the comments of Fowden, "Pagan Holy Man," 54–59, on the tendency of the fourth-century followers of Iamblichus to refuse to take up this role. They seem to be exceptional, however. Both their contemporary Themistius (*Or.* 28.341d) and later Platonists like Damascius (*Isid.* 26B; 124), and Simplicius (*In Ench.* 64.53–65.11) advocate for a robust public role.

4. This was famously argued by Plato in the *Republic*, though the idea has Pythagorean and Stoic echoes as well. One of the most famous late antique discussions of the principle is Simplicius, *In Ench.* 64.35–41.

5. An idea expressed most clearly in Simplicius, *In Ench.* 64.53–65.11.

6. *In Ench.* 65.4–8.

7. A point made explicitly by Marinus in *Proc.* 15. This was also a behavior attributed to Isidore and Marinus by Damascius (*Isid.* 15 A-B [Isidore] and 100 A [Marinus]).

8. Simplicius, *In Ench.* 61.10–62.49 (honors), 62.50–63.23 (offices). These are comments on Epictetus, *Ench.* 24 (Lemma xxxii).

9. Simplicius, *In Ench.* 65.30–38.

10. *Isid.* 100 A.

11. *Isid.* 112 A–B.

12. On Uranius, see Agathias, 2.29.1–32.2, and the discussion of J. Walker, "The Limits of Late Antiquity: Philosophy between Rome and Iran," *Ancient World* 33 (2002): 45–69.

13. On Themistius's career see the discussions of Watts, *Final Pagan Generation*; P. Heather and D. Moncur, *Politics, Philosophy, and Empire: Select Orations of Themistius* (Liverpool, 2001); R. Penella, *Private Orations of Themistius* (Berkeley, 2000); and J. Vanderspoel, *Themistius and the Imperial Court* (Ann Arbor, 1995).

14. For Themistius' grandfather, see *Or.* 5.63d and the discussion of this passage in Vanderspoel, *Themistius*, 32–33. For his father's position in Constantinople, see *Or. Const.* 22b–23b, 28d. For Themistius's training in the city, see *Oration* 23 and the discussion of Vanderspoel, *Themistius*, 35. On the view that Themistius was not native to Constantinople, see, too, Penella, *Private Orations*, 1–2 (argued on the basis of *Or.* 17.214).

15. For Themistius's time in Nicomedia, see Vanderspoel, *Themistius*, 42–49.

16. The date of 347 has been proposed on the basis of *CTh* 11.36.8, a law that places Constantius in Ancyra on March 8, 347. For arguments in favor of this date, see Vanderspoel, *Themistius*, 48, 73–77; Heather and Moncur, *Politics, Philosophy, and Empire*, 4, 69–71. Allusions within the speech to a coin type issued in early 348, however, seem to push the date of the speech to the spring of that year.

17. This identity is claimed immediately, at *Or.* 1.1a. For discussion, see Heather and Moncur, *Politics, Philosophy, and Empire*, 73–77.

18. Most of these orations are translated and discussed at length in Heather and Moncur, *Politics, Philosophy, and Empire*.

19. For discussion, see Vanderspoel, *Themistius*, 88–89.

20. On the senatorial expansion and equivalence, see Heather and Moncur, *Politics, Philosophy, and Empire*, 122–23; P. Heather, "New Men for New Constantines," 11–33. For his role, see Themistius, *Or.* 34.14.

21. *CTh* 6.4.12. The specific office mentioned here is the praetorship, the key office that began the public career of senatorial youths.

22. Watts, *Final Pagan Generation*, 192–94.

23. The next such figure was Flavius Messius Phoebus Severus, consul of the West in 470 (*PLRE* II 1005–6; cf. R. S. Bagnall, et al., *Consuls of the Later Roman Empire* [Atlanta, 1987], 470). His philosophical credentials are discussed by Damascius (*Isid.* 51 C–D, 77 A).

24. These are charges that Themistius addresses at length in *Orations* 17, 31, and 34. For more on the controversy surrounding his appointment, see Heather and Moncur, *Politics, Philosophy, and Empire*, 287–98.

25. At the beginning of every regime from Jovian to Theodosius I, it seems that Themistius offered a speech in support of the new emperor that mixed in criticism of the previous regime. On this, see Heather and Moncur, *Politics, Philosophy, and Empire*, 24–38.

26. Julian gently accuses Themistius of flattery unbecoming a philosopher (*Letter to Themistius*, 254b). For a broader discussion of Julian's interactions with Themistius, see S. Elm, *Sons of Hellenism, Fathers of the Church* (Berkeley, 2012), 96–106.

27. See, for example, Gregory Nazianzen *Ep.* 24 B–C. For discussion of Gregory's blending of philosophical and rhetorical tropes in this letter, see B. Storin, "The Letters of Gregory Nazianzus: Discourse and Community in Late Antique Epistolary Culture," PhD diss., Indiana University, 2011, 228–29.

28. See, for example, Ammianus, 22.7, 29.1; Eunapius, *VS* 473–81.

29. Eunapius, *VS* 473.

30. Eunapius, *VS* 475.

31. Eunapius tells this story at *VS* 476–77.

32. Eunapius, *VS* 477.

33. For additional discussion of this story and the role Maximus's wife played in it, see Chapter 7.

34. Eunapius, *VS* 478–80. For his execution, see also Ammianus, 29.1.42; Libanius, *Or.* 1.158; Zosimus, 4.15.1; Socrates Scholasticus, *HE* 3.1.

35. Socrates, *HE* 7.15.2. The next clause reads, "she had no shame to be in the midst of men." It is possible that we should take Socrates's statement here to mean that, as a woman, she was modest, and for this reason she had no cause to be ashamed when speaking before men. If this meaning is intended, however, Socrates almost certainly is alluding to both the supposed limits of women's public roles and the modesty expected of a philosopher. If there was no comment about the philosophical propriety of her public activities implied, both the statement about her education and the following comment about everyone being amazed by her prudence would not otherwise be relevant to this clause. On this comment, see too Harich-Schwartzbauer, *Hypatia*, 200–201.

36. Socrates, *HE* 7.15.3.

37. *Isid.* 43E.

38. *Isid.* 43E.

39. *Isid.* 43E. The word Damascius uses is προσαγορεύοιτο, which here has the sense of a patroness receiving her clients, granting favors, and offering assistance.

40. *Ep.* 46. For the dating, see Roques, *Études*, 220.

41. For discussion of this letter, see Harich-Schwartzbauer, *Hypatia*, 81–85.

42. On the contexts in which letters were delivered, the so-called "letter event," see Storin, "Letters of Gregory," 80–146.

43. Ammianus, 14.6, points to the degeneration of this custom in the city of Rome in the later fourth century, though this is likely more for rhetorical effect than a reflection of an actual change in behavior.

44. Synesius, *Ep.* 81.17–18.

45. *Ep.* 81.19–20.

46. This is *Ep.* 101. For Pylamenes, see Roques, *Études*, 117–36.

47. On this, see A. Petkas, "The Place of Philosophy: Landscapes and Audiences of the Works of Synesius of Cyrene," PhD diss. in preparation, Princeton University, Chapter 2. I thank Mr. Petkas for sending me an in progress copy of this chapter and allowing me to cite it.

48. *Ep.* 101.41–43.

49. *Ep.* 101.45–49.

50. *Ep.* 101.48–51. This echoes Plato, *Letter* 7.326b, as well as *Rep.* 9.592a–b, and the discussions of Epictetus mentioned above.

51. *Ep.* 103.

52. This was possibly as early as 406–407. For this dating, see T. D. Barnes, "When Did Synesius Become Bishop of Ptolemais?," *GRBS* 27 (1986): 325–29.

53. *Ep.* 105.

54. *Ep.* 62.

55. These are *Epp.* 18–21.

56. Petkas, "The Place of Philosophy," Chapter 2.

57. On the *De Regno* see Cameron and Long, *Barbarians and Politics*, 103–42; H. Ziche, "Barbarian Raiders and Barbarian Peasants: Models of Ideological and Economic Integration," in *Romans, Barbarians, and the Transformation of the Roman World*, ed. R. Mathisen and D. Shanzer (Aldershot, 2011), 199–219, at 199–201; C. Amande, "Il Lexikon di Sinesio: Presentazione ed esemplificazioni dal *De regno*," in *Synesios von Kyrene: Politik-Literatur-Philosophie*, 66–72.

58. *De Regno* 10–11.

59. *De Regno* 12.

60. *De Regno* 13–17

61. *De Regno* 24–32.

62. Cameron and Long, *Barbarians and Politics*, 107–21, are correct in seeing the chamberlain Eutropius and the Gothic commander Alaric as Synesius's targets.

63. For the revolt of Gaïnas, see Socrates, *HE* 6.6; Sozomen, *HE* 8.4; Zosimus, 5.13, as well as the discussion of M. Kulikowski, *Rome's Gothic Wars* (Baltimore, 2007), 168–70.

64. *Ep.* 73.3–4.

65. *Ep.* 78.

66. *Ep.* 133.

67. *Ep.* 133.37–50.

68. *Ep.* 108.

Chapter 7

1. G. Ménage, *Historia mulierum philosopharum* (Paris, 1690). The current translation of this work is G. Ménage, *A History of Women Philosophers*, trans. B. H. Zedler (New York, 1984). For discussion of its genesis, see S. Ronchey, "Hypatia the Intellectual," in *Roman Women*, ed. A. Fraschetti (Chicago, 1999), 160–89, at 168.

2. See, for example, K. Wider, "Women Philosophers in the Ancient Greek World: Donning the Mantle," *Hypatia* 1.1 (1986), 21–62. For Pythagorean women in

particular, see the discussion of S. Pomeroy, *Pythagorean Women: Their History and Writings* (Baltimore, 2013), 1–18.

3. None of the four women discussed in this chapter figure into Wider's survey, for example.

4. This is not surprising. Few of her fellow mathematicians are mentioned in historical sources unless they were also accomplished philosophers. Much of this has to do with the tendency for fourth-, fifth-, and sixth-century Platonists to write biographies of their intellectual ancestors that explained how their lives embodied the philosophical principles the school taught. Alexandrian mathematicians like Pappus and Pandrosion did not belong to this intellectual ancestry, and this meant that their lives were not germane to the projects Platonic biographers undertook.

5. The manuscripts of the *Collectio* make it clear that Pandrosion was a woman, but earlier editions of the text amended the manuscripts so that they referred to her as a man. For discussion of this issue and its correction see Deakin, *Hypatia*, 132; Cuomo, *Pappus of Alexandria*, 127 n. 2.

6. For example, *Collectio* 3. Praef.1=Hultsch 30.3ff, where Pappus defines the term πρόβλημα for Pandrosion.

7. The Greek terms are πρόβλημα (problem) and θεωρήμα (theorem). For this passage, see also Cuomo, *Pappus of Alexandria*, 170ff.

8. Pappus, *Collectio* 3.Praef.=Hultsch 30.17–19.

9. Pappus, *Collectio* 3.Praef.=Hultsch 30.19–21.

10. μέγας τις γεωμέτρης εἶναι δοκῶν 30.23

11. On this, see Deakin, *Hypatia*, 131–32.

12. *Collectio* 3.11.28=Hultsch 68.17–70.8.

13. Deakin, *Hypatia*, 131–32.

14. Described in *Ep.* 154 and Chapter 5.

15. For discussion of this, see Chapter 3.

16. Sosipatra, known only from Eunapius's *Lives of the Sophists*, gets nine Loeb pages in that text. This is far more than survives for Hypatia and is perhaps the most extensive ancient portrait of any female philosopher. It is not likely that Hypatia influenced the portrait of Sosipatra, in spite of the arguments of Penella, *Greek Philosophers and Sophists*, 61–62.

17. For this intellectual line serving as the basis of Eunapius's text, see Watts, "Orality and Community Identity," 334–61.

18. Eunapius, *VS* 467.

19. Eunapius, *VS* 467–68.

20. Eunapius, *VS* 469. On this narrative, see R. Pack, "A Romantic Narrative in Eunapius," *TAPA* 83 (1952), 198–204; and S. Iles Johnston, "Sosipatra and the Theurgic Life: Eunapius Vitae Sophistorum 6.6.5–6.9.24," in *Reflections on Religious Individuality: Greco-Roman and Judaeo-Christian Texts and Practices*, ed. J. Rüpke and W. Spickermann (Berlin, 2012), 99–118, at 101–5.

21. Eunapius, *VS* 469.

22. Eunapius, *VS* 469.

23. Eunapius uses the Greek term συνουσίαν to describe the meetings from which these students came, a word that suggests an intimate gathering of teacher and students.

24. Eunapius, *VS* 469.

25. Eunapius, *VS*. 469–70.

26. Eunapius, *VS* 470. For the significance of her clairvoyance, see Iles-Johnston, "Sosipatra," 106–7.

27. Eunapius, *VS* 471.

28. For Antoninus, see Eunapius, *VS* 471–72 and the discussion of his career in Chapter 4. For his role in Eunapius's portrait of Sosipatra, see Iles-Johnston, "Sosipatra," 111–12.

29. Eunapius styles them *daimones* at *VS* 468. For the particular significance of Sosipatra not being trained by Iamblichus or his disciples, see Iles-Johnston, "Sosipatra," 108–11.

30. For a discussion of the nature of her circle and her known students, see Dzielska, *Hypatia*, 28–43.

31. It has even been argued that she is presented as a godlike figure (Iles-Johnston, "Sosipatra," 106).

32. Other female teachers are known to have taught publicly in the Roman period, though their instruction seems mainly to have been confined to lower-level teaching like grammar. For a discussion of these figures, see Cribiore, *Gymnastics of the Mind*.

33. Synesius, *Ep.* 16.

34. For further discussion of this, see Fowden, "Pagan Holy Man," 39.

35. The *Life of Proclus* is organized around the scale of virtues first developed by Plotinus and later elaborated by Porphyry and Iamblichus. For how the scale of virtues is reflected in the text, see Blumenthal, "Marinus' *Life of Proclus*," 471–93.

36. *Proc.* 28. For Chaldean top-spinning, see *Or. Chald*, fr. 206 des Pl. ex hoc 1.

37. For Nestorius, see Chapter 4.

38. *Proc.* 28.

39. For the extent of Syrianus's instruction, see *Proc.* 26.

40. For a discussion of the political climate in fifth-century Athens and the ways in which it might have influenced philosophical behavior, see Watts, *City and School*, 101–9.

41. At *VS* 477 and 478–79.

42. See Chapter 6.

43. *VS* 477 (trans. Wright).

44. *VS* 479.

45. Maximus participated in public performances in which he denied practicing theurgy (*VS* 480). He also agreed to interpret the oracle that ultimately led to the Theodorus incident, an event that led to his execution (*VS* 480–81; cf. Ammianus, 29.1).

46. For male teachers advertising their celibacy, see Damascius celebrating the philosopher Theosebius for refraining from sexual acts *(Isid.* 46 D).

47. I thank Mariah Smith for this insight.

48. For the important role that clothing played in advertising the interior development of a woman, see the important study of Kate Wilkinson (*Women and Modesty in Late Antiquity* [Cambridge, 2015]), particularly her discussion in Chapter 2 of the book.

49. *Isid.* 43 A. The entire passage reads περιβαλλομένη δὲ τρίβωνα ἡ γυνὴ καὶ διὰ μέσου τοῦ ἄστεως ποιουμένη τὰς προόδους ἐξηγεῖτο δημοσίᾳ τοῖς ἀκροᾶσθαι βουλομένοις ἢ τὸν Πλάτωνα ἢ τὸν Ἀριστοτέλην ἢ τὰ ἄλλου ὅτου δὴ τῶν φιλοσόφων.

Chapter 8

1. For Theophilus officiating at Synesius's wedding, see Synesius, *Ep.* 105.69–70 and the discussion in Chapter 4.

2. He did this, he says, "so that, whatever happens, no one will have a right to accuse me before God or man or Theophilus" of taking the position under false pretenses. Synesius, *Ep.* 105.8.

3. Theophilus's mentoring of Cyril is suggested by John of Nikiu, 79.12, and by Cyril himself in his *Letter to Acacius of Beroea* (*Ep.* 33.7; cf. the translation of J. A. McGuckin, *St. Cyril of Alexandria: The Christological Controversy* [Leiden, 1994], 336–42). It is stated explicitly in the *Synaxarion* of the Coptic Church (Abib 3).

4. Socrates, *HE* 7.7.

5. Socrates, *HE* 7.7. For Cyril's actions in this crisis, see S. Wessel, "Socrates's Narrative of Cyril of Alexandria's Episcopal Election," *JThS* 52 (2000): 102–3; T. D. Barnes, "Review: C. Haas, *Alexandria in Late Antiquity* (Baltimore, 1997)," *JThS* 49 (1998): 363–65.

6. On the role of Novatians in Socrates's history, see M. Wallraff, "Socrates Scholasticus on the History of Novatianism," *Studia Patristica* 29 (1997): 170–77.

7. Socrates, *HE* 7.7. On Socrates use of this passage as part of a larger discussion of Cyril's character, see E. Watts, "Interpreting Catastrophe: Disasters in the Works of Pseudo-Joshua the Stylite, Socrates Scholasticus, Philostorgius, and Timothy Aelurus," *JLA* 2 (2009): 79–98, at 83–85. It is worth noting that actions were also taken against Novatians in Rome not long before this (Socrates, *HE* 7.9).

8. See, for example, *Ep.* 12.

9. Socrates, *HE* 7.13 provides the details.

10. For the possible involvement of the Jewish community in the succession struggle, see Haas, *Alexandria in Late Antiquity*, 298–301.

11. John of Nikiu, 84.95, says explicitly that Jewish leaders refused to agree to Cyril's demands because they "gloried in the support of the prefect, who was with them."

12. See, for example, Socrates, *HE* 7.13; John of Nikiu, 84.96–99.

13. John of Nikiu, 84.99, says that the Jews involved in the earlier violence were expelled. Socrates Scholasticus (7.13) says all Jews were expelled, but this point is clearly exaggerated. Socrates uses it to contrast Cyril's inability to work with Jews with the Constantinopolitan bishop Atticus's success in converting one of the Alexandrian Jewish refugees to Christianity. For the contrast between Atticus and Cyril as a thematic element of Socrates's text, see Watts, "Interpreting Catastrophe," 84–85.

14. Socrates, *HE* 7.13

15. The most memorable such incident involved the bishop Ambrose publicly confronting the emperor Theodosius I about a massacre of people in Thessaloniki. For the event, see Sozomen, *HE* 7.25, and the discussion of McLynn, *Ambrose of Milan*, 315–29.

16. Socrates, *HE* 7.14.

17. This step of proclaiming a Christian rioter a martyr is paralleled in other contexts, including a man who died while participating in an anti-pagan riot in North Africa. On this incident, see Augustine, *Ep.* 16.2 and the discussion of Shaw, *Sacred Violence*, 236–37.

18. Socrates, *HE* 7.14.

19. The Athanasian festal letters suggest that the average tenure of an Egyptian prefect from 328 to 373 was about eighteen months. This likely remained the standard

in the 410s as well. For this, see A. H. M. Jones, *The Later Roman Empire 284–602* (Norman, OK, 1964), 381.

20. The Riot of the Statues in Antioch in 387 had led to the entire city council being imprisoned in the council building while an investigation of the event was conducted. On this, see Libanius, *Or.* 22.29–31; Chrysostom, *Hom. de Stat.* 17.2.

21. Haas, *Alexandria in Late Antiquity*, 312–13; Dzielska, *Hypatia*, 88–90.

22. Damascius, *Isid.* 43E.

23. M. Vinzent ("'Oxbridge' in der ausgehenden Spätantike," 72–73) revived the idea that Cyril was a student of Hypatia. Against this, see M. O. Boulnois, *Le paradoxe trinitaire chez Cyrille d'Alexandrie: Herméneutique, analyses philosophiques et argumentation théologique* (Paris, 1994), 394–97.

24. This is suggested by John of Nikiu, 84.88. For a more detailed discussion of the complexity of this text and the different layers of evidence it uses, see Chapter 9.

25. *Isid.* 43E.

26. Socrates (HE 7.15) mentions a "slander" against her, the content of which is likely reflected in John of Nikiu, 84.88.

27. John of Nikiu, 84.88.

28. Such talk could find one in violation of *CTh* 9.4.1, a law issued in 393 CE by the emperor Theodosius I that provides for the investigation of the circumstances under which someone might "disparage Our times." If talk turned to a possible attack on Orestes, this could be punished as a criminal conspiracy under *CTh* 9.14.3, a law of 397 CE.

29. See, for example, Damascius, *Isid.* 42G; Socrates, *HE* 5.16.

30. The link between Hypatia's murder and the Serapeum destruction in the mind of her killers is implied by John of Nikiu's statement (84.103) that her death purged the city of paganism and marked Cyril as a new Theophilus. It is worth emphasizing that, despite some popular ideas, women and men seem to have been more or less equally likely to have suspicions of witchcraft arise against them in antiquity. On this, see F. Graf, "Untimely Death, Witchcraft, and Divine Vengeance: A Reasoned Epigraphical Catalog," *ZPE* 162 (2007): 139–50.

31. Peter is called a reader by Socrates but a presbyter by John of Nikiu.

32. This is described in Chapter 1.

33. For the distinction between what citizens of a city received and what migrants could claim, see P. Brown, *Poverty and Leadership in the Later Roman Empire* (Hanover, NH, 2002), 3–5. For the necessity of such distributions, see the vital study of P. Garnsey, *Famine and Food Supply in the Greco-Roman World: Responses to Risk and Crisis* (Cambridge, 1988).

34. F. Nau, "Histoire des solitaires égyptiens," no. 214, *Revue de l'Orient chrétien* 13 (1908): 282. Note as well the discussions of Brown, *Power and Persuasion*, 92; *Poverty*, 12.

35. Their function as hospital attendants is defined in *CTh* 16.2.43. For the group and its character see Haas, *Alexandria in Late Antiquity*, 235–38. They were, Haas writes (237), "recruited from desperate elements among the population."

36. This was less true of lower-class groups of youths, who, in some parts of the Roman world, may have been more prone to physical fights with each other that sometimes resulted in deaths. For a discussion, see Shaw, *Sacred Violence*, 235–59. The targets of these groups occupy a very different social strata than Hypatia. On the different susceptibilities to violence among elites in late antiquity see C. Grey, "Shock, Horror, or Same Old Same Old? Everyday Violence in Augustine's Africa," *JLA* 6 (2014), 216–32, at 223.

37. Ammianus, 27.3. For this incident, see C. Sogno, *Q. Aurelius Symmachus: A Political Biography* (Ann Arbor, 2006), 52–53; Matthews, *Western Aristocracies*, 19–20.

38. For Alexandria's reputation, see Dio Chrysostom, *Or.* 32.35–6. For this speech and its context, see C. P. Jones, *The Roman World of Dio Chrysostom* (Cambridge, 1978), 36–44.

39. For the death of George of Capadocia, see *Historia Acephala* 2.8–10; Socrates, *HE* 3.2; Sozomen, *HE* 5.7. The emperor Julian blamed the lynching on Alexandrian pagans (*Ep.* 60, c.f. Socrates, *HE* 3.3), perhaps with reason. For discussion, see T. D. Barnes, *Athanasius and Constantius* (Cambridge, MA, 1993), 155. For the death of Proterius, see Evagrius, 2.8; Zacharias, *HE* 4.1–2; *Life of Peter the Iberian*, 64–68; Theophanes, *AM* 5950.111.2–3. For discussion, see Haas, *Alexandria in Late Antiquity*, 317–18; Davis, *Early Coptic Papacy*, 88–89. Callistus, the *praefectus augustalis* of Alexandria in 422, was murdered, but the assailants seem to have been his own slaves and not a mob (Theophanes, *AM* 5914.84).

40. All sources agree that Hypatia was attacked while in public. Socrates (*HE* 7.15) describes her being pulled from her carriage. John of Nikiu (84.101) says that the mob found her seated on a chair, which could mean either a litter or the *thronos* used by teachers in their classrooms. Damascius (*Isid.* 43E) says that she was attacked as she left her house.

41. No less a figure than Pyrrhus of Epirus was killed by roof tiles (Plutarch, *Pyrrhus*, 34.2). For roof tiles as a weapon, see W. D. Barry, "Roof Tiles and Urban Violence in the Ancient World," *GRBS* 37 (1996): 55–74.

42. Damascius, *Isid.* 43 E.

43. Socrates, *HE* 7.15.

44. On this ritual, see Haas, *Alexandria*, 87–89. For Agathocles, see Polybius, 15.33.9. His body was not cremated, however. The Christian martyrs are described by Eusebius, *Ecclesiastical History*, 6.41.1ff; and George's death is recorded, most memorably, by Socrates, *HE* 3.2 and Philostorgius, *HE* 7.2.

45. This is suggested by John's terming Hypatia's murder the destruction "of the last remains of idolatry in the city" (John of Nikiu, 84.103).

46. *HE* 7.15.

47. See, for example, Philostorgius, 8.9; Malalas, 13.39. These authors are discussed in more detail in Chapter 9.

48. For this law, see *CTh.* 16.2.42. This change lasted only two years. See Haas, *Alexandria in Late Antiquity*, 314–15.

49. Damascius, *Isid.* 43H.

50. *Proc.* 10.

51. For this process, see Watts, *City and School*, 204–9.

52. On Alexandrian philosophy following the closing of the Athenian school, see Watts, *City and School*, 232–56.

53. See, for example, Themistius, *Oration* 5 (delivered to highlight religious tolerance under the emperor Jovian).

54. Meeting with governors: Olympiodorus (*In Alc.* 2.80–82) suggests his presence at an event welcoming the governor Hephaestus to Alexandria in 546. Advocating for local causes: *Proc.* 15.

55. See, for example, Damascius, *Isid.* 106A–B. This passage and Hypatia's legacy within these later pagan philosophical circles will be discussed in the next chapter. For these traditions, see Watts, *Riot in Alexandria*, 56–57. For the larger context, note

as well P. Athanassiadi, "Persecution and Response in Late Paganism: The Evidence of Damascius," *JHS* 113 (1993): 1–29.

56. See, for example, *Isid.* 69A–D, 77A, 115. For discussion, see Watts, *Riot in Alexandria*, 55; and R. von Haehling, "Damascius und die heidnische Opposition im 5 Jahrhundert nach Christus" *JAC* 23 (1980): 82–95.

57. See, for example, Ammonius, described by Damascius as "sordidly greedy" and seeing "everything in terms of profit" (*Isid.* 118B) for making an agreement that permitted him to continue teaching amid an imperial investigation in the 480s. For discussion, see Watts, *City and School*, 222–25; R. Sorbaji, "Divine Names and Sordid Deals in Ammonius' Alexandria," in *Philosophy and Science in Late Antiquity*, ed. A. Smith (Swansea, 2005), 203–14.

Chapter 9

1. *HE* 5.Pro.10–11. For discussion of this idea in Socrates's text, see G. Chesnut, *The First Christian Histories: Eusebius, Socrates, Sozomen, Theodoret, and Evagrius* (Macon, GA, 1986), 192–97; T. Urbainczyk, *Socrates of Constantinople* (Ann Arbor, 1997), 69–81.

2. M. Walraff, *Die Kirchenhistoriker Sokrates Untersuchungen zu Geschichtsdarstellung, Methode und Person* (Göttingen, 1997), 235–57; M. Walraff, "Socrates Scholasticus," 170–77; Urbainczyk, *Socrates*, 26–28.

3. Watts, "Interpreting Catastrophe," 83–87.

4. Socrates, *HE* 7.10.

5. For Socrates's view of Alexandria, see also Harich-Schwartzbauer, *Hypatia*, 179–83.

6. For the Roman narrative, see Watts, "Interpreting Catastrophe," 85–86.

7. Κατὰ δὴ ταύτης τότε ὁ φθόνος ὡπλίσατο (Socrates, *HE* 7.15).

8. Socrates finished his text sometime between 439 and 443. For this dating, see Chesnut, *First Christian Histories*, 175 n. 1; Urbainczyk, *Socrates*, 19–20; and (arguing for 439) Alan Cameron, "The Empress and Poet: Paganism and Politics at the Court of Theodosius II," *YCS* 27 (1982): 217–89, at 256.

9. On the circulation of Synesius's letters in the mid-fifth century, see Maldonado, "The Letter Collection of Synesius."

10. This is Book 8, Chapter 9. Philostorgius's text concludes with the elevation of Valentinian III in 425, suggesting that the work was composed not long after this date. For this date and the larger literary context of his work, see E. Argov, "Giving the Heretic a Voice: Philostorgius of Borissus and Greek Ecclesiastical Historiography," *Athenaeum* 89 (2001): 497–524, at 497–502; and A. E. Nobbs, "Philostorgius' View of the Past," in *Reading the Past in Late Antiquity*, ed. G. Clarke (Rushcutters Bay, 1990), 251–64, at 256–57.

11. Philostorgius, *HE* 8.9.

12. On Photius's involvement in drafting this epitome, see P. Batiffol, *Quaestiones Philostorgianae* (Paris, 1891), 31. This idea has been generally accepted, though one should also note the doubts cast by Argov, "Giving the Heretic a Voice," 520–23. For a discussion of Philostorgian fragments beyond the epitome, see Nobbs, "Philostorgius' View of the Past," 254–55.

13. On this text, see Harich-Schwarzbauer, *Hypatia*, 217–30. For the dating and context of this project, see Alan Cameron, "Cassiodorus Deflated," *JRS* 71 (1981): 183–86, at 185.

14. Malalas, *Chron*.14.12. For a more detailed assessment of this passage, see Harich-Schwarzbauer, *Hypatia*, 335–40.

15. The dates of Hesychius are difficult to determine. We are told that he was active during the reign of Anastasius, but the surviving fragments of his *Onomatologus* include information that must be Justinianic. For more on the biography and literary interests of Hesychius, see A. Kaldellis, "The Works and Days of Hesychios the Illoustrios of Miletos," *GRBS* 45 (2005): 381–403.

16. *Suda* Y.166 lines 1–11. Harich-Schwarzbauer (*Hypatia*, 323–34) sees nearly all of this material coming from Hesychius. Much less is attributed to Hesychius in the edition of K. Müller, *Fragmenta historicorum Graecorum* (*FHG*), Vol. 4 (Paris, 1841–1870), 145–77, which seems more likely to be correct. This point is discussed below.

17. Damascius "dedicated the composition to a certain Theodora, a Hellene too by religious persuasion, not unacquainted with the disciplines of philosophy, poetics, and grammar, but also well versed in geometry and higher arithmetic, Damascius himself and Isidore taught her and her younger sisters at various times" (Photius, 181.3–10, trans. Athanassiadi).

18. On the text's preservation, note the comments of Athanassiadi, *Damascius: The Philosophical History*, 61–62.

19. The various attempts to reconstruct the text include those of R. Asmus, *Das Leben des Philosophen Isidoros* (Leipzig, 1911); C. Zintzen, *Vitae Isidori Reliquiae* (Hildsheim, 1967); and Athanassiadi, *Damascius: The Philosophical History*.

20. Not well read: *Isid*. 37E; Ineffective teacher: *Isid*. 37D–E; Prickliness: *Isid*. 15A–B; Unfair attacks on others: *Isid*. 32B.

21. Isidore fled the Athenian Platonic school rather than take over as the successor of Marinus because he thought that the situation could not be improved by his leadership (*Isid*. 151B–E). For discussion, see Watts, *City and School*, 122–23.

22. "God wanted to show that [Isidore] was a soul rather than a combination of soul and body, and that he had not deposited philosophy in this combination but had established it in the soul alone" (*Isid*. 14). Note also *Isid*. 71B.

23. For a discussion of collective biography more generally, see P. Cox Miller, "Strategies of Representation in Collective Biography: Constructing the Subject as Holy," in *Greek Biography and Panegyric*, ed. T. Hägg and P. Rousseau (Berkeley, 2000), 209–54.

24. *Isid*. 40A–B.

25. *Isid*. 42A–F.

26. *Isid*. 43E; 43A.

27. *Isid*. 43E.

28. *Isid*. 43E.

29. *Isid*. 106A.

30. See for example, Simplicius, *Commentary on Aristotle's Physics*, 795.15–17. Note, too, the discussions of Polymnia Athanassiadi, "The Oecumenism of Iamblichus: Latent Knowledge and Its Awakening," *JRS* 85 (1995): 244–50, at 247; and "Dreams, Love and Freelance Divination: The Testimony of Iamblichus," *JRS* 83 (1993): 115–30, at 128–29.

31. *Suda* Y.166, lines 1–11.

32. διετέλει παρθένος.

33. This explanation is suggested by Harich-Schwarzbauer, *Hypatia*, 326.

34. One of the exceptions to this trend is Nicephorus Callistus Xanthopulus, whose *Ecclesiastical History* reproduced the text of Socrates and the character of

Hypatia that he had created. This account is found in *Historia Ecclesiastica*, Bk. 14, Ch. 16.

35. Theophanes, *AM* 5906.

36. Socrates is treated in the 28th chapter. The *Life of Isidore* is briefly treated in Chapter 181 and reproduced at great length in Chapter 242.

37. See, for example, *Bib.* 242.164.

38. *Historia Romana* 8.3 at p. 294, ln. 2–5.

39. For John's reliance upon John Malalas and John of Antioch, see A. Carile, "Giovanni di Nikius, cronista bizantino-copto del VII secolo," *Felix Ravenna* 121-2 (1981), 103–55, at 113–14; and M. H. Zotenberg, *La Chronique de Jean, Évêque de Nikiou* (Paris, 1879), 11–15. John's use of Socrates for fourth and fifth-century material is not as well recognized. There are many examples of this dependence. *Chronicle*, 78.18 f, on Magnentius comes from *HE* 2.25. *Chron.* 78.22 contains a list of bishops and details quoted from *HE* 2.36. *Chron.* 78.24–25 on Liberius and Felix (bishops of Rome in Arian controversy) is derived from *HE* 2.37. *Chron.* 83.32 on the appointment of Nectarius to see of Constantinople derives from *HE* 5.8. *Chron.* 83.58 on the use of underground cellars to commit robberies appears to come from *HE* 5.18. *Chron.* 84.72 on Maximian as patriarch of Constantinople resembles *HE* 7.35.

40. John of Nikiu, 79.3–4, *The Chronicle of John, Bishop of Nikiu*, trans. R. Charles (Oxford, 1916). For discussion of this tradition and its sources, see Watts, *Riot in Alexandria*, 203–5.

41. *Chron.* 89.37–57. These parallel the particular emphasis placed upon Severus's time in Egypt by, for example, the *History of the Alexandrian Patriarchs* (e.g., the life of Patriarch Timothy III) and the *Coptic Synaxary*. This dependence is further demonstrated by a fragmentary Sahidic chronicle that significantly overlaps with John's text and may be an independent reflection of John's Egyptian source materials. On this text, see R. Charles, *Chronicle of John*, iv–v.

42. *Chron.* 51.18, which draws upon the Coptic text edited by H. L. Jansen, *The Coptic Story of Cambyses' Invasion of Egypt* (Copenhagen, 1950).

43. John's dependence is especially evident in his description of Cyril's anti-Jewish actions, which is preserved only in Socrates and not in any other source John is known to have used. This is John, *Chron.* 84.89–98. In its details, it mirrors Socrates, *HE* 7.13.

44. John of Nikiu, 84.87, trans. Charles.

45. John of Nikiu, 84.97, trans. Charles.

46. John of Nikiu, 84.98, trans. Charles.

47. John of Nikiu, 84.100, trans. Charles.

48. John of Nikiu, 84.101–2, trans. Charles.

49. John of Nikiu, 84.103, trans. Charles.

50. This charge of sorcery laid out in John of Nikiu probably represents the slander that Socrates Scholasticus describes as leading to her death (*HE* 7.15). On this point, compare Dzielska, *Hypatia*, 91.

51. It is notable in this instance that the only church John of Nikiu describes is dedicated to the martyr St. George.

52. In Zotenberg, *La Chronique de Jean, Évêque de Nikiou*.

53. There exists an extensive bibliography on the controversy that exploded at Chalcedon in 451. See, among many others, P. Blaudeau, *Alexandrie et Constantinople (451-491): De l'Histoire à la Géo-Ecclésiologie* (Rome, 2006); Gaddis, *There Is No Crime*, 299–322; and W. H. C. Frend, *The Rise of the Monophysite Movement* (Cambridge, 1972).

54. The last clearly pagan teacher in Alexandria was Olympiodorus, who remained active until at least 565 CE, based on the date of March/April 565 for a set of published lectures he gave on Aristotle's *Meteorology* (established by Neugebauer, *History of Ancient Mathematical Astronomy*, 1043–45). For discussion of his career, see Watts, *City and School*, 232–37, 251–55.

Chapter 10

1. The first scholarly work of any sort devoted to her career was a Latin dissertation completed in Jena in 1689. This is D. J. A. Schmid, *De Hipparcho, duobus Theonibus doctaque Hypatia* (Jena, 1689).

2. The *Tetradymus* also contained essays called "Hodegus," "Clidophorus," and "Magoneutes." Toland's Hypatia work was republished as a standalone book in 1753. On the confrontation between Dr. Henry Sacheverell and William Whiston that inspired Toland's project see the comments of Toland (preface to the *Tetradymus*, pp. 7–8) and the discussion of E. Watts, "Hypatia and her 18th Century Reception," in *The Context and Legacy of Hypatia of Alexandria*, eds. D. LaValle and A. Petkas, forthcoming.

3. Toland, *Hypatia: Or, the History of a most beautiful, most vertuous, most learned, and every way accomplish'd Lady; who was torn to Pieces by the* CLERGY *of Alexandria, to gratify the Pride, Emulation, and Cruelty of their* ARCHBISHOP, *commonly but undeservedly stiled St. Cyril*, quoted here from the reprinted London edition of 1753, p. 3.

4. Toland, *Hypatia*, 5.

5. Toland, *Hypatia*, 7.

6. Toland, *Hypatia*, 22.

7. The one exception is John of Nikiu, whose text would not make it to Europe until the late nineteenth century.

8. See, for example, his comment on page 22: "A Lady of such uncommon Merit and Accomplishments as Hypatia . . . could not possibly fail being sometimes importuned with Addresses of Gallantry."

9. Toland, *Hypatia*, 30.

10. Tolans, *Hypatia*, 36.

11. T. Lewis, *The History of Hypatia, A Most Impudent School-Mistress of Alexandria: Murder'd and Torn to Pieces by the Populace, in Defence of Saint Cyril and the Alexandrian Clergy. From the Aspersions of Mr. Toland* (London, 1721).

12. Lewis, *Hypatia*, 3.

13. The full title is "Dissertation sur Hypacie, où l'on justifie Saint Cyrille d'Alexandrie sur la mort de cette Sçavante," and it appears in *Continuation des Mémoires de Litterature et d'Histoire* 5.1 (1728), 139–186. It is followed immediately by a letter of praise written by Mademoiselle B., published on pages 187–191.

14. "Dissertation sur Hypacie," 139.

15. "Dissertation sur Hypacie," 143.

16. "Dissertation sur Hypacie," 141.

17. These arguments appear on pages 177–83.

18. "Dissertation sur Hypacie," 184.

19. "Dissertation sur Hypacie," 186.

20. The censorship laws in France during this time mean that the use of pseudonyms is extremely common in *Continuation des Mémoires de Litterature et*

d'Histoire. There is no way to determine the identity of Mademoiselle B., though it does seem likely that she was wealthy and well educated. Her letter also displays no real knowledge of Greek, which may be the reason why she needed to commission the Dissertation.

21. "Lettre de Mademoiselle B. à M. G. sur la Dissertation précedente," *Continuation des Mémoires de Litterature et d'Histoire* 5.1 (1728), 187–191.

22. "Lettre de Mademoiselle B.," 191.

23. The anonymous letter of response is found in "Lettre à l'Auteur de la Dissertation sur Hypacie, inserée dans le Tome V de ces Mémoires, page 139," *Continuation des Mémoires de Literature et d'Histoire* 6.1 (1729), 97–106. The letter consists of a discussion of the scholarship connected to the spurious letter to Cyril that was once attributed to Hypatia. The "Dissertation" is engaged with directly by Voltaire as late as the 1770s.

24. Cyril is blamed by, among others, Diderot in the article "Éclecticisme," *in Encyclopédie*, Vol. 5, pp. 282–83, part of a longer piece that draws upon the earlier work of J. Brucker, *Historia critica philosophiae* (Leipzig, 1742–1744); Voltaire, "Examen important de Milord Bolingbroke ou le tombeau de fanatisme," in *Oeuvres complètes de Voltaire: Nouvelle édition*, Vol. 26 (Paris, 1879), 283–290 (originally written in 1736); Voltaire, "Lettre XIV—A. M. Covelle, citoyen de Genève, par M. Baudinet," included within *Questions sur les Miracles*, in *Oeuvres complètes de Voltaire: Nouvelle édition*, Vol. 19 (Paris, 1860), 382–83 (originally compiled in 1765); E. Gibbon, *The Decline and Fall of the Roman Empire*, Chapter 47.5.

25. Among the most vocal defenders of Cyril was the unnamed author of *Histoire critique de l'éclectisme, ou des nouveaux Platoniciens* (Paris, 1766), a two-volume response to the "Éclecticisme" article in the *Encyclopédie*. The defense of Cyril covers pages 286–301, the final 15 pages of the first volume, and includes a full bibliography of both contemporaries who blamed Cyril and those who defended him.

26. "Hipathie" in *Dictionnaire philosophique*, pp. 392–93=*Questions sur l'encyclopédie*, Vol. 9 (1772), 138–40. The article was accessed from the reproduction found in *Oeuvres complètes de Voltaire: Nouvelle édition*, Vol. 13 (Paris, 1860), 585–86.

27. This, incidentally, evokes a real controversy between Madame Dacier, Antoine Houdar de la Motte, and the abbé Jean Terrasson about the relative merits of Homer versus eighteenth-century French tastes. The real controversy ended in 1716, not with Dacier's murder, but with a congenial supper at which Dacier and la Motte drank to Homer's health.

28. p. 393.

29. D. Saluzzo Roero, *Ipazia ovvero delle filosofie*, Vols. 1–2 (Turin, 1827).

30. "L'opera può chiamarsi romanzo in versi." Saluzzo Roero, *Ipazia*, Vol. 1, 12. The criticism of Toland is on page 10.

31. On the contrast with Emerson, see S. Roberson, "Degenerate Effeminacy and the Making of a Masculine Spirituality in the Sermons of Ralph Waldo Emerson," in *Muscular Christianity: Embodying the Victorian Age*, ed. D. Hall (Cambridge, 1994), 150–73. The passage defining "muscular Christianity" comes from Kingley's Christmas sermon at Cambridge in 1864, quoted by Roberson at 150.

32. On Kingsley's antipathy towards ideas of celibacy, see V. Lankewish, "Love among the Ruins: The Catacombs, the Closet, and the Victorian 'Early Christian' Novel," *Victorian Literature and Culture* 28 (2000): 239–73.

33. All references to Kingsley's Hypatia come from the two-volume publication of 1854 (*Hypatia: Or, New Foes with an Old Face* [London]). Before its publication as a

book in 1853, Hypatia was first serialized in *Fraser's Magazine* in 1852. For this period in Kingsley's life, see L. Uffelman, *Charles Kingsley* (Boston, 1979), 18–23.

34. Kingsley, *Hypatia*, xix.

35. Such as the "negress" servant who appears in Vol. 1, pp. 115–18.

36. Kingsley, *Hypatia*, Vol. 2, 377.

37. Including a Spanish translation, *Hipatia, ó, Los últimos esfuerzos del paganism en Alejandría* (Madrid, 1857).

38. E. Bowers, *The Black Agate; or Old Foes with New Faces* (Philadelphia, 1859). The text of the play is accessible online at http://babel.hathitrust.org/cgi/pt?id=hvd. hx5c5r;view=1up;seq=19. Bowers play was first performed on September 5, 1859, at Philadelphia's Academy of Music. See A. Howe Kritzer, *Plays by Early American Women, 1775-1850* (Ann Arbor, 1995), 373.

39. G. Stuart Ogilvie, *Hypatia: A Play in Four Acts* (London, 1894). The play opened at London's Haymarket Theater on January 2, 1893.

40. Julia Margaret Cameron's photo of Marie Spartali, reproduced in C. Ford, *Julia Margaret Cameron: 19th Century Photographer of Genius* (London, 2003).

41. "Così finisce il sogno della ragione hellenica/ Così, sul pavimento di Cristo," M. Luzi, *Ipazia: Poemetto Drammtico* (Milan, 1972), 45, ln. 9–10.

42. A. Zitelmann, *Hypatia* (Weinheim and Basel, 1989).

43. "Certo la persecuzione contro Ipazia mosse anche in gran parte da questa proterva e superstiziosa tendenza antifeminile," C. Pascal, *Figure e caratteri (Lucrezio, L'Ecclesiaste, Seneca, Ipazia, Giosue Carducci, Giuseppe Garibaldi)* (Milan, 1908), 143–96, at 179.

44. U. Molinaro, "A Christian Martyr in Reverse. Hypatia: 370–415 A.D.: A Vivid Portrait of the Life and Death of Hypatia as Seen through the Eyes of a Feminist Poet and Novelist," *Hypatia* 4.1 (1989): 6–8.

45. Molinaro, "Hypatia," 7.

46. Molinaro, "Hypatia," 7–8.

47. Molinaro, "Hypatia," 8.

48. U. Eco, *Baudolino* (Milan, 2000). The *Favola di Venezia* appeared in Italian in 1977. The most recent edition appeared in 2009.

49. See, for example, M. Lackey, E. Flint, and D. Freer, *The Shadow of the Lion* (Riverdale, NY, 2002).

50. Ursule Molinaro, though, had made it a prominent theme in her short piece about Hypatia.

Reconsidering a Legend

1. The moment of transition is impossible to determine, but it does seem that the city's pagan population sensed a shift during the episcopate of George the Cappadocian (356-361). For a discussion of this period, the looting of the Caeseareum church in June of 356, and the murder of George in 361, see Haas, *Alexandria in Late Antiquity*, 280–95, as well as Athanasius, *Hist. Ar.* 56 col. 761a (on the Caesareum looting).

2. For an appraisal of Julian's religious reforms and additional bibliography, see Watts, *Final Pagan Generation*, 105–15.

3. See, for example, Pascal, *Figure e Caratteri*, 179; Molinaro, "Hypatia," 8.

4. This is part of a broader pattern in the fourth-century Roman world. See Sandwell, *Religious Identity*.

5. For the Pachomian monastery on the Serapeum site in the suburb of Canopus, see Eunapius, *VS* 472; and the Coptic *Storia della Chiesa di Alessandria*, II.12.21–24; as well as the discussion of J.-L. Fournet and J. Gascou, "Moines pachômiens et batellerie," in *Alexandrie medieval 2*, ed. C. Decobert (Cairo, 2002), 23–45. For the remaking of the Alexandrian Serapeum site, see Rufinus, *HE* 11.27–28; *Storia della Chiesa* II.14.10–16.2; Sozomen, *HE* 7.15; Eunapius, *VS* 472. On this process more generally, see Watts, *Riot in Alexandria*, 196–8.

6. M. Whitby, "John of Ephesus and the Pagans: Pagan Survivals in the Sixth-Century," in *Paganism in the Later Roman Empire and Byzantium*, ed. M. Salaman (Kraków, 1991), 111–31. For the tenth century, note Constantine Porphyrogenitus, *de Admin.*, 1.50.

7. On the closing of the Athenian school, see Watts, *City and School*, 111–41.

Bibliography

Agusta-Boularot, S., and M. Bousbaa. "Une inscription inedited de Cherchell (Algérie): *Volusia Tertullina grammat(ica)." L'Africa Romana* 11 (1994): 164–73.

Amande, C. "Il Lexikon di Sinesio: presentazione ed esemplificazioni dal *De regno."* In *Synesios von Kyrene: Politik-Literatur-Philosophie*, edited by H. Seng and L. M. Hoffmann, 66–72. Turnhout, 2012.

Anonymous. "Dissertation sur Hypacie, où l'on justifie Saint Cyrille d'Alexandrie sur la mort de cette Sçavante." *Continuation des Mémoires de Litterature et d'Histoire* 5.1 (1728): 139–86.

Anonymous. "Lettre de Mademoiselle B. à M. G. sur la Dissertation précedente." *Continuation des Mémoires de Litterature et d'Histoire* 5.1 (1728): 187–91.

Anonymous. "Lettre à l'auteur de la Dissertation sur Hypacie, inserée dans le Tome V de ces Mémoires, page 139." *Continuation des Mémoires de Litterature et d'Histoire* 6.1 (1729): 97–106.

Anonymous. *Histoire critique de l'éclectisme, ou des nouveaux platoniciens.* 2 vols. Paris, 1766.

Argov, E. "Giving the Heretic a Voice: Philostorgius of Borissus and Greek Ecclesiastical Historiography." *Athenaeum* 89 (2001): 497–524.

Asmus, R. *Das Leben des Philosophen Isidoros.* Leipzig, 1911.

Athanassiadi, P. "Dreams, Love and Freelance Divination: The Testimony of Iamblichus." *Journal of Roman Studies* 83 (1993): 115–30.

Athanassiadi, P. "Persecution and Response in Late Paganism: The Evidence of Damascius." *Journal of Hellenic Studies* 113 (1993): 1–29.

Athanassiadi, P. "The Oecumenism of Iamblichus: Latent Knowledge and Its Awakening." *Journal of Roman Studies* 85 (1995): 244–50.

Athanassiadi, P. "The Chaldean Oracles: Theology and Theurgy." In *Pagan Monotheism in Late Antiquity*, edited by P. Athanassiadi and M. Frede, 149–84. Oxford, 1999.

Athanassiadi, P. *Damascius: The Philosophical History.* Athens, 1999.

Bagnall, R. S. et al. *Consuls of the Later Roman Empire.* Atlanta, 1987.

Baltes, M. "Plato's School, The Academy." *Hermathena* 155 (1993): 5–26.

Barnes, T. D. "When Did Synesius Become Bishop of Ptolemais?" *Greek, Roman, and Byzantine Studies* 27 (1986): 325–29.

Barnes, T. D. "Himerius and the Fourth Century." *Classical Philology* 82 (1987): 202–25.

Barnes, T. D. *Athanasius and Constantius.* Cambridge, MA, 1993.

Barnes, T. D. "Review: C. Haas, *Alexandria in Late Antiquity* (Baltimore, 1997)." *Journal of Theological Studies* 49 (1998): 363–65.

Barry, W. D. "Roof Tiles and Urban Violence in the Ancient World." *Greek, Roman, and Byzantine Studies* 37 (1996): 55–74.

Batiffol, P. *Quaestiones Philostorgianae.* Paris, 1891.

Belenkiy, A. "An Astronomical Murder?" *Astronomy and Geophysics* 51.2 (2010): 9–13.

Bernard, A. "Theon of Alexandria and Hypatia." In *The Cambridge History of Philosophy in Late Antiquity.* Vol. 1, edited by L. Gerson, 417–36. Cambridge, 2010.

Blaudeau, P. *Alexandrie et Constantinople (451–491): De l'histoire à la géo-ecclésiologie.* Rome, 2006.

Blumenthal, H. "Marinus' *Life of Proclus*: Neoplatonist Biography." *Byzantion* 54 (1984): 471–93.

Boulnois, M. O. *Le paradoxe trinitaire chez Cyrille d'Alexandrie: Herméneutique, analyses philosophiques et argumentation théologique.* Paris, 1994.

Bowers, E. *The Black Agate, or Old Foes with New Faces.* Philadelphia, 1859.

Bradley, K. "Wet-Nursing at Rome: A Study in Social Relations." In *The Family in Ancient Rome: New Perspectives*, edited by B. Rawson, 201–29. London, 1986.

Breccia, E. *Catalogue générale des antiquité égyptiennes du Musée d'Alexandrie (nos. 1–568): Inscrizione greche e latine.* Cairo, 1911.

Bregman, J. *Synesius of Cyrene, Philosopher Bishop.* Berkeley, 1982.

Brown, P. *The Body and Society: Men, Women, and Sexual Renunciation in Early Christianity.* Boston, 1988.

Brown, P. *Power and Persuasion in Late Antiquity.* Madison, WI, 1992.

Brown, P. *Poverty and Leadership in the Later Roman Empire.* Hanover, NH, 2002.

Brucker, J. *Historia critica philosophiae.* Leipzig, 1742–1744.

Butler, A. J., and P. M. Fraser. *The Arab Conquest of Egypt.* 2nd ed. Oxford, 1978.

Cameron, A. "Palladas and Christian Polemic." *Journal of Roman Studies* 55 (1965): 17–30.

Cameron, A. "Iamblichus at Athens." *Athenaeum* 45 (1967): 143–53.

Cameron, A. "Cassiodorus Deflated." *Journal of Roman Studies* 71 (1981): 183–86.

Cameron, A. "The Empress and Poet: Paganism and Politics at the Court of Theodosius II." *Yale Classical Studies* 27 (1982): 217–89.

Cameron, A. *The Last Pagans of Rome.* Oxford, 2012.

Cameron, A. "The Empress and the Poet." In *Wandering Poets and Other Essays*, 37–80. Oxford, 2016.

Cameron, A. "Hypatia: Life, Death, and Works." In *Wandering Poets and Other Essays*, 185–203. Oxford, 2016.

Cameron, A. "Palladas: New Poems, New Date?" In *Wandering Poets and Other Essays*, 91–112. Oxford, 2016.

Cameron, A. *Wandering Poets and Other Essays on Late Greek Literature and Philosophy*. Oxford, 2016.

Cameron, A., and J. Long. *Barbarians and Politics at the Court of Arcadius*. Berkeley, 1993.

Carile, A. "Giovanni di Nikius, cronista bizantino-copto del VII secolo." *Felix Ravenna* 121–122 (1981): 103–55.

Castelli, E. "Virginity and Its Meaning for Women's Sexuality in Early Christianity." *Journal of Feminist Studies in Religion* 2 (1986): 61–88.

Charles, R. *The Chronicle of John, Bishop of Nikiu*. Oxford, 1916.

Chesnut, G. *The First Christian Histories: Eusebius, Socrates, Sozomen, Theodoret, and Evagrius*. Macon, GA, 1986.

Cooper, K. *The Virgin and the Bride: Idealized Womanhood in Late Antiquity*. Cambridge, MA, 1999.

Cox Miller, P. "Strategies of Representation in Collective Biography: Constructing the Subject as Holy." In *Greek Biography and Panegyric*, edited by T. Hägg and P. Rousseau, 209–54. Berkeley, 2000.

Crespo Ortiz de Zarate, S. *'Nutrices' en el imperio romano*. 2 vols. Valladolid, 2005–2006.

Cribiore, R. *Writing, Teachers and Students in Graeco-Roman Egypt*. Atlanta, 1996.

Cribiore, R. *Gymnastics of the Mind: Greek Education in Hellenistic and Roman Egypt*. Princeton, 2001.

Cribiore, R. *The School of Libanius in Late Antique Antioch*. Princeton, 2007.

Cribiore, R. "Spaces for Teaching in Late Antiquity." In *Alexandria Auditoria of Kôm el-Dikka and Late Antique Education*, edited by T. Derda, T. Markiewicz, and E. Wipszycka, 143–50. Warsaw, 2007.

Cuomo, S. *Pappus of Alexandria and the Mathematics of Late Antiquity*. Cambridge, 2000.

Davis, S. *The Early Coptic Papacy: The Egyptian Church and its Leadership in Late Antiquity*. Cairo, 2004.

Deakin, M. *Hypatia of Alexandria: Mathematician and Martyr*. Amherst, NY, 2007.

Delia, D. "The Population of Roman Alexandria." *Transactions of the American Philological Association* 118 (1988): 275–92.

Delia, D. "From Romance to Rhetoric: The Alexandrian Library in Classical and Islamic Traditions." *American Historical Review* 97 (1992): 1449–67.

Dillon, J. *The Middle Platonists, 80 B.C. to A. D. 220*. 2nd ed. Ithaca, 1996.

Dillon, J. *The Heirs of Plato: A Study of the Old Academy*. Oxford, 2003.

Dillon, J. "Review of H. D. Saffrey and A. Segonds, *Jamblique: Réponse à Porphyre (De mysteriis). Collection des universités de France, Série grecque, 496* (Paris, 2013)." *Bryn Mawr Classical Review* 2013.11.41. http://bmcr.brynmawr.edu/2013/2013-11-41.html.

Duffy, J. "Byzantine Medicine in the Sixth and Seventh Centuries: Aspects of Teaching and Practice." *Dumbarton Oaks Papers* 38 (1984): 21–27.

Dzielska, M. *Hypatia of Alexandria*. Translated by F. Lyra. Cambridge, MA, 1995.

Eco, U. *Baudolino*. Milan, 2000.

Edwards, M. *Neoplatonic Saints: The Lives of Plotinus and Proclus by their Students*. Liverpool, 2000.

Elm, S. *Sons of Hellenism, Fathers of the Church*. Berkeley, 2012.

Erskine, A. "Culture and Power in Ptolemaic Egypt: The Museum and Library of Alexandria." *Greece and Rome* 42 (1995): 38–48.

Evans Grubbs, J. *Women and the Law in the Roman Empire*. London, 2002.

Évrard, E. "A quel titre Hypatie enseigna-t-elle la philosophie?" *Revue des Études Grecques* 90 (1977): 69–74.

Ford, C. *Julia Margaret Cameron: 19th Century Photographer of Genius*. London, 2003.

Fournet, J.-L., and J. Gascou. "Moines pachômiens et batellerie." In *Alexandrie médiévale 2*, edited by C. Decobert, 23–45. Études alexandrines 8. Cairo, 2002.

Fowden, G. "Bishops and Temples in the Eastern Roman Empire, AD 320–435." *Journal of Theological Studies* 29 (1979): 53–78.

Fowden, G. "The Pagan Holy Man in Late Antique Society." *Journal of Hellenic Studies* 102 (1982): 33–59.

Fowden, G. "The Athenian Agora and the Progress of Christianity." *Journal of Roman Archeology* 3 (1990): 494–500.

Franēk, J. "Philosophical Parrhesia as Aesthetics of Existence." *Continental Philosophy Review* 39 (2006): 113–34.

Frankfurter, D. "The Consequences of Hellenism in Late Antique Egypt: Religious Worlds and Actors." *Archiv für Religionsgeschichte* 2 (2000): 162–94.

Frantz, A. *The Athenian Agora XXIV: Late Antiquity 267–700*. Princeton, 1988.

Fraser, P. M. "A Syriac *Notitia Urbis Alexandrinae*." *Journal of Egyptian Archeology* 37 (1951): 103–8.

Fraser, P. M. *Ptolemaic Alexandria*. Oxford, 1970.

Frend, W. H. C. *The Rise of the Monophysite Movement*. Cambridge, 1972.

Gaddis, M. *There is No Crime for Those Who Have Christ*. Berkeley, 2005.

Galvão-Sobrinho, C. *Doctrine and Power: Theological Controversy and Christian Leadership in the Later Roman Empire*. Berkeley, 2013.

Garnsey, P. *Famine and Food Supply in the Greco-Roman World: Responses to Risk and Crisis*. Cambridge, 1988.

Garnsey, P. "Roman Patronage." In *From the Tetrarchs to the Theodosians*, edited by S. McGill, C. Sogno, and E. Watts, 33–54. Cambridge, 2010.

Gibson, C. "Alexander in the Tychaion: Ps.-Libanius on the Statues." *Greek, Roman, and Byzantine Studies* 47 (2007): 431–54.

Gibson, C. "The Alexandrian Tychaion and the Date of Ps.-Nicolaus *Progymnasmata*." *Classical Quarterly* 59 (2009): 608–23.

Graf, F. "Untimely Death, Witchcraft, and Divine Vengeance: A Reasoned Epigraphical Catalog." *Zeitschrift für Papyrologie und Epigraphik* 162 (2007): 139–50.

Grey, C. "Shock, Horror, or Same Old Same Old? Everyday Violence in Augustine's Africa." *Journal of Late Antiquity* 6 (2014): 216–32.

Haas, C. *Alexandria in Late Antiquity: Topography and Social Conflict*. Baltimore, 1997.

Haas, C. "John Moschus and Late Antique Alexandria." In *Alexandrie médiévale 2*, edited by C. Decobert, 47–59. Études alexandrines 8. Cairo, 2002.

Hahn, J. *Gewalt und religiöser Konflikt: Studien zu den Auseinandersetzungen zwischen Christen, Heiden, und Juden im Osten des Römischen Reiches (von Konstantin bis Theodosius II.)* Berlin, 2004.

Hahn, J. "The Conversion of the Cult Statues: The Destruction of the Serapeum 392 AD and the Transformation of Alexandria into the 'Christ Loving' City." In *From Temple to Church: Destruction and Renewal of Local Cultic Topography in Late Antiquity*, edited by J. Hahn, S. Emmel, and U. Gotter, 335–63. Leiden, 2008.

Hanlein-Schäfer, H. *Veneratio Augusti, eine Studie zu den Templen des ersten römischen Kaisers*. Rome, 1985.

Harich-Schwarzbauer, H. *Hypatia: Die spätantiken Quellen. Eingeleitet, kommentiert, und interpretiert*. Bern, 2011.

Heath, T. L. *Euclid: The Thirteen Books of the Elements*. Cambridge, 1909.

Heather, P. "New Men for New Constantines?" In *New Constantines: The Rhythm of Imperial Renewal in Byzantium, 4th–13th Centuries*, edited by P. Magdalino, 11–34. Aldershot, 1994.

Heather, P., and D. Moncur. *Politics, Philosophy, and Empire: Select Orations of Themistius*. Liverpool, 2001.

Heiberg, J. L., ed. *Apollonii Pergaei quae Graece exstant cum commentariis antiquis*. Vol. 2. Leipzig, 1893.

Howe Kritzer, A. *Plays by Early American Women, 1775–1850*. Ann Arbor, 1995.

Iles Johnston, S. "Sosipatra and the Theurgic Life: Eunapius Vitae Sophistorum 6.6.5–6.9.24." In *Reflections on Religious Individuality: Greco-Roman and Judaeo-Christian Texts and Practices*, edited by J. Rüpke and W. Spickemann, 99–118. Berlin, 2012.

Jansen H. L. *The Coptic Story of Cambyses' Invasion of Egypt*. Copenhagen, 1950.

Johnson, A. *Religion and Identity in Porphyry of Tyre: The Limits of Hellenism in Late Antiquity*. Cambridge, 2013.

Jones, A. *Pappus of Alexandria: Book 7 of the Collection*. Vol. 1. New York, 1986.

Jones, A. H. M. *The Later Roman Empire 284–602*. Norman, OK, 1964.

Jones, C. P. "A Friend of Galen." *Classical Quarterly* 17 (1967): 311–12.

Jones, C. P. *The Roman World of Dio Chrysostom*. Cambridge, 1978.

Kahlos, M. *Vettius Agorius Praetextatus: A Senatorial Life in Between*. Rome, 2002.

Kaldellis, A. "The Works and Days of Hesychios the Illoustrios of Miletos." *Greek, Roman, and Byzantine Studies* 45 (2005): 381–403.

Kaster, R. A. *Guardians of Language: The Grammarian and Society in Late Antiquity.* Berkeley, 1988.

Keenan, J. "'Die Binnenwanderung' in Byzantine Egypt." *Greek, Roman, and Byzantine Studies* 51 (2011): 57–82.

Kingsley, C. *Hypatia: Or, New Foes with an Old Face.* London, 1854.

Kulikowski, M. *Rome's Gothic Wars.* Baltimore, 2007.

Lackey, M., E. Flint, and D. Freer. *The Shadow of the Lion.* Riverdale, NY, 2002.

Laes, C. *Children in the Roman Empire.* Cambridge, 2011.

Lamberton, R. "The Schools of Platonic Philosophy of the Roman Empire: The Evidence of the Biographies." In *Education in Greek and Roman Antiquity*, edited by Y. L. Too, 433–58. Leiden, 2001.

Lankewish, V. "Love among the Ruins: The Catacombs, the Closet, and the Victorian 'Early Christian' Novel." *Victorian Literature and Culture* 28 (2000): 239–73.

Lewis, N. "*Literati* in the Service of Roman Emperors: Politics before Culture." In *Coins, Culture and History in the Ancient World: Numismatic and Other Studies in Honor of Bluma L. Trell*, edited by L. Casson and M. Price, 149–66. Detroit, 1981.

Lewis, T. *The History of Hypatia, A Most Impudent School-Mistress of Alexandria: Murder'd and Torn to Pieces by the Populace, in Defence of Saint Cyril and the Alexandrian Clergy. From the Aspersions of Mr. Toland.* London, 1721.

Luzi, M. *Ipazia: Poemetto drammatico.* Milan, 1972.

Majcherek. G. "The Late Roman Auditoria: An Archeological Overview." In *Alexandria Auditoria of Kôm el-Dikka and Late Antique Education*, edited by T. Derda, T. Markiewicz, and E. Wipszycka, 11–50. Warsaw, 2007.

Maldonado, D. "The Letter Collection of Synesius of Cyrene." In *Late Antique Epistolography*, edited by C. Sogno, B. Storin, and E. Watts, Berkeley, 2016.

Mansfeld, J. *Prolegomena: Questions to Be Settled before the Study of an Author or Text.* Leiden, 1994.

Mansfeld, J. *Prolegomena Mathematica: From Apollonius of Perge to Late Neoplatonism.* Leiden, 1998.

Maspero, J. "Horapollon et la fin du paganisme Égyptien." *Bulletin de l'Institut Français d'Archéologie Orientale* 11 (1914): 163–95.

Matthews, J. F. *Western Aristocracies and Imperial Court, A.D. 364–425.* Oxford, 1975.

McGuckin, J. A. *St. Cyril of Alexandria: The Christological Controversy.* Leiden, 1994.

McKenzie, J. *The Architecture of Alexandria and Egypt, 300 BC–700 ad.* New Haven, 2007.

McKenzie, J., S. Gibson, and A. T. Reyes. "Reconstructing the Serapeum in Alexandria from the Archeological Evidence." *Journal of Roman Studies* 94 (2004): 73–121.

McLynn, N. *Ambrose of Milan: Church and Court in a Christian Capital.* Berkeley, 1994.

Ménage, G. *A History of Women Philosophers.* Translated by B. H. Zedler. New York, 1984.

Molinaro, U. "A Christian Martyr in Reverse: Hypatia: 370–415 A.D.: A Vivid Portrait of the Life and Death of Hypatia as Seen through the Eyes of a Feminist Poet and Novelist." *Hypatia* 4.1 (1989): 6–8.

Monserrat, D. "Heron 'Bearer of *philosophia*' and Hermione *grammtike*." *Journal of Egyptian Archeology* 83 (1997): 223–26.

Morley, N. *Metropolis and Hinterland: The City of Rome and the Italian Economy 200 B.C.–A.D. 200.* Cambridge, 1996.

Morris, I. *Why the West Rules—For Now.* New York, 2010.

Nau, F. "Histoire des solitaires égyptiens." *Revue de l'Orient Chrétien* 13 (1908): 46–67; 266–97.

Neugebauer O. *A History of Mathematical Astronomy.* Philadelphia, 1975.

Nobbs, A. E. "Philostorgius' View of the Past." In *Reading the Past in Late Antiquity,* edited by G. Clarke, 251–64. Rushcutters Bay, Australia, 1990.

Norman, A., ed. and trans. *Libanius: Autobiography and Selected Letters.* Vol. 2. Cambridge, MA, 1990.

Ogilvie, G. Stuart. *Hypatia: A Play in Four Acts.* London, 1894.

O'Meara, D. *Pythagoras Revived: Mathematics and Philosophy in Late Antiquity.* Oxford, 1989.

Pack, R. "A Romantic Narrative in Eunapius." *Transactions of the American Philological Association* 83 (1952): 198–204.

Parkin, T. *Old Age in the Roman World.* Baltimore, 2003.

Pascal, C. *Figure e caratteri (Lucrezio, L'Ecclesiaste, Seneca, Ipazia, Giosue Carducci, Giuseppe Garibaldi).* Milan, 1908.

Penella, R. "When was Hypatia Born?" *Historia* 33 (1984): 126–28.

Penella, R. *Greek Philosophers and Sophists.* Leeds, 1990.

Penella, R. *Private Orations of Themistius.* Berkeley, 2000.

Pépin, J. *Théologie cosmique et théologie chrétienne.* Paris, 1964.

Petit P. *Les étudiants de Libanius.* Paris 1957.

Petkas, A. "The Place of Philosophy: Landscapes and Audiences of the Works of Synesius of Cyrene." PhD diss. in preparation, Princeton University.

Pomeroy, S. *Pythagorean Women: Their History and Writings.* Baltimore, 2013.

Praechter, K. "Die griechischen Aristoteleskommentatoren." *Byzantinische Zeitschrift* 18 (1909): 516–38.

Rabe, H. *Syriani in Hermogenem commentaria.* 2 vols. Leipzig, 1892–1893.

Rawson, B. *Children and Childhood in Roman Italy.* Oxford, 2003.

Rist, J. M. "Hypatia." *Phoenix* 19 (1965): 214–25.

Roberson, S. "Degenerate Effeminacy and the Making of a Masculine Spirituality in the Sermons of Ralph Waldo Emerson." In *Muscular Christianity: Embodying the Victorian Age,* edited by D. Hall, 150–73. Cambridge, 1994.

Robertson Brown, A. "Banditry or Catastrophe? History, Archaeology, and Barbarian Raids on Roman Greece." In *Romans, Barbarians, and the Transformation of the Roman World,* edited by R. Mathisen and D. Shanzer, 79–96. Aldershot, 2011.

Rodziewicz, M. *Les habitations romaines tardives d'Alexandrie à la lumière des fouilles polonaises à Kom el-Dikka, Alexandrie III*. Warsaw, 1984.

Rome, A. "Le troisième livre sur l'Almagest par Théon et Hypatie." *Annales de la Société Scientifique de Bruxelles* 46 (1926): 1–14.

Ronchey, S. "Hypatia the Intellectual." In *Roman Women*, edited by A. Fraschetti, 160–89. Chicago, 1999.

Roques, D. "La Famille d'Hypatie." *Revue des Études Grecques* 108 (1995): 128–49.

Roques, D. *Synésios de Cyrène, Tome II Correspondance*. Paris, 2003.

Russell, N. *Theophilus of Alexandria*. London, 2007.

Saffrey H. D., and A. Segonds, *Jamblique: Réponse à Porphyre (De mysteriis)*. Collection des universités de France, Série grecque, 496. Paris, 2013.

Saffrey H. D., and L. G. Westerink. *Théologie Platonicienne*. Paris, 1968.

Saluzzo Roero, D. *Ipazia ovvero delle filosfie*, Vols. 1–2. Turin, 1827.

Sandwell, I. *Religious Identity in Late Antiquity: Greeks, Jews, and Christians in Antioch*. Cambridge, 2007.

Scheidel, W. *Death on the Nile: Disease and the Demography of Roman Egypt*. Leiden, 2001.

Scheidel, W. "Germs for Rome." In *Rome the Cosmopolis*, edited by C. Edwards and G. Woolf. 158–76. Cambridge, 2003.

Scheidel, W. "Human Mobility in Roman Italy, I: The Free Population." *Journal of Roman Studies* 94 (2004): 1–26.

Scheidel, W. "Demography, Disease, and Death." In *The Cambridge Companion to Ancient Rome*, edited by P. Erdkamp, 45–59. Cambridge, 2013.

Schmid, D. J. A. *De Hipparcho, duobus Theonibus doctaque Hypatia*. Jena, 1689.

Schmitt, T. *Die Bekehrung des Synesios von Kyrene: Politik und Philosophie, Hof und Provinz als Handlungsräume eines Aristokraten bis zu seiner Wahl zum Metropoliten von Ptolemaïs*. Munich-Leipzig, 2001.

Seng, H., and L. M. Hoffmann, eds. *Synesios von Kyrene: Politik-Literatur-Philosophie*. Turnhout, 2012.

Shaw, B. "'With Whom I Lived:' Measuring Roman Marriage." *Ancient Society* 32 (2002): 195–242.

Shaw, B. *Sacred Violence and Sectarian Hatred in the Age of Augustine*. Cambridge, 2011.

Shaw, G. "Theurgy: Rituals of Unification in the Neoplatonism of Iamblichus." *Traditio* 41 (1985): 1–28.

Shepardson, C. *Controlling Contested Places: Late Antique Antioch and the Spatial Politics of Religious Controversy*. Berkeley, 2014.

Simmons, M. B. *Universal Salvation in Late Antiquity: Porphyry of Tyre and the Pagan-Christian Debate*. Oxford, 2015.

Sogno, C. *Q. Aurelius Symmachus: A Political Biography*. Ann Arbor, 2006.

Sogno, C., B. Storin, and E. Watts, eds. *Late Antique Letter Collections: A Critical Introduction and Reference Guide*. Berkeley, 2016.

Sogno, C., B. Storin, and E. Watts. "Collected Epistolography in Late Antiquity." In *Late Antique Letter Collections: A Critical Introduction and Reference Guide.* Berkeley, 2016.

Sorabji, R. "John Philoponus." In *Philoponus and the Rejection of Aristotelian Science,* edited by R. Sorabji, 1–40. London, 1987.

Sorbaji, R. "Divine Names and Sordid Deals in Ammonius' Alexandria." In *Philosophy and Science in Late Antiquity,* edited by A. Smith, 203–14. Swansea, 2005.

Storin, B. "The Letters of Gregory Nazianzus: Discourse and Community in Late Antique Epistolary Culture." PhD diss., Indiana University 2011.

Stowers, B. "Eudocia: The Making of a Homeric Christian." PhD diss., University of Cincinnati, 2008.

Tanaseanu-Döbler, I. *Konversion zur Philosophie in der Spätantike: Kaiser Julian und Synesios von Kyrene.* Stuttgart, 2005.

Tanaseanu-Döbler, I. "Synesios und die Theurgie." in *Synesios von Kyrene: Politik-Literatur-Philosophie,* edited by H. Seng and L. M. Hoffmann, 201–30. Turnhout, 2012.

Taormina, D. *Plutarcho di Atene.* Rome, 1989.

Tarán, L. *Asclepius of Tralles, Commentary to Nicomachus' Introduction to Arithmetic.* Philadelphia, 1969.

Tardieu, M. "La Gnose Valentinienne et les Oracles Chaldaïques." In *The Rediscovery of Gnosticism.* Vol. 1, edited by B. Layton, 194–237. Leiden, 1980.

Tarrant, R. "Socratic *Synousia*: A Post-Platonic Myth?" *Journal of the History of Philosophy* 43 (2005): 131–55.

Toland, J. *Hypatia: Or, the History of a most beautiful, most vertuous, most learned, and every way accomplish'd Lady; who was torn to Pieces by the* CLERGY *of Alexandria, to gratify the Pride, Emulation, and Cruelty of their* ARCHBISHOP, *commonly but undeservedly stiled St. Cyril.* London, 1753.

Uffelman, L. *Charles Kingsley.* Boston, 1979.

Urbainczyk, T. *Socrates of Constantinople.* Ann Arbor, 1997.

Van Hoof, L. "The Letters of Libanius." In *Late Antique Letter Collections,* edited by C. Sogno, B. Storin, and E. Watts. Berkeley, 2016.

Vanderspoel, J. *Themistius and the Imperial Court.* Ann Arbor, 1995.

Virlouvet, C. *Tessera frumentaria: Les procédés de la distribution du blé public à Rome à la fin de la République et au début de l'Empire.* Rome, 1995.

Vollenweider, S. "Ein Mittleres zwischen Vater und Sohn. Zur Bedeutung des Neuplatonikers Porphyrios für die Hymnen des Synesios." In *Synesios von Kyrene: Politik-Literatur-Philosophie,* edited by H. Seng and L. M. Hoffmann, 183–200. Turnhout, 2012.

Voltaire, "Hipathie." In *Dictionnaire philosophique. Oeuvres complètes de Voltaire: Nouvelle édition.* Vol. 13, 585–86. Paris, 1860.

Voltaire, "Lettre XIV—A. M. Covelle, citoyen de Genève, par M. Baudinet." In *Questions sur les miracles. Oeuvres complètes de Voltaire: Nouvelle édition.* Vol. 19, 382–83. Paris, 1860.

Voltaire, "Examen important de Milord Bolingbroke ou le tombeau de fanatisme." In *Oeuvres complètes de Voltaire: Nouvelle édition*. Vol. 26, 283–90. Paris, 1879.

von Haehling, R. "Damascius und die heidnische Opposition im 5 Jahrhundert nach Christus." *Jahrbuch für Antike und Christentum* 23 (1980): 82–95.

Walker, J. "The Limits of Late Antiquity: Philosophy between Rome and Iran." *Ancient World* 33 (2002): 45–69.

Wallraff, M. "Socrates Scholasticus on the History of Novatianism." *Studia Patristica* 29 (1997): 170–77.

Walraff, M. *Die Kirchenhistoriker Sokrates Untersuchungen zu Geschichtsdarstellung, Methode und Person.* Göttingen, 1997.

Watts, E. *City and School in Late Antique Athens and Alexandria.* Berkeley, 2006.

Watts, E. "Creating the Academy: Historical Discourse and the Shape of Community in the Old Academy." *Journal of Hellenic Studies* 127 (2007): 106–22.

Watts, E. "Interpreting Catastrophe: Disasters in the Works of Pseudo-Joshua the Stylite, Socrates Scholasticus, Philostorgius, and Timothy Aelurus." *Journal of Late Antiquity* 2 (2009): 79–98.

Watts, E. *Riot in Alexandria.* Berkeley, 2010.

Watts, E. "Doctrine, Anecdote, and Action: Reconsidering the Social History of the Last Platonists (c. 430–c. 550 CE)." *Classical Philology* 106 (2011): 226–44.

Watts, E. "Damascius' Isidore: A Perfectly Imperfect Philosophical Exemplar." *Byzantina et Slavica Cracoviensia* 7 (2014): 159–68.

Watts, E. *The Final Pagan Generation.* Berkeley, 2015.

Watts, E. "Athens, Educational Reform and Philosophy." In *Athens in Late Antiquity*, edited by I. Tanaseanu-Döbler and S. Anghel, forthcoming.

Wessel, S. "Socrates's Narrative of Cyril of Alexandria's Episcopal Election." *Journal of Theological Studies* 52 (2000): 98–104.

Westerink, L. G. "Deux commentaires sur Nicomaque: Asclépius et Jean Philopon." *Revue des Études Grecques* 77 (1964): 526–35.

Whitby, M. "John of Ephesus and the Pagans: Pagan Survivals in the Sixth Century." In *Paganism in the Later Roman Empire and Byzantium*, edited by M. Salaman, 111–31. Kraków, 1991.

Wider, K. "Women Philosophers in the Ancient Greek World: Donning the Mantle." *Hypatia* 1.1 (1986): 21–62.

Wilkinson, Kevin. "Palladas and the Age of Constantine." *Journal of Roman Studies* 99 (2009): 26–60.

Wilkinson, Kate. *Women and Modesty in Late Antiquity.* Cambridge, 2015.

Ziche, H. "Barbarian Raiders and Barbarian Peasants: Models of Ideological and Economic Integration." In *Romans, Barbarians, and the Transformation of the Roman World*, edited by R. Mathisen and D. Shanzer, 199–219. Aldershot, 2011.

Zintzen, C. *Vitae Isidori reliquiae.* Hildsheim, 1967.

Zitelmann, A. *Hypatia.* Weinheim and Basel, 1989.

Zotenberg, M. H. *La Chronique de Jean, évêque de Nikiou.* Paris, 1879.

Index

Iamblichus (Iamblichan Neoplatonism), 32–33, 35, 42–48, 50, 51–56, 58–61, 77, 82, 97, 117, 120, 128
intellectual family, 65–78, 85–87, 96–99, 103, 117–18, 140, 146
    differences between *akroatai* and *zēlotai,* 66
    inner circle of, 66–70, 72, 98, 119
intellectuals, 2, 13
    education of the children of, 21–24
    education of the daughters of, 21–24, 97–98
    higher education of, 24–30
    interaction with the public, 18–19, 61–62, 63, 78, 79, 103, 114, 116–18, 151
    pagan, 118–19, 134
    women as, 18–19, 21, 23, 25–28, 38–39, 55, 75, 91, 93–106, 125, 131, 135–38, 144, 146, 149–51, 155
Isidore of Alexandria, 118, 125–30, 136, 144

John, bishop of Nikiu, 116, 131–34
John Chrysostom, 47, 145
John Malalas, 125, 131
John Philoponus, 30, 154
Judaism, 7, 46
    Alexandrian Jews, 16, 81, 108–10, 132–33, 140–41
    anti-Semitism, 142, 186n43
Julian, emperor, 27, 52, 56, 82–83, 101–2, 104, 150, 167n27, 177n26, 183n39
Julius Caesar, 9, 14
Justinian, 115, 118, 127, 131, 154

Kingsley, Charles, 140–42

Leontius (in *Life of Isidore),* 126–27
Letter collections, 67–74, 76, 85–91, 99, 124. *See also* Hypatia
Lewis, Thomas, 136–37
Libanius, 38, 52, 65, 161–62n12–13, 166n6
Longinus (Athenian philosopher), 53

Mademoiselle B., 137–39
Marinus (Athenian Platonist), 76, 80–81, 97, 100, 126
mathematics, 21, 23–24, 26–35, 37–41, 49–50, 51, 94–97, 99, 103, 117–18, 127, 150, 185n17

geometry, 23, 28, 124, 130, 185n17
intersection between philosophy and, 27–35, 39–41, 44, 49–50, 51, 97, 103, 117–18, 128, 154–55
Maximus of Ephesus, 82–85, 88, 94, 98, 101–2, 104
    wife of, 94, 100–2, 104
medicine, study of, 28, 29
Molinaro, Ursule, 144–45

Neoplatonism, 4, 32–35, 41, 43, 128
    concepts of, 41–42
    theurgy in, 42–43, 45–48, 53–57, 61, 82, 100–1, 114, 166n9, 168n35, 180n45
    See also Iamblichus
Nestorius (Iamblichan Neoplatonist), 53, 100
Nestorius (Nestorianism), 122, 134
Nicaeus (letter carrier between Hypatia and Synesius), 68, 70, 86
Nicander (Constantinopolitan sophist), 71–72
Nicomachus of Gerasa, 29, 30, 32–35
    Introductio Arithmetica, 29–30, 32
    Theologoumena Arithmeticae, 29, 32, 34–35
Numenius of Apameia, 32–33

Olympius (student of Hypatia), 46, 90–91
Olympus (Iamblichan Neoplatonist), 46, 55–56, 58–59, 61, 114, 127–28, 151, 153, 168n35
Orestes, prefect of Egypt, 2–3, 108–15, 121, 123, 132, 141, 144, 146, 153
Origen (student of Ammianus Saccas), 33–34

paganism (traditional religion), 4–5, 7, 9, 15, 17–18, 42, 46–47, 49–50, 54–59, 61, 63, 78, 91, 111, 113–20, 127, 131–34, 137, 144, 146, 149–54
    laws against (anti-paganism), 51–52, 56–59
    pagan intellectuals (*see* intellectuals)
    sacrifice in, 55–57, 83
    theurgy (*see* Neoplatonism)
Pamprepius (Egyptian poet), 80–81
Pandrosion, 94–97, 102–4, 106

Synesius of Cyrene, 45–46, 49–50, 51–55,
    62, 66–73, 76, 85–93, 96, 107–8, 141,
    146, 152–53
    correspondence between Hypatia and
    (*see* Hypatia)
    De Regno, 89
    Dion, 70–71
    Hymns, 45, 47–49
Syrianus, 27, 30, 38, 54–55, 76, 100–1

Temple of Serapis in Canopus, 55, 60, 98
Theagenes, senator of Athens, 80–81
Themistius, 21, 45, 81–82
Theodosius II, 3, 25, 56, 59, 82, 110, 132, 139
Theon (father of Hypatia), 21, 26, 27,
    30–31, 34–35, 37–38, 40, 63–64, 69,
    96, 123–25, 127, 129, 144

retirement of, 37–39, 49
Theophilus, patriarch of Alexandria,
    57–58, 60–61, 62
Theosebius (Alexandrian
    philosopher), 76
theurgy. *See* Neoplatonism
Timothy, 108
Toland, John, 135–41, 145, 147
Troilus (official), 90

Uranius (sophist), 80–81

Valens, 24, 83, 101–2
Valentinian I, 24
Voltaire, 139

Zitelmann, Arnulf, 143